"This easy-to-read book has marvelously blended the glory of sex with the realities of life. It addresses real people in a real world without compromising God's wonderful design and purpose for His gift of sex. . . .

There is no question that this groundbreaking work by Dr. William Cutrer and Sandi Glahn is the answer for those who wish to take the subject of sex out of the closet while keeping it out of the gutter. It will help those who read it address their actions and attitudes regarding sex in light of God's unique purpose for humankind. It will also provide hope, encouragement, and direction for those who are open and willing to bring their sexuality under the lordship of Jesus Christ."

from the foreword by Dr. Tony and Lois Evans
Oak Cliff Bible Fellowship
Dallas, Texas

"*Sexual Intimacy in Marriage* is scientifically accurate, biblically based, intensely practical, and written with a large dose of humor. The book should be bought and read together by every Christian couple desiring to improve their marriage."

Dr. David Stevens
President, Christian Medical & Dental Associations

"This book provides knowledge on one of the most important yet least talked about aspects of marriage. It is practical and biblical—author Bill Cutrer's medical expertise makes the book especially helpful."

Drs. Les and Leslie Parrott
Seattle Pacific University
authors of *Saving Your Marriage Before It Starts*

"Ignorance is often the greatest enemy to happiness and satisfaction in the area of romance within marriage. *Sexual Intimacy in Marriage* goes a long way toward dealing with our need for information, helping couples to enjoy their sex life together to the fullest. If you want to be the 'lover' your mate desires and needs, you will be blessed by this book."

Daniel L. Akin
Dean, School of Theology
The Southern Baptist Theological Seminary
Louisville, Kentucky

"Superbly witty and well-written, *Sexual Intimacy in Marriage* is a reliable, informative, and practical guide to human sexuality for married and soon-be-be-married couples. Authors Bill Cutrer and Sandra Glahn have developed an excellent resource that will help partners more fully understand God's intentions for the sexual relationship."

Carol B. Hanshew
Director, Life & Health Resources
Christian Medical & Dental Associations

SEXUAL *Intimacy* IN MARRIAGE

SEXUAL *Intimacy*
IN MARRIAGE
SECOND EDITION

WILLIAM CUTRER, M.D.
SANDRA GLAHN

kregel
PUBLICATIONS

Grand Rapids, MI 49501

Sexual Intimacy in Marriage

© 1998, 2001 by William Cutrer and Sandra Glahn
Second Edition

Published by Kregel Publications, a division of Kregel, Inc., P.O. Box 2607, Grand Rapids, MI 49501. For more information about Kregel Publications, visit our Web site: www.kregel.com.

Cover design: John M. Lucas
Cover photo upper right: © Photodisc
Cover photo lower left: © Peter Griffith / Masterfile

Library of Congress Cataloging-in-Publication Data
Cutrer, William.
    Sexual intimacy in marriage / William Cutrer and Sandra Glahn.
       p.   cm.
    Includes bibliographical references.
    1. Sex instruction. 2. Sex in marriage. 3. Sex—Religious aspects—Christianity. 4. Marriage—Religious aspects—Christianity. 5. Intimacy (Psychology) I. Glahn, Sandra. II. Title.
HQ31.C985   1998   306.7—dc21   97-34279
                                       CIP

ISBN 0-8254-2366-x

To my dear wife, Jane;
my son, Bill, and his wife, Elisabeth;
my daughter, Jennie, and her husband, Casey;
and my youngest son, Bob—
with deep gratitude to God
for richly blessing my life with each of them.

Bill Cutrer

To Gary, the love of my life,
and our daughter, Alexandra,
through whom God has brought us
many of His sweetest blessings.

Sandra Glahn

CONTENTS

ACKNOWLEDGMENTS

The authors gratefully acknowledge the kind permission of Grolier Incorporated to reproduce the diagrams on pages 24, 33, and 212, which are taken from the *Encyclopedia Americana,* 1985 Edition. Copyright by Grolier Incorporated. Used by permission.

Unless otherwise noted, Scripture quotations are from the *New American Standard Bible* (NASB) © 1960, 1977 by the Lockman Foundation.

Scripture quotations marked NIV are from the *Holy Bible, New International Version*® © 1973, 1984 by International Bible Society. Used by permission of Zondervan Publishing House. All rights reserved.

Scripture quotations marked AMP are from the *Amplified Bible* © 1962, 1964 by Zondervan Publishing House. Used by permission.

Scripture quotations marked NKJV are from the *New King James Bible Version* © 1979, 1982 by Thomas Nelson, Inc., Publishers.

The authors and publisher are not engaged in rendering medical or psychological services, and this book is not intended as a guide to diagnose or treat medical or psychological problems. If medical, psychological, or other expert assistance is required by the reader, please seek the services of your own physician or certified counselor.

FOREWORD

Most books on the subject of sex suffer from one of two possible extremes. Some are so overly spiritual that they ignore the human realities of the issue. These works bypass the mental and emotional aspects of sex in favor of esoteric explanations that real people living in a real world can hardly relate to.

On the other extreme are books that address the subject of sex as if it has little or no relationship to the Divine. It is so secularized as to be purely biological and animalistic. With no sense of covenant or of the spiritual uniqueness of sex within the context of marriage, people are left to focus on the physical at the expense of the spiritual.

Sexual Intimacy in Marriage does not suffer from either of these extremes. This easy-to-read book has marvelously blended the glory of sex with the realities of life. It addresses real people in a real world without compromising God's wonderful design and purpose for His gift of sex. The book holds in highest esteem the institution of marriage, and the sexual relationship is given its proper place within the context of marriage.

There is no question that this groundbreaking work by Dr. William Cutrer and Sandi Glahn is the answer for those who wish to take the subject of sex out of the closet while keeping it out of the gutter. It will help readers address their actions and attitudes regarding sex in light of God's unique purpose for humankind. It will also provide hope, encouragement, and direction for those who are open and willing to bring their sexuality under the lordship of Jesus Christ.

The involvement in this project of Dr. Bill Cutrer makes this work all the more special to us. He has served for several years as gynecologist for the women of the Evans' household and also has taught a Christian approach to medical health at our annual Church Development Conference. His medical expertise, combined with his Christian training and commitment, give him a unique blend of skillful hands and a tender heart—a blend that has greatly benefited our own family and marriage relationship.

In *Sexual Intimacy in Marriage* we finally have a book that places the sensitive subject of sex on a low enough shelf for people to reach, yet on a high enough shelf for God to be honored by it. After you read this book, you will understand why marriage is the only context in which authentic sexual intimacy is possible. In addition, you will discover a practical approach to many of the sexual problems and challenges that confront married couples. Most importantly, you will grow in your love for the Creator, who has given us such a wonderful gift to enjoy.

Dr. Tony and Lois Evans

1

IN THE SECRET PLACE

Every couple, at some time in their relationship if not throughout their years together, will encounter sexual difficulties or transitional times requiring adaptation, change, and flexibility. One of the most damaging beliefs is, "We are the only ones having trouble; everyone else has a perfect love life." That is totally false. Consider a few examples, from my experience (Dr. Bill's), of things that can go wrong.

- Trina and Jim were flying home from their honeymoon when Jim said, "After we settle into a routine and stop having sex every single day . . ." Before he could finish, Trina burst into tears. "Why can't we have sex every day?" she wanted to know.
- After their disastrous honeymoon, a couple came for help. "I didn't expect sex to be so painful," the wife told me. "Besides, he wants it every day. I'm afraid he might be some kind of pervert."
- Lonnie frequently climaxed too early, leaving his wife unsatisfied and frustrated. He came to me wondering what he might be able to do about it.
- Tom told his wife, "I'm kind of bored with our love life." His wife, visualizing a variety of more romantic atmospheres, said, "Great! Let's change it." She was stunned when he entered the bedroom that night wearing only toy guns and a cowboy hat.

- Kathie, the wife of an oral surgeon, could have appeared on the cover of *Glamour* magazine, yet her husband rarely noticed her. Like many workaholics' wives, Kathie's feelings about sex had progressed from normal desire to compelling need. She purchased an entire wardrobe from Victoria's Secret, but she still couldn't seem to get her husband's attention.

- Fred and Dana found themselves facing sexual difficulties for the first time in their marriage. During Dana's pregnancy, they experienced the normal challenges in maintaining a strong love life. They tried to make the most of it and find humor in their troubles. Yet after the baby arrived, Dana felt exhausted and remained uninterested in sex. Fred felt replaced by the baby and told his wife she'd demoted him from "the king" to "a serf."

- Becky and Brad had received premarital counsel that told them the goal of sex should be simultaneous orgasm. The pressure Becky felt over her inability to "time it right" made her unable to reach orgasm at any point in their lovemaking.

Do any of those scenarios sound familiar? They're all common. We may feel isolated in our struggles and consider our own experiences unique, thus hesitating to seek help. Yet what is most personal is usually most universal. Fortunately, help is available.

Whether we believe men and women are basically the same or fundamentally different, we would all agree that male and female anatomies differ. The perspective of this book is that God has created the male and female bodies to beautifully complement each other. While we have termed this a "Christian guide to sexual intimacy," perhaps we need to clarify that there is no such thing as "Christian sex." There is only sex in which the participants are Christians. They may or may not reflect a Christian worldview, just as Christian artists do not use Christian easels or Christian paintbrushes, yet they may be used to illustrate a New Testament story such as the Prodigal Son.

For me (Dr. Bill) this handbook comes out of more than fifteen years of medical practice as an obstetrician/gynecologist. As I conducted premarital exams and counseling, I was struck by the lack of information among couples preparing to pledge themselves to one another "for better or for worse." Many of these young (and sometimes not so young) people staggered in a fog of misinformation and partial truths about sex, hoping that everything would "work out." After reviewing the accuracy, practicality, and depth of the information that is disseminated as premarital counseling by many pastors, I was disappointed. In the area of sexuality and marital intimacy, it seemed that many counselors were wasting the couple's time, perpetuating harmful myths or, even more sadly, guiding them incorrectly.

After retiring from medical practice, I served the Lord as a full-time pastor. Only then could I fully appreciate the difficulty of the task. The problem, which for many may prove insurmountable, is the limits on information the pastor has. Not all pastors are aware of several areas of information necessary for successfully guiding a couple in their expressions of intimacy. Just to help in establishing a physically functional relationship, a counselor needs to be able to draw upon (1) a detailed sexual history, (2) a physical examination, and (3) a thorough understanding of medications either partner may require. These logically precede recommendations and guidance.

Yet a pastoral counselor will probably feel uncomfortable asking "at what age did you become sexually active," or other detailed sexual history questions. In addition, he or she cannot touch a muscle and say, "This is the one you need to relax when sex is uncomfortable." The counselor also may not realize that the wife's birth control pills have diminished her sexual interest, a piece of information that could save months of counseling that tries to pinpoint sources of suppressed anger or a "sex is wrong" mentality.

Pastoral staff should ideally incorporate godly physicians to participate in premarital evaluation and education. Following the initial medical evaluation and subsequent "green light," the counselor can then effectively guide the couple through the theological and marital issues in the ongoing relationship. A team ministry approach can help solve some of the devastating real-life situations related in the chapters ahead. My desire is that this work will bridge that medical/ministry boundary, and as such, it will prove a helpful guide for opening dialogue between ministry personnel and couples seeking the fullest expression of marital love.

Believing that God intends sex to be not only fulfilling and unifying but also great fun within the bounds of marriage, we have purposely taken a rather lighthearted approach. However, we realize there is nothing funny about sexual difficulties. It is our hope and prayer that the information presented in this way can both heal and prevent some of the physical and emotional pain that can make sexual intimacy less than the joyful, satisfying experience God intended.

> "O my dove, in the clefts of the rock,
> In the secret place of the steep pathway,
> Let me see your form,
> Let me hear your voice;
> for your voice is sweet,
> And your form is lovely."
> —Song of Solomon 2:14

2

WHAT IS SEX?

I have come into my garden.
—Song of Solomon 5:1

W hat is sex? It might seem silly to even ask the question. Is there anything about sex we haven't already learned from Dr. Ruth, Howard Stern, or the ever-increasing number of television and radio talk shows? *The Joy of Sex* has more name recognition than *The Joy of Cooking*. The bestseller *Everything You Wanted to Know About Sex But Were Afraid to Ask* has been around for more than a generation and has spawned countless variations of its title. We live in a society saturated with messages about sex from the daily newspaper to billboards, magazines, television, movies, and the Internet. Yet most people talk a better game than they know.

Still, textbook knowledge is not the only limitation. Data indicate that the nature of sexual dysfunction in even physician couples, who are trained in anatomy and physiology, is not fundamentally different from that of other professionals.[1] So while we need more than an understanding of physiology, we begin there.

Consider the couple whose story begins with a routine appointment in my (Dr. Bill's) office. They had been married for about a year when the wife, realizing her period was several weeks late, came for a pregnancy test. It proved to be positive.

As they answered questions about their medical history, she revealed that she had never had a gynecological exam. They had moved to the United States from another culture where they did not do them for the sake of modesty. So I decided to do a sonogram first since it is less threatening. I would show them the pregnancy sac to break the ice and then do the examination. The equipment required a full bladder, which she did not have. This rendered the abdominal sonogram useless, so I explained that I could do a vaginal sonogram. They agreed.

I prepared the instrument which, although quite slender, was no doubt terrifying to her. I talked about the procedure in an effort to get her to relax, but it didn't help. I was seeing nothing on the screen, so now besides being uncomfortable, they were becoming concerned about the baby because I couldn't image anything. An experienced gynecologist, I prided myself in knowing anatomical geography and in my uncanny ability to find the vagina with a sonogram probe in a darkened room.

But it was not happening. I could not find this woman's vagina. I told my nurse that we needed to do a speculum exam to see what was happening. (I can usually do the sonogram without actually touching a nervous patient and develop some rapport with the "baby pictures," but all the usual techniques were failing.) This patient was now doubly anxious, being for the first time in the "dorsal lithotomy" posture (that very exposed gynecological exam position). The nurse handed me a normal marital speculum.

I found no vaginal opening.

I thought, *This lady is pregnant. There must be access somewhere, somehow.* I got the small pediatric speculum and began just below the urethra. I found the vagina completely covered by a thick hymen except for a small opening the size of a Q-tip. I could explore the vagina only with a Q-tip; not even my little finger could pass.

In short order I deduced that intercourse had really been *outercourse*, that no penetration had ever occurred. Some tenacious and goal-oriented sperm had found its way—and a long way it is—from the vaginal opening all the way up the vagina to a fallopian tube. I told them I had discovered a minor abnormality and asked her to dress and join me in my office.

I tried to frame an opening line more sensitive than "Guess what— you only *thought* you were having sex." I asked the husband if he had noticed any difficulty with intercourse, imagining that only Microman would have had any success. He said no. He had found it to be "most pleasurable." I remember how that remark surprised me!

In my kindest and most doctorlike voice, I explained the situation and the surgical remedy that could wait until the time of delivery, if they wished. She did need to have a Pap smear, which had never been done. Since she hadn't had multiple partners, she was not at a high risk for disease. In fact, she'd had *no* partners in the usual sense of the word. So I felt comfortable waiting. The husband, whose mind had begun to run full throttle, began to put two and two together (which of course he had been unable to do as yet!) and asked if I could do the surgery sooner. I agreed to fix the congenital intact hymen.

I used a laser technique, then told them to wait six weeks. For them this was no hardship since they still didn't know what they were missing. They dutifully waited the six weeks (unlike most of my patients).

When they returned, I saw a glow radiating from their faces during the visit following the "doctor's clearance to proceed." I didn't have to ask if everything was fine. His silly grin screamed it. She shyly smiled and said, "Everything is wonderful. We didn't know it could be like this." The increased elasticity and lubrication of pregnancy prevented any first-time difficulties, and wedded bliss took on a new and more profound meaning.

What is sexual intercourse? Unlike this couple, you probably know that, from a purely technical viewpoint, it is the insertion of the penis *inside* the vagina, generally followed by ejaculation. It represents a beautiful example of skillful engineering on the part of the divine Creator. Normally for conception to occur, sperm must make it into the vagina, and sexual intercourse is usually how that happens.

Yet sex involves more than the textbook definition of sexual intercourse. It involves the physical expression of love and pleasure. So it may or may not include intercourse, ejaculation, or orgasm. These are possible options, but not requirements.

Even if we know this basic information, we probably have a clouded understanding of our bodies and what physical intimacy involves. We draw many, if not most, of our attitudes and perceptions of sexuality from the erotic images of American culture. Yet developing sexual intimacy involves understanding anatomy, physical response cycles, marriage, and communicating with all five senses. Each of these will be covered in the following pages.

Because understanding your own body and your spouse's body is essential to developing sexual intimacy, we will begin with some foundational common ground—understanding anatomy.

3

THE MALE ANATOMY

His hands are rods of gold set with beryl;
His abdomen is carved ivory inlaid with sapphires.
His legs are pillars of alabaster
Set on pedestals of pure gold. . . .
—Song of Solomon 5:14–15

irst we'll discuss what's "down there"—the *genitalia*. This is not a fancy term for "citizens of Genit." It's the plural form of "genital," which means "relating to reproduction or generation." It has come to be a general term for the sex organs, both male and female. Once we look at the individual parts, we'll move on to look at how they work together. The point of this chapter isn't to prepare you to pass a medical school exam but rather to provide accurate information that will make the process of intimacy easier to understand. Also, by using the correct terms, you can be more specific with your spouse in guiding your lovemaking toward greater mutual fulfillment.

Gonads

These structures produce reproductive cells (either sperm or eggs) and thus include the male testicles and female ovaries. The male gonads are enclosed in the *scrotum,* which is a sac suspended between the thighs. The process of producing mature sperm cells begins at approximately age twelve, although the exact time varies from individual to individual. This period of development is called puberty, a time when adolescents

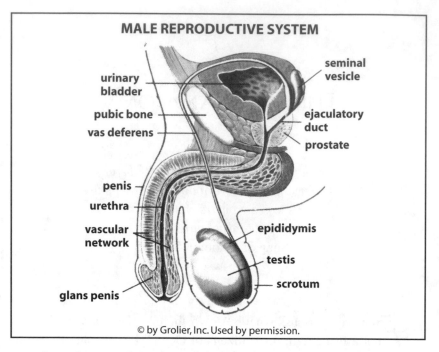

MALE REPRODUCTIVE SYSTEM

urinary bladder

pubic bone

vas deferens

penis

urethra

vascular network

glans penis

seminal vesicle

ejaculatory duct

prostate

epididymis

testis

scrotum

© by Grolier, Inc. Used by permission.

experience hormonal storms and their moms and dads may feel like they are living in parental purgatory.

Epididymis

A tiny, twisting segment of the tube that carries the sperm from the testicle to the portion of the tube called the *vas deferens*.

Vas deferens

This is the next portion of the sperm-carrying tube connecting the epididymis to the seminal vesicles. When a man has a vasectomy, his physician removes a portion of the "vas," thus preventing sperm from passing from the testicle to the ejaculate. Although a high percentage of vasectomies can be reversed by re-opening the vas, antibodies may have developed that have incapacitated the sperm. We'll talk more about vasectomy in appendix B, which deals with contraception.

Seminal vesicles

Two reservoirs where sperm get stored until the time of ejaculation, or release. The majority of the fluid contained in the ejaculate is secreted here. Thus, after vasectomy there is still a release of milky fluid, just no sperm (although vasectomy is not 100 percent foolproof).

Penis

The male sex organ that is visible and external. At the time of sexual stimulation, blood rushes into its network of blood vessels. At the same time, small valves automatically close, preventing blood from circulating back into the body. As stimulation continues and blood flows in, the penis fills up, tightens, and stands rigid or "erect." Under normal conditions, when either stimulation ceases or ejaculation takes place, the small valves gradually open, and the excess blood flows back into the circulatory system.

Some imaginative folks have theorized that so much blood is collected here during sexual excitation that the man could pass out; this has never actually been reported. The amount of blood normally collected is, in fact, quite small. The ejaculation of the semen is called *orgasm*. Popular language often uses the term *climax,* among others.

It may be helpful here to note that most women don't gain the majority of their sexual satisfaction from the penis being in the vagina, no matter what size the penis is.

In most men, the penis responds pleasurably to being stroked. The loose skin around its shaft forms what looks like a seam down the back side of the penis. For some this is the part most responsive to caressing.

A growing number of surgeons now promise to substantially lengthen and widen a man's penis with penile surgery or *phalloplasty.* The procedure, which costs thousands of dollars, takes around an hour to perform, is presently unregulated, and doesn't always work. The FDA, which oversees breast implants, doesn't monitor the surgery because no implant or drug is involved. One man who has had the surgery observes, "It preys on men with low self-esteem."[1] Others report satisfactory results. Men considering phalloplasty may need to consider the greater issues of spiritual maturity and relational confidence before going ahead with surgery.

On average, the relaxed penis is about 3-1/2 to four inches long; an erect penis is about five to 6-1/2 inches long, but there is variation from man to man. Sexual difficulties due to male penis diameter and/or length are virtually never a problem except for young, small, or nervous women.

Contrary to popular thought, penis size has little to do with sexual pleasure or satisfaction for most women—or men for that matter. The vagina
changes to accommodate a rather wide range of penis sizes. As someone
has put it, "It's not the length of the wand; it's the magic in the act."

In addition, sexual researchers have found that the size of an unaroused
penis does not relate proportionately to its size when erect. In other words,
"a small, flaccid penis generally enlarges to a greater extent at the time
of arousal than does a larger flaccid penis. In its erect state there is little
difference in size between one penis and another, even though they may
differ significantly in size when they are unaroused."[2]

Glans penis

The head of the penis is called the *glans penis* and is a little larger than the
shaft of the penis. The glans penis contains a heavy concentration of nerve
endings that play a major role in the sexual arousal of the male. In fact, the
concentration is so heavy that many men would prefer very gentle or even
indirect stimulation here, as is true of women with the clitoris.

While the nerve endings that register touch are the same as those in
other parts of the body, they form a more dense concentration here. Usually, at birth, the glans penis is encircled with a thick layer of skin called
the *prepuce* or foreskin. Circumcision is a procedure that removes a portion of this foreskin.

Circumcision is ordinarily a simple operation in which a surgeon cuts
the top of the foreskin away, thus freeing the glans penis from its covering. Many couples choose to have their infants circumcised within days
of birth for religious, social, or ethnic reasons. Doctors no longer consider this a medical necessity and many hospitals have moved away from
routine circumcision.

Circumcision easily allows effective personal hygiene, although careful
attention will normally suffice for both circumcised and uncircumcised
men. Two opposite views of circumcision have been suggested—that
circumcision enhances or that it inhibits sexual control and pleasure.
However, neither theory has strong supporting evidence.

Prostate

Normally the prostate is a golf ball-sized, walnut-shaped gland. It tends
to enlarge as men age. Like the appendix, it appears to have little vital

function. It secretes fluid into the ejaculate and serves as the counterpart to the same female mucus secreting glands (Skene's glands). As men age, the risk of prostate cancer increases. Prostate removal does not necessarily have to interfere with normal sexual functioning.

Semen

The thick, white sperm-containing fluid that is ejaculated. Most of the liquid of the ejaculate originated in the seminal vesicles and the prostate gland.

Testosterone

The primary male hormone responsible for the growth of facial hair, change of voice at puberty, muscular structure and development, sex-drive, and aggressive tendency in males. One man we know, upon learning that men make about fifteen times more testosterone than women, walked around with his arms outstretched as a victor proclaiming, "The man—fifteen, maybe twenty. The woman? One." (We noticed he made no comment when he heard that women produce ten times more estrogen than men.)

Females produce this hormone as well but in far smaller amounts. Injecting similar amounts of testosterone into a woman may cause her to grow facial hair, acquire a deepened voice, develop greater muscle tone, and increase her libido. (And it might have her acting like a man as well.)

So the obvious question: Why is testosterone not prescribed to increase sex drive in women? One husband was so bold as to ask if some could be slipped into his wife's drink. Actually, it *is* available and present in some forms of estrogen replacement therapy to restore female testosterone to an age-appropriate level. It's also available for replacement in castrate males. Yet widespread, long-term use is limited primarily because of its side effects. Simply put, most women don't want oily skin, a beard, mustache, or a bass voice.

One of my patients unintentionally took twice the prescribed dosage of testosterone. She came back to report, "Now I finally understand how men feel." She had been chasing her husband around the house for several weeks. At first he felt deeply gratified, but finally in a state of total exhaustion, he sent her back to me for deliverance.

Men have relatively boring, straightforward hormonal dominance as opposed to the female's beautifully complex hormonal cycle. Not only do men produce roughly fifteen times the amount of testosterone women do, as noted above, men also make estrogen in small amounts—only about one tenth the amount that women make. Men who have undergone sex-change operations (a practice that we don't endorse) take estrogen to fill out their hips and breasts, make their voices higher, help them lose facial hair, and basically to "feminize" them.

In addition to the 15:1 ratio of male to female testosterone, males also experience so-called testosterone storms, which apparently have no sexual equivalent in the female. During "storms," men will charge concrete walls if necessary to be with their women. Testosterone can be elevated by sight, scent, exercise, pornography, or any number of factors.

Testosterone production reaches its peak around age twenty, and maintains that level until about forty. After that it slowly drops until it is close to zero by age eighty. The decrease in testosterone does not need to affect a man's sexual pleasure although it may affect functioning.

What does all this mean practically? I have talked to numerous wives whose husbands' desires fell within normal ranges, yet the wives feared they had married weirdoes or perverts. I have often needed to assure newlyweds that it is natural and healthy for the husband to have a robust and seemingly endless sexual interest in his beautiful bride.

4

THE FEMALE ANATOMY

Hurry, my beloved,
And be like a gazelle or a young stag
On the mountains of spices.
—Song of Solomon 8:14

The week I (Sandi) got married, the mother of a friend told me, "Don't read anything about sex. If you do, it will take away the mystery. Why not just do what comes naturally? My husband taught me everything I know. That's *his* job."

Fortunately, my own mother had a much different view. While attending a seminar on "Talking to Your Kids About Sex," I discovered that I was the only woman present who had ever engaged in candid discussions about sexual issues with either of my parents. They provided books and explanations and used the appropriate terms for body parts long before I reached puberty, holding to the belief that knowledge is always preferable to ignorance.

We women tend to know less about our anatomies than men know about theirs because more of ours is internal. Yet by learning all she can about herself as God made her, a woman also enhances her ability to know her husband. In fact the word "know" frequently has sexual connotations in biblical writings. Abraham knew Sarah. Joseph did not know Mary before the birth of Jesus.

As the writer of Proverbs tells us, "To get wisdom, get understanding." God included an entire book of the Bible, Song of Solomon, that is devoted to helping us appreciate the delicate, God-given gift of our sexuality. This portion of the Scriptures coupled with some basic instruction about our anatomies can reduce a great number of misunderstandings and hurt feelings. (Dr. Bill will take over at this point, describing the female anatomy.)

Breast

The female breasts are milk-producing glands that allow most mothers to provide nourishment to their babies. Breast size and tenderness for an individual woman may vary greatly during the various phases of the monthly cycle, and it is also fairly common for a woman's breasts to differ in size. Some asymmetry is normal. The larger breast is usually on the dominant hand side. Thus, if a woman is right handed, the right breast will often be the larger.

During self-examination, a woman may notice small nodules or lumps. At one time doctors referred to them as the results of "fibrocystic disease," but because eighty to 85 percent of women have them, they are now referred to as fibrocystic change. Often, if a woman with a history of fibrocystic change finds a lump and waits through the menstrual cycle, the lump will disappear completely. If it does, it is not problematic. If it remains, she should seek medical consultation. Caffeine, which affects glandular tissue, can increase breast discomfort.

Almost every woman, if she presses hard enough, may find a tiny bit of secretion from her nipples. Often women on birth control pills will have a slight milky discharge that can result from using the pill. Vigorous direct stimulation over time can cause a milky secretion also.

As a rule, have any discharge evaluated, especially if it is bloody. In addition, pursue aggressive follow-up of lumps. Approximately one in nine women will have a diagnosis of breast cancer during her lifetime. This represents a drastic increase in this generation, for reasons we don't fully understand. Because of this risk, I strongly recommend breast self-exam and mammography, when appropriate. (Organizations differ in their recommendations regarding mammography, based on age and family history, so check with your doctor.) Self-examination may be the most important three or four minutes of a woman's month.

Check for any lumps, hard knots, swelling, dimpling, or thickening. Also look for any abnormal changes of size, shape, color, or discharge.

Because hormones can affect the breast, the best time to do the exam is seven to ten days after the start of your menstrual cycle, when swelling is minimal. Postmenopausal women should do their self-examinations on the same day of each month.

The American Cancer Society approves several methods of breast self-exam, but we will include only one to be done in the shower, as soapy water can heighten the sensitivity of your fingers. Raise your right arm behind your neck and using the finger pads (not tips), roll and press the breast area firmly against the chest wall. Repeat this process raising your left arm behind your neck and checking your left breast area. Be sure to cover the whole breast in circular motion, from the center out, or vertically in strips. Do so thoroughly and consistently.

Be sure to examine the chest area above each breast and also under the arms. In addition, be sure to gently squeeze each nipple, checking for any discharge.

For most women, the breasts play an important role in sexual stimulation. We should note here, however, that breast *size* has little to do with responsiveness or sexuality. Both small-breasted and large-breasted women have an equal capacity for sexual intensity. Usually the only

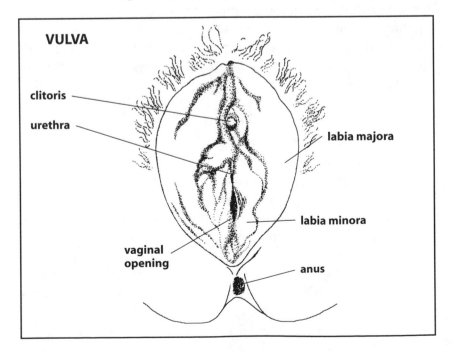

major difference in responsiveness is based on how a woman feels about herself. Many of my patients have confided their dissatisfaction with breast size, yet anything from a AA cup to a DD can be perfectly functional and appealing.

Vulva

Not to be confused with Volvo, a brand of car, these two names are often unintentionally confused, resulting in embarrassment for the man who knows cars better than he knows his wife. Vulva is the term for the entire female external (outside) genital area.

Labia majora

These are the large outer vaginal "lips." Their size and shape can vary from quite flat to rather full and prominent. This area does not have an abundant nerve supply but provides protection and cushion to the underlying structures.

Labia minora

The smaller internal vaginal "lips." These are the delicate non-hair-producing tissues that provide a covering for the clitoris. Before childbearing changes them, they meet in the midline to cover the urethra and the vaginal opening. When the legs are spread or sometimes following childbirth, the middle separates, exposing the underlying structures, the urethra and vagina.

Vagina

Many envision this "tunnel of love" as a tubular (tampon-shaped) organ with the cervix at the far end. In fact, the vagina is two flat walls that meet with the cervix protruding through the far end of the top before childbearing. Intercourse takes place below the cervix, rather than pointing into it.

This anatomical design allows a woman to cough or sneeze without the enormous intra-abdominal pressure that could cause the uterus to push out or make the bladder leak. Those who have experienced pregnancy or have recently given birth appreciate what can happen to the bladder (it "leaks") when the growing uterus distorts these normal structural relationships.

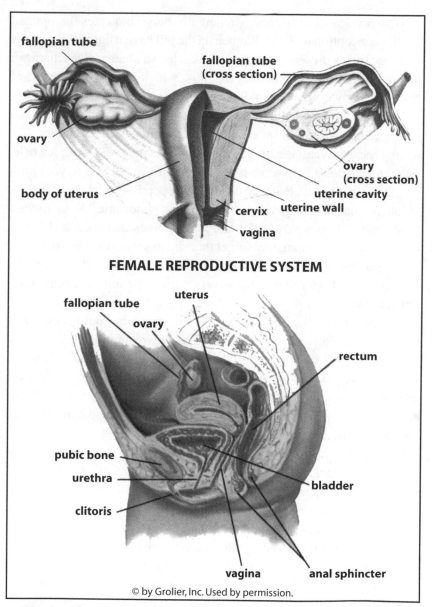

FEMALE REPRODUCTIVE SYSTEM

© by Grolier, Inc. Used by permission.

The healthy vagina fends off infections through its own acid-base balance. Because of this, douching is unnecessary for the average woman unless her physician directs her to do so for a specific problem or for hygiene during the menstrual flow. Mild vinegar-and-water solutions bought over the counter are safe if used correctly and reasonably.

At midcycle, a heavy clear, stretchy discharge indicates the optimal time for conception to occur. Women on the pill have a light white, sticky discharge that is present throughout the cycle. An abnormal discharge or itch can signal the presence of vaginitis, which has an assortment of causes and may produce pain. Physicians cannot tell accurately without using a microscope whether yeast or abnormal bacteria are present, and the treatment is different for each of these. While we use antibiotics for treating bacteria, yeast is a fungus and antibiotics may well make it worse. Yeast creams don't help some types of vaginitis at all. So see your physician if you have an abnormal discharge or persistent itching.

Another cause of vaginitis is "lost tampon syndrome." Sometimes a string tears off, and part of the tampon becomes detached and left in the vagina. Or a woman may forget that she has used two at a time and only removes one. The diagnosis is quite easy since the discharge produces a foul odor that remains very noticeable until the remaining part is removed.

A woman whose husband engages in frequent, vigorous oral sex will sometimes develop a condition termed as vulvovaginitis secondary to saliva. She may come to the office with significant genital inflammation, but use of the microscope reveals no yeast or infection. We usually recommend abstaining from oral sex for a while in addition to washing and immediately drying off. Sometimes steroids are also helpful in reducing the inflammation.

In my practice, some women came in with what they feared to be a yeast infection, and I was faced with the unpleasant task of telling them they had the herpes virus. Before AIDS, this was one of the most devastating diagnoses our patients could receive, second only to cancer. At present, herpes is a lifetime disease for which there is no cure.

Herpes is a small virus that can escape the condom in overflow or be secreted without external signs or ulcers. Even if couples use all the precautions, they still have a one in ten chance per year that the noninfected partner will contract it. In other words, if you marry someone with herpes, in all likelihood you eventually will get it too. A blood test is available, but it cross-reacts with the strain of herpes virus that causes fever blisters, which 70 percent of the population have. So results usually come back positive even if the patient does not have genital herpes.

No one recommends that you have sex when your spouse has active herpes; usually the tender ulcers make intercourse unappealing anyway.

Cervix

The cervix, the so-called door to the womb, is the lowermost portion of the uterus, which opens into the vagina. This organ dilates or stretches during labor to allow the passage of a baby into the birth canal (which is another name for the vagina and surrounding structures at the end of pregnancy). The cervix is also the tissue that is sampled during the Pap smear to check for cancer of the cervix. It contains an unusual and unique complement of nerve fibers that register pain when stretched (as in labor) yet can be cut, pierced, burned, and biopsied with relatively little discomfort.

Clitoris

This is the only organ in human anatomy whose sole purpose is to receive sexual pleasure. A small, approximately pea-size organ, the clitoris contains the high concentration of nerve fibers that transmit pleasurable sensation in most women. It is similar developmentally to the male's glans penis or head of the penis, and it is located in front just beneath the point where the labia minora join.

This organ is perhaps the most important (yet poorly understood and difficult to find) female structure. When couples came to the office having difficulties with intercourse or orgasm, I would invite the husband (with his wife's permission) to enter the exam room and be a part of the consultation. More often than not, his understanding of anatomy and function proved remarkably confused, and many misunderstandings could be clarified and corrected. Wives likewise had limited knowledge of the location of their body parts and how they were supposed to function. This is the major reason for including this explanation of anatomic details and why we have included some self-exploration exercises in the appendix corresponding to this chapter. Experience tells me that this topic and the explanation of orgasm may be the only part of this chapter many people will read!

The clitoris has a dense concentration of nerve endings that God designed to produce sexual arousal when stimulated. It differs from the penis in that it has no opening and it does not directly play a part in the process of reproduction. It is the external trigger that sets off sexual arousal and orgasm for many women.

Some doctors say that clitoral stimulation *has* to happen for orgasm to occur. For example, one writes: "These nerve endings must be stimulated directly by physical contact for a woman to become sexually aroused high enough to have an orgasm. . . . There must be uninterrupted stimulation of the clitoris and the area close to the clitoris for a wife to have an orgasm."[1] This is not true. Some woman have reported having orgasms while reading novels or receiving back rubs. Yet for *most* women, clitoral stimulation must occur. The nerve endings are so sensitive, however, that many women report that they prefer stimulation *around* the clitoris, not directly on it. The flat portion of the palm works better here than fingers for some couples.

Hymen

This is ordinarily a thin membrane or portion of tissue that, during the intrauterine development of the baby girl, completely covers the vaginal opening. As a young girl matures and the vaginal opening enlarges, the hymen normally perforates or splits creating a window of varying size that allows the menstrual fluid to escape at puberty.

The hymen carries potential for difficulty. If it does not perforate at all (which is unusual), a young girl will have "cycles" but no blood will pass, and it will collect in the vagina until detected. Because the vagina is a sterile area before the hymen perforates, this does not pose a medical risk.

More often, though, the hymen will perforate sufficiently to allow menstrual flow but will not comfortably permit tampon insertion or intercourse. Women who develop thick, rigid hymens (although menstrual flow and tampon insertion may present no problem) may find intercourse painful or impossible. This can be readily solved with stretching exercises (included in the workbook section) or surgical removal of the remnant of the hymen. This procedure has proved to be a marriage saver and a boost to a couple's enjoyment of sexual activity. Repetitive, painful intercourse creates some negative associations for the wife that may require many successful encounters to fully erase after correction of the problem.

The couple whose story we shared in chapter 2 had difficulty because the hymen made it impossible to permit intercourse. A hymeneal problem cannot *always* be determined during the premarital exam, though it often can. It may take attempting intercourse to find out if the vaginal opening will comfortably adapt. Of course, it is better to correct any problems "pre-need," but many have been repaired after a couple has had less-than-satisfactory attempts at intercourse. If you have difficulty with intercourse, seek medical attention to keep from developing an emotional aversion to sexual intimacy.

It is important to understand that the initial discomfort should go away quickly, within two to four weeks, with stretching. Sadly, many women are unsure about what is normal and have understood that pain is "part of the duty," distasteful as it may be. I have seen cases where years down the marital road, the couple has never experienced even minimally pleasurable sex, and the wife considers orgasm a figment of the novelist's imagination. Once vaginal diameter accommodates penetration, lubrication and elasticity play an even greater role. These generally cannot happen with fear and/or discomfort present.

During the premarital visit, a family or Ob/Gyn physician should make a thorough examination, particularly of the hymen, checking for thickness and whether it is completely intact or has ruptured through the normal course of events. Even an Ob/Gyn doctor is unavoidably at a bit of a disadvantage because he or she examines only the female, and a key consideration is comfortable fit.

Urethra

The external opening and short tube in the female that leads from the bladder to the exterior of the body. In the male the urethra likewise drains the bladder and is of variable length.

Uterus

Generally known as the womb, this smooth, involuntary muscular organ contains the growing baby in pregnancy. The lining of the uterus under the stimulation of the female hormones prepares each month to receive a pregnancy. When pregnancy does not occur, the thickened lining sloughs off, passes through the cervix, and exits through the vagina as the "menstrual flow." This process occurs slowly so that the blood has time to clot within the uterus and the clots have time to dissolve before passing out of the uterus. Thus none are visible externally. If the flow is a bit more vigorous, the blood will clot in the uterus and pass as clots into the vagina. This is also completely normal. The passage of clots through the cervix is the cause of menstrual cramps. Women with heavy flooding, numerous clots, and incapacitating cramps should seek medical attention.

Since this organ is mostly muscular, it contracts rhythmically with orgasm. Some women feel this sensation is pleasurable; others hardly notice it. This has significance for those considering surgical removal of the uterus (hysterectomy). Knowing in advance that the operation may affect orgasm can help alleviate concern and surprise. It has been suggested that a woman can exercise her uterus for greater sexual enjoyment. For the record, this is a myth. In the workbook we have provided an exercise that women *can* do to aid in increasing sexual pleasure.

Ovaries

The paired "egg producing" organs of the female. They vary in size depending on the day of a woman's menstrual cycle. At their smallest, they are about the size of a walnut, and with normal monthly follicle development, one may reach approximately twice that size. At birth, a little girl has all the eggs she will ever use, stored in approximately 300,000 to 400,000 follicles, tiny cysts in the ovaries. Only about 300 to 400 of these will ever mature and release from the ovary during the monthly ovulation cycle, unlike the male's sperm, which a healthy man produces daily.

Each month a number of potential eggs from this vast group will begin the egg maturation process. This happens at the culmination of puberty, which takes place over several years and usually begins between ages nine and thirteen. It involves the development of cysts, fluid-filled sacs in which the egg develops. The most responsive of these prospects goes on to maturity and is expelled from the small cyst, a process called "ovulation" or egg release. Occasionally several eggs may be released in one cycle, increasing the possibility of fraternal (non-identical) twins or triplets.

In a normal, functioning ovary, a cyst develops each month on one side or the other and grows until it is approximately two centimeters in length (a bit less than an inch). This normal cyclical enlargement in the ovary can cause discomfort during lifting, exercise, and sexual activity. At ovulation, the cyst "ruptures" to release the egg, causing sharp pain— known as *mittleschmertz*—at midcycle in some women. This is a normal process but it can cause discomfort. Occasionally it will rupture across a blood vessel and leak blood into the abdominal cavity. The resulting pain and sufficient bleeding may, on rare occasions, require hospitalization and/or surgery for pain relief. This occurrence is rare considering the number of "ovulatory events." I have seen three to five in my years of practice. If this happens, it does not alter fertility nor affect lovemaking, and for most women it heals on its own.

Some women with highly irregular cycles need to be more careful about going on the pill—by irregular I mean one cycle of perhaps thirty-five days, the next twelve, then sixty. This may indicate a significant ovarian malfunction. These nonovulatory cycles can allow cysts to form that are larger and more tender than average and require medical evaluation.

Fallopian tubes

These come in pairs. They are connected at one end to the top corners of the uterus and delicately extend to an opening right next to the ovaries. They function by picking up the egg released by an ovary and moving it gently down (not like a drainpipe, but with tiny hairlike structures called cilia) to the portion of the tube where the sperm may fertilize the egg. This structure can be interrupted surgically by cutting, tying, cauterizing with electricity (tubal, tubal ligation, tubes tied) or other available techniques as a permanent method of birth control.

Pubococcygeus (PC) muscles

These are involuntary muscles that extend from the pubic bone in front to the tailbone in back. They surround the vagina, urethra, and anus, and in concert with several other muscles provide support to the floor of the pelvis. This design helps prevent any organs from making their way down the birth canal and "hanging out." Additionally, with exercise and learning

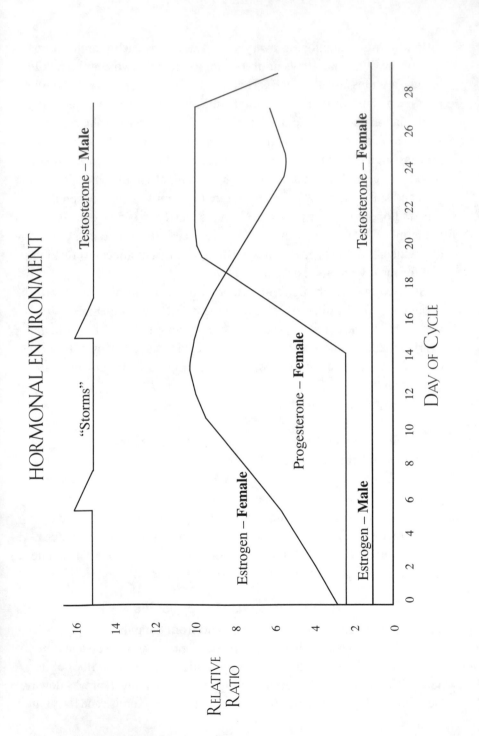

HORMONAL ENVIRONMENT

"Storms"

Testosterone – **Male**

Estrogen – **Female**

Progesterone – **Female**

Estrogen – **Male**

Testosterone – **Female**

RELATIVE RATIO

0 2 4 6 8 10 12 14 16 18 20 22 24 26 28

DAY OF CYCLE

0 2 4 6 8 10 12 14 16

to control these muscles, the vaginal diameter can be managed to generate pleasurable friction during intercourse.

Thoughts or touch can trigger the tightening of these muscles. Voluntary tightening can increase sexual pleasure. But the strong, involuntary tightening of these muscles is called vaginismus, or muscular spasms of the vagina. Usually triggered by pain, vaginismus can be brought about by unwanted penetration, a "bad fit," or painful memories. We generally recommend time, tenderness, and intimacy exercises to remedy this situation.

Women can do exercises to strengthen these muscles and thus increase sexual pleasure. We have included them in the workbook section corresponding to this chapter.

Menstrual cycle

The monthly process triggered by the brain and messenger hormones from the pituitary, a small gland at the base of the brain. It includes maturation and release of the egg and preparation of the uterine lining for the arrival and implantation of an embryo. In the absence of pregnancy, the cycle concludes with the sloughing and discharge of the lining cells of the uterus, called menstrual flow or menstruation.

This entirely normal process is cloudy and mysterious in the minds of many husbands who prefer to escape to the solitude and darkness of their "caves" during their wives' dreaded "time of the month." For some men, overcoming the embarrassment of buying tampons for their wives may be their idea of sacrificial love, but there is no substitute for comprehending this process and communicating a sense of understanding and support to one's spouse.

Simple education about hormonal events that trigger this normal variation can help alleviate fear and trepidation. It can also promote a compassionate understanding of emotional peaks and valleys that are quite normal, and to a considerable degree, inescapable. This beautiful cycle is a complex symphony of hormonal crescendo and decrescendo that carries the woman physically and emotionally through the month.

The average woman cycles between twenty-five and thirty-five days. The twenty-eight-day lunar month is selected as the "norm," but many women experience regular cycles on a different set schedule. The fixed portion of the cycle is the portion following ovulation, lasting twelve to fourteen days. Thus, the major variable is the number of days prior to ovulation, which can range from ten to twenty-one days and still be entirely normal. This is vital to understanding the fertile period and anticipating those hormonal times when the husband's thoughtfulness may be met with what seems to be semiautomatic weaponry.

Estrogen, the dominant female hormone, has its major peak around ovulation and a secondary, smaller peak later in the cycle. Estrogen is responsible for the "feminization" of the female adolescent. This includes fatty breast and hip deposits, maturation of the genital organs, and a gentle increase in the libido.

Thus, strictly from the hormonal stimulus, women generally have a stronger sexual desire around the time of ovulation. This "window" of opportunity lasts approximately twenty-four to forty-eight hours. Many husbands have asked how to open this "window" for longer stretches of time. However, the hormonal environment plays only one small part in creating the romantic atmosphere that supports satisfying marital intimacy. In other words, acting with kindness can open other "windows" of sexual interest, desire, and passion.

The second, milder elevation of estrogen often gets lost in the strong surge of progesterone, the powerful hormone that follows ovulation. Progesterone, the "pro-gestational" or "pro-pregnancy" hormone, reaches a high level seven to ten days after ovulation. If pregnancy occurs, it will remain high in normal situations. Besides the positive effect of preparing the uterus for pregnancy, progesterone causes bloating, fullness, and a general crankiness that for some women can be overwhelming each month in the premenstrual phase.

The premenstrual portion of the cycle can be so difficult for some women that the diagnosis of "premenstrual syndrome" or PMS is used. Symptoms go beyond the normal cyclical bloating and moodiness to depression, rage, sleeplessness, and other significant life-disrupting symptoms. A myriad of theories has been advanced to explain this perplexing collection of symptoms. Only in the past generation has this "syndrome" been appreciated as a reality and not as "just all in her head." Multiple therapies with variable success attest to the fact that medical science has yet to fully unravel the tangled yarn of this problem. Most physicians will chart the symptoms with a "PMS diary" and then continue to track the significant problems during therapy to see which ones improve. Vitamin therapy with or without minerals, thyroid, progesterone, and antidepressant mood-elevating drugs have been tried. Each regimen has enjoyed some success, but some patients do not respond at all.

We now have evidence that different women metabolize or break down progesterone via different enzyme pathways, producing different end products. The chemicals result in sleepiness for one, rage in another, and depression in yet another. If this theory proves true, it would explain why progesterone therapy makes some women better and some worse. Those with the enzyme that breaks down progesterone into a compound causing drowsiness will do much better than those with the enzyme pathway that produces a compound causing restlessness, anger, or depression. If medical science can develop a compound that will block the harmful pathway, many women may finally find relief from this debilitating condition.

Others suggest that a defect in the production or secretion of serotonin, a chemical in the brain, causes some of the difficulties associated with PMS. Further investigation is currently underway.

When we look at our parts individually and as they function together, we see behind them an intelligent and wise Creator. We move now to look at how He, in His wisdom, created them to work together as "two become one."

5

THE SEXUAL RESPONSE CYCLE

I have come into my garden, my sister, my bride;
I have gathered my myrrh along with my balsam.
I have eaten my honeycomb and my honey;
I have drunk my wine and my milk.
—Song of Solomon 5:1

B eth gets home from work first, so she starts dinner. Nicholas arrives and gives her a little peck on the cheek. He plays with the kids; then they have supper. Nick helps the oldest child finish her homework, then he and Beth put the children to bed. While she does the dishes, he sits down, hunts for the remote, and reads the paper. They spend the remainder of the evening channel surfing. At 10:30, he collects all the garbage for tomorrow's pickup. They watch the 11:00 news, then it's bedtime. He pads off to the bathroom, does his little chores, and changes into his bedtime attire. She does the same thing and they climb in bed. They read for a while, perhaps, then he reaches over and turns off his light. She reads awhile longer, then finally reaches over and turns off her light. Everything is still. And then suddenly, in the dark, there it is. A cold hand on her breast. Then Nick kisses her ear. Seven minutes later, everything is over. Nick snores while Beth stares at the ceiling. Again. The next morning, Nick wonders why Beth just lies there when they make love.

Nick isn't a clod, and Beth isn't uninterested; they are both uninformed. Neither of them is demonstrating an understanding of the differences in how men and women generally view the sexual process. Their love life reflects how little they genuinely "know" each other. So what do they and others in the same situation need to know? Here are some differences in how men and women view the sex process. Please note that these are *generalizations*. Men and women vary in their responses.

- Men are primarily quick to respond physically; women are moved along more gently. Some have said "Men are like light bulbs; women are like electric irons," or "Men are like gas stoves, and women are like crock pots."
- To a man, sex is primarily about meeting mostly physical needs with some emotional needs; to a woman, sex is primarily about meeting mostly emotional needs with some physical needs (this may become more balanced through the process of aging). Thus a husband can come home, slam the door, and ask, "Howz about it?" Rarely do we hear of such behavior from wives. As one writer observes, "For most men, being sexual is a way of being intimate. Women usually see sex as a precursor to being intimate. It sounds terribly traditional and old-fashioned, but still it is true: when men feel lonely and hurt, they want to be held and make love. When women feel hurt, they want to be understood and talked to. This difference is very confusing and causes incredible problems between couples."[1]

"According to the men I interviewed, when it comes to sex, a deep emotional bond has definite physical benefits," says Peter Wish, Ph.D., a Florida sex therapist. "Some women just can't achieve orgasm unless they know they're in a love relationship. While that's not true for many men, an emotional bond can definitely add to a man's physical pleasure."

Missy, who came to know the Lord after she got married, admits, "Before I was a Christian, I was very promiscuous. I had multiple sexual encounters, and I faked orgasm every time. Not until I married did I actually experience one. I had to have love and security and a patient husband for sex to 'work right' for me."

In addition, enjoying sex may be hard for a woman if she feels angry or distracted. But some men can stop in the middle of a loud argument— in which anger permeates the air—and desire sex; then they can return to the fight. A woman has a harder time shifting gears into sexual mode and then resuming the argument afterward.

"Most of us have a difficult time responding sexually when we're angry and upset, particularly if the problem hasn't yet been resolved," writes Vickie Kraft in *The Influential Woman*. "This is true because most women really love with their whole being while most men seem to be more compartmentalized. Your husband may not even like you on a given day but he probably will manage to maintain his interest in the sexual relationship anyway."[2]

Even Christian men at marriage conferences admit that they could be tempted to have sex with a total stranger; their wives stand aghast. They cannot understand how it is possible for a man to be so tempted sexually by somebody he doesn't love or even know.[3]

Men and women appear to have some disparity in the degree of emotional involvement necessary to engage in or enjoy sex, although the gap may be narrowing. One recent study found that in a test group of 1,049 men and women aged eighteen to sixty-five, nearly eight out of ten respondents said it is difficult to have sex without emotional involvement. While most women have traditionally linked sex with feelings of affection, more men are now agreeing. In 1984, 59 percent of men studied said they found it difficult to have sex without having a love relationship with the woman involved. A staggering 71 percent of men studied in America in 1994 said that the emotional side of sex was very important. In both studies, 86 percent of women said they felt this way.[4]

- A man can separate love from sex; a woman has more difficulty doing so. For her, affection and physical expression are more intertwined. At times a woman longs much more for the closeness and intimacy of the sex act than she does for the thrill of it, while a man more often longs for the thrill, while he enjoys the closeness and intimacy. This may change a bit with age, too. In one study, men under thirty-five reported liking intercourse more than foreplay, but once they reached thirty-five, a higher percentage of men reported liking foreplay more.[5]
- Men tend to be event-oriented. Many husbands can see their wives in anything or nothing, and they want sex. Conversely, women tend

to be process-oriented. Sex for them is not an event but an environment. Thus mood and surroundings may play bigger roles.

- Although men become aroused in a variety of ways, visual stimulation is the favorite. In other words, they are stimulated *primarily* by sight. They like to see women in sexy attire, and they like to see naked women. Many wives readily testify that their husbands enjoy watching them undress and that, upon seeing their wives naked, men become aroused in a few seconds. A lot of women find this hard to understand because they experience arousal so differently. Women respond, though generally more gently, to stimuli from any or all of the senses with the addition of gentleness and affection. According to researchers, "Men are usually much more intensely aroused by sexually viewing women than are females viewing men. . . . Females are usually much more excited at being seen by men than males are at being viewed by women. Many women deny that being viewed has sexual meaning for them; they say that they wish only to 'be attractive.' So if a man goes beyond sexual delight and into sexual leering, women will likely feel hurt and resentful."[6]
- Men tend to hunger for a variety of sexual practices while women tend to want variety of mood and atmosphere. A man will fantasize about having sex in every room of the house or every seat of the car in every position possible. The woman's perspective is often closer to, "That's not even *comfortable!* But would you like me to light some candles and put on some soft music?"

Now that we understand some general emotional and intellectual differences in how men and women approach sex, it's also important to understand how their bodies experience different physical changes during the act of lovemaking. Masters and Johnson have assigned four labels to describe the textbook outline of what is "supposed to happen" during the phases of the normal sexual response cycle: Excitement, Plateau, Orgasm, and Resolution. We will now discuss these with accompanying time frames and intervals. But we have broken them into five categories with lighthearted labels that we feel reflect more of the "art" of lovemaking than the clinical science: Sex is a Mood-Making, Heart-Shaking, Earth-Quaking, Out-of-Body, Near-Death experience.

Imagine sitting in a room with four other people. All of you receive the latest Spiegel catalog and are asked to choose the most beautiful model and the nicest outfit. Of course, you would probably choose different "favorites." In the same way, imagine walking into the Hermitage Museum in St. Petersburg, Russia. If you spent thirty seconds looking at each of the Rembrandts, Picassos, DaVincis, and all the other works of art, it would take several years to see it all. Imagine being told to choose the most beautiful painting. It would be the best painting *to you*, but there would be no one *right* answer for everyone. Yet people often try to classify sex as "normal frequency" and "normal order of events." Everyone is different. Not only is variation enormous from person to person, but variations also occur within an individual during the course of a lifetime. So always keep in mind that what works for you as a couple is what's "normal" for you.

And now for the first stage:

Mood-Making

If we equate sex with dining, this would be the hors d'oeuvres. Others have labeled this "excitation" or "arousal." It's that time of initial interest, the warm, fuzzy glow of attraction. As we said, all five of our senses can serve as channels to arousal. A marathon runner may jog past a home where he or she always smells bacon frying; it may stir the desire to stop in for breakfast. In the same way, our sexual appetites receive stimuli. Something visual may trigger it—someone or even some*thing* attractive. The moon over the ocean or a light snowfall might "put you in the mood." A sound might start it—someone's voice, a song, or a word. It could be a smell such as the scent of a favorite perfume. (In some cultures, sweat would make this list.) Sometimes a thought or a memory can set the process in motion. And, of course, touch arouses—sometimes it's as simple as casually brushing against someone's arm and realizing, "This person is a member of the opposite sex." It might be a passing moment of "connection"; or it could become more significant and sustained. God made us such that different body parts and shapes appeal to different appetites, so we have no "standard" for what everyone considers universally attractive.

Advertisers, of course, attempt to connect their products with that positive sense of arousal. Consider, for example, a TV commercial that takes us through the thought processes of a couple of strangers who meet on an elevator. As they ride together on the elevator, they notice they are wearing the same brand of jeans, and they progress mentally from romance to a wedding and childbirth before they ever reach the ground floor.

Do you know the cologne she likes? Use it. Do you know the color he likes? Wear it (or if he likes nudity, don't wear it and think of the money you will save). Consider lighting and location. Do the ocean or the mountains "do it for you"? These things are all a matter of taste. Men tend to be more adventurous, experimental, even territorial. Women tend to be more attuned to atmosphere for the stirring of desire. Do you know and do those things that entice each other's imagination? Expand those thoughts to incorporate all the senses.

In Song of Solomon 1:13, the bride says this to her groom:

"My beloved is to me a pouch of myrrh
Which lies all night between my breasts."

In Solomon's day a woman often wore a small pouch of myrrh around her neck at night. The perfume would provide a lingering fragrance as she slept. Her sense of smell would remind her of him all night long. Thus, she connected this aroma with her love for him. Her culture placed great emphasis on bringing all five senses to bear in their lovemaking, with scent emphasized most.

Gender differences may play a role here, too. We are not suggesting these are necessarily *innate* differences. But if a woman has been home with toddlers all day, she may need "all-day foreplay"—not physical fondling, but a kiss in the morning, a call at noon, then the sight of her hubby cleaning house, shopping, or doing chores unexpectedly. These actions sometimes serve as much better turn-ons than seeing him emerge from the bathroom in a pair of silk boxers. As author Kathy Peel has written, "Going to the grocery store on his way home, asking if he could build some shelves in my closet, helping me refinish the garage sale treasures to brighten our tiny house, listening to me, caring about what was important in my life—if he wanted me to be in the mood at night, he needed to do what he could to make the day go well." Add romantic dinners, flowers, poetry, and active listening—these provide the affectionate, nongenital contact she needs to fill her mind and imagination with thoughts of her man.

Aside from mental stirring or stimulation, physical changes take place. In males, penile erection is the dominant symptom. The penis becomes erect and hard, and muscles under the skin around the testicles contract, causing them to draw up against his body more tightly. The erection may persist and escalate or diminish as he "deals with" the stimuli. For example, when a woman with flowing, dark hair spins around, if she turns out to be the creepy Crypt keeper from television's "Tales of the Crypt," it can literally "kill the mood." Or the stop light changes and he must drive on, leaving the beautiful girl and his fantasy evaporating with the exhaust fumes.

Usually when a woman is stimulated, she experiences lubrication of the vaginal opening (tiny beads like perspiration form). She may lubricate in response to an attractive man and not even be aware of it. One or both of her nipples may also become erect. And she may have clitoral swelling or "congestion" caused by blood and fluid collecting in the sexual organs. The labia majora and minora swell, and heart and breathing rates generally increase.

God designed our genitals to become aroused. What we *do* with that arousal is our responsibility. It's one thing to appreciate beauty when you see it. But it's another to drive around the block to get a better look. "We can learn to enjoy the eyes, the hair, the smile, the strength of shoulders and arms, the curve of hips and legs, without leering and lusting," explains author Richard Foster. "They are lovely gifts from the Creator's hand. How dare we despise them!"[7]

The enjoyment of beauty does not need to be wicked; it simply needs to be controlled—and it can be. We can appreciate the lovely form of biceps or breast without falling headlong into uncontrolled passion.

Arousal whets the sexual appetite in the same way that a banquet table covered with food gets the gastric juices flowing. It does not necessarily require "gorging," but it gently or not-so-gently turns the mind toward sexual fulfillment. Sometimes sight is enough.

Later in Song of Solomon, we read what he says about his beloved, the Shulammite. He begins in 6:13 by speaking to the maidens who admire her:

"How you gaze upon Shulamith as at the
dance of Mahanaim!"

Then in 7:1 he addresses his bride:

"How beautiful are your feet in sandals,
O prince's daughter!
The curves of your hips are like jewels,
The work of the hands of an artist."

Leading Bible authorities believe that "curves of your hips" here refers to the swaying motion as she dances before Solomon.[8]

Dancing as part of the process of arousal? Perhaps. Variety on many
levels is important. Even if you tend to be unadventuresome, it's good
for you, once in a while, to try the sexual equivalent of a raw oyster,
sushi, Borscht, or even if you're really a roast beef-and-potatoes kind of
person, a taco.

A woman at one of my (Dr. Bill's) marriage seminars questioned her
husband's spirituality because he had requested colorful, revealing lingerie. Since this was during the holiday season, I said, "Nobody wants
all his or her Christmas presents wrapped in brown paper." We're guessing that neither the "thong" nor the string bikini was invented by women,
certainly not by those who wanted to hide extra weight. But couples
should seek plenty of creativity and variety here.

The need for interesting attire is important for men to consider, too.
While males generally find themselves attracted to bikinis on women,
many women say "gross" when they see men wearing Speedo bathing
suits. Yet though there appears to be no exact parallel for "what works,"
women do have *some* visual orientation—find out what she considers
fun or interesting and wear it.

In Song of Solomon 4:9, the groom writes,

"You have made my heart beat faster
with a single glance of your eyes,
With a single strand of your necklace."

If "fed," it leads to the next stage.

Heart-Shaking

We often call this foreplay. In lovemaking, this process begins with gentle physical stimulation of sensitive areas—kissing, hugging, fondling, and caressing. It involves an increasing level of arousal, intensity of feelings, and a desire for further physical contact. Kissing is a good indicator of a couple's level of ongoing passion. In the beginning of Song of Solomon 1:2, we read this:

> "May he kiss me with the kisses of his mouth!
> For your love is better than wine."

Wine works as an "uninhibitor." Once touch begins, if both partners are willing, their expression of physical love makes them share more vulnerably than a glass of wine could. In fact, the Hebrew word for "love" used here often refers to physical expressions of romantic, sexual love. Sustaining this stage usually requires physical contact—effective, pleasurable stimulation.

Earth-Quaking

Others label this "excitation" or the "plateau." The key problem with the "plateau" label is that it gives the impression that things stay the same. Geographically, it's more like driving up and down some hills than cruising along the rim of the Grand Canyon. This stage varies considerably in length and degree. During the third part of the sexual process, the same physical changes continue, but with greater intensity. It's like the title of a song that Carole King sang in the 70s, "I Feel the Earth Move."

If we use the food analogy, this would be the dining itself. Some days you like home cooking; other times you want a Big Mac and fries. Other occasions might require beef Wellington. But all can be satisfying and pleasurable, and each "dinner" can last variable lengths of time. Like a menu, it may include a variety of options (different positions, locations, and ambiance). You don't want the same steak cooked the same way every night. You have your favorites, but when you have them three times a week, you long for some variety.

During a given encounter, a woman may experience a short, intermediate or long "earth-quaking" stage. The length of this period doesn't matter. To the best of my knowledge, medically and theologically, there are no awards or prizes for the shortest or longest plateau phases. It is a matter of an individual's unique design. It may be variable, unpredictable, or prolonged even beyond "normal" experience, assuming the spouse can maintain the endeavor the desired length of time. She may not even be desirous of orgasm on some occasions and be quite content to remain for long periods of time in this pleasurable "zone."

In men, this stage can last for as little as three to five minutes. It is important to understand that this is not a race; no one wins any ribbons for "doing it" quickly. It's not like steer roping where you try to be the fastest to "get the job done." Nor is it like bull riding where an eight-second ride is okay. Control is the key. During this time the erection is most firm and achieves its greatest size. Men release small amounts of seminal fluid during this phase preceding ejaculation.

Some studies would indicate that the number one sexual difficulty among married couples is "premature ejaculation" (PE). We must clarify that these couples define PE, not as a "formal, medical sexual dysfunction," but as times when "he ejaculates before she is ready for him to." This being the case, it is nearly universal that a man will experience it sometimes, perhaps even often.

Some women have a short plateau phase. However, most women report, "It takes me too long." At one conference when the men were asked how long they thought this stage generally lasted for wives, they answered "hours!" Most women need an average of ten to fifteen minutes of uninterrupted stimulation, which includes contact with the clitoris, to reach orgasm. And many women need even more time than this. This stage may lead to orgasm, but orgasm is not inevitable, required, or even absolutely desired in every instance for either men or women.

One woman reported, "It takes thirty to forty minutes, sometimes more. I get self-conscious because I'm taking so long. Then that slows me down because I'm distracted." The ten- to fifteen-minute figure is an average range or guideline; it's merely a scientific observation based on intervals that women have reported. (Of course, it's also true that humans compulsively alter the facts in relation to sexual performance and prowess.)

While we don't condone the lifestyle described by another woman,

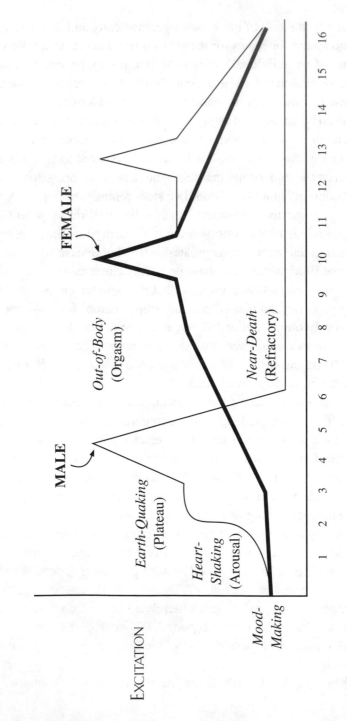

she makes an important point about the plateau phase: "When I slept with guys before I got married, I faked orgasm within five to seven minutes. I didn't know that there's a long plateau of ten to fifteen minutes for most women. I had been married for a while before I ever had an orgasm, and part of the delay was that we expected it to take less time. The women my husband had been with were also 'fast.' Now I wonder, *Have I ruined sex for my partners who are probably all now husbands? Are they expecting their wives to orgasm every time, and in five minutes?* The women my husband slept with before we got married were pretty similar. I wonder if they faked it, too. We both had expectations that it would go a lot faster for me, and probably part of why I never had an orgasm until I'd been married for a while was because we simply hadn't 'stayed with it' long enough."

Making love is an art. In the same way that a person who completes a "paint-by-number" picture has made a picture without any personal technique, so the person who understands all the statistics about sex does not necessarily become a good lover. Nor do the statistics indicate couples are "bad" lovers because they have sex less frequently or it takes longer for them. Sex is very personal. More important than knowing what is "usual" and "average" is knowing what works for you. God designed us to have art and mystery. We're each unique, so enjoy the experience and grow *together.*

Out-of-Body

This is orgasm, climax, or "dessert." Some describe it as explosive, rhythmic pelvic muscle contractions. Others describe a more gradual elevation of variable intensity and duration. It's extremely pleasurable by design (though the range of individual experiences may include "good," "great," or "so what?").

During orgasm, men ejaculate, releasing about a teaspoonful of semen that normally contains several million sperm. The heart rate elevates, breathing quickens, and the end of the world as we know it approaches. He experiences multiple rhythmic contractions of the vesicles within the prostate gland, ejaculatory ducts, and muscles in the pelvis and penis. His sensations feel more localized than hers, with intense feelings directed toward the pelvis and penis.

A woman experiences the involuntary contraction of her muscles surrounding the outer portion of the vagina, which includes a thrusting of the pelvis. Contractions of other body muscles may also occur. This whole-body event generally brings intense pleasure and relief. Most women do not technically ejaculate, though the rhythmic contractions of the pelvis, the heart rate, and breathing are similar. Generally women return to the "earth-quaking" or plateau phase after climax. Some can stay stimulated, desiring perhaps further sexual attention.

"Do women really have orgasms?" This question comes up frequently in the premarriage counselor's office. The answer is yes. Unfortunately, some wives don't even realize they've had them. If you are relaxed and satisfied after sexual relations, you may have had one, though it may have been a quiet one. Sex expert Jennifer Korneich, author of *Mindblowing Sex in the Real World* (HarperCollins), says men call in to her talk show asking "How can I make sure she's had an orgasm?" The answer is that she herself may not know.

Some women (and a few men) think orgasm is overrated and not worth the effort. Like desserts with varying calorie counts, orgasms come in many varieties, some "better than others." You don't always have to have dessert. But if you do, it can be as plain as applesauce with cookies or as exotic as flaming bananas Foster.

Near-Death

This is the resolution or refractory period. While "near death" may seem like an unusual label, it's been around for a while: "The mythical connection between sex and death in European culture gave rise to the term *le petit mort*, or 'the little death.' . . . Read *The Canonization*, by the 16th- and 17th-century poet John Donne, and you'll find reference to the superstition that each orgasm subtracts a day from one's life."[9]

At the time of orgasm, the body experiences the release of endorphins, a potent morphine/narcoticlike substance within the brain. Endorphins are addictive in that they create a desire for more. They also relieve minor aches and pains. (Thus, as has often been said, "Sex is good for what ails you.") For most, they produce a contented afterglow, as the satisfied lovers enjoy the pleasurable sensation of intimacy—relaxed, refreshed, and renewed.

However, if endorphin levels are high, they can make a person quite drowsy, so that postfiesta becomes a siesta. The sensation of drowsiness peaks one to two minutes after orgasm and subsides over the next quarter of an hour. This is "near death" in that endorphins can cause a comalike syndrome, especially in men. (Okay, we confess—we've exaggerated—they do remain conscious.) During this time, lasting ten minutes to a lifetime (it seems), the husband becomes physically incapable of achieving a significant functional erection. Wives, don't dial 911—just make sure he's breathing (some men may not be brought around by anything but an ensuing football kickoff). Or better still, knowing his partner may as yet feel unsatisfied, he will focus his time and attention on her need.

Most women have a deep desire for affection during this time, and some desire multiple orgasms. But men usually become totally uninterested in sex within a minute or two of climax. Some men will jump up and take a shower, others roll over and fall asleep while their wives lie there feeling unhappy. Most men cannot immediately have another erection and orgasm, and will relax and go to sleep more quickly than their wives. Men need to be sensitive here; and wives need to understand that a husband's drowsiness isn't rejection.

For a woman, engorgement returns to normal more gradually than for her husband. The process happens still more slowly if she has not experienced orgasm. Sometimes the husband can bring his wife to orgasm for the first or multiple times by other types of stimulation after he has ejaculated.

Not everyone falls asleep after sex. As one man noted, "Some nights after sex I immediately fall asleep, and other nights, as with any other athletic activity, I'm energized and ready to get some work done." Women report similar experiences.

I did have one case of a female patient claiming to pass out, but if she truly did, I don't think it was due to an endorphin rush. It started when I overheard my secretary handling a call: "Do you want me to call an ambulance? . . . Unconscious? . . . What happened?"

The man on the phone told her, "We were making love—vigorously. And now she's unconscious."

"Is she breathing?"

"Yes, I think so."

"Good. I'll get the doctor."

When I took the phone to handle this "medical crisis," the patient was awakening. I tried to provide some reassuring words to her partner until she could speak to me. When she did, I asked her questions such as "Do you know your name?" "What's the date?" and "Who is the president of the U.S. today?" Then in the solemn tone of a trained medical professional, I asked if she often passed out during romantic activities. She replied (with her partner obviously nearby), "Oh, no. No one has ever excited me like that." This was their first time together, and apparently the combination of hyperventilation, breath holding, and a tight torso squeeze from her partner had made her lose consciousness.

Every time this patient called or stopped in at the office, comments about her partner's incredible technique surfaced. He shattered the mystery one day when he arrived with her, and to everyone's disappointment, he turned out to be a rather average-looking guy. But clearly, in her heart and mind, he was Superman.

And somewhere out there I'm guessing that yet another myth is being propagated by a couple who believe that passing out is an indication of great sex rather than an indication that the brain needs oxygen.

So there we have it, the five stages that make up a mood-making, heart-shaking, earth-quaking, out-of-body, near-death experience.

Unfortunately, all too often, the man experiences all five of these stages while the woman receives little pleasure. An understanding of how we think and experience sex can greatly enhance enjoyment for both partners. Researchers have documented much more technical information than we have provided, but in all my years as a doctor, nobody seemed particularly interested in which muscles contracted, why the testicles elevate at orgasm, which veins congest permitting erection, or anything like that. The questions they asked me were generally more practical. Do we need to make simultaneous orgasms our goal? Are "quickies" okay? How can we increase the percentage of times we both experience orgasm? Those practical matters, covered in the next chapter, are indeed the issues that can make or break truly satisfying sexual intimacy.

THE WEDDING NIGHT
AND BEYOND

Your lips, my bride, drip honey;
Honey and milk are under your tongue,
And the fragrance of your garments is like the fragrance of Lebanon.
—Song of Solomon 4:11

B onnie and Steve are pretty good at caring and communicating, and they have what they describe as a "decent" love life together, which involves having sex about twice a week. However, Bonnie is rarely interested initially, and she almost never initiates. Steve's parameters for what he's comfortable doing during lovemaking are wider than hers. She sometimes feels self-conscious that she is not the lover he wants her to be, both because she feels uncomfortable with some of what he wants her to do and also because it takes her longer to reach orgasm than she would like, when she does at all. Steve, on the other hand, gets there rapidly and often finishes just as she is "getting warmed up." They frequently resort to "quickies" rather than endure the frustration of "it happened again."

If it's any consolation, Bonnie and Steve are in good company.

As we said earlier, everyone has sexual difficulties. Why? Because we live in a fallen world. Others take advantage of our nature—our baser desires—appealing to our greed, lust, and self-indulgence; and we cooperate with them! Thus we have distorted views of physical intimacy. When Russia opened to the non-Communist world after seventy years, the first Western influences to race in were the black market, MTV, and prostitution. A growing percentage of the Internet is devoted to pornography or "chat rooms" where people can write their fantasies to strangers.

Most guys learn about sex from less-than-accurate sources such as locker rooms, "adult" reading material, and Internet chat rooms. "Studs" bombard each other with information having a 98 percent margin for error, then mix in the "Hollywood Factor." That is, they buy in to the belief that movies accurately depict reality, and come to believe most people must be having sex on the floor of the office copy room, in elevators, or hanging from chandeliers.

Next, there are influences from our individual backgrounds over which we have little control. If your parents were Lucy and Ricky Ricardo, you thought married couples slept in twin beds, and you figured conception was a miraculous deal. (Most couples act as though they never have sex, so kids assume their parents only made love the number of times necessary to produce the children in the home.)

Most of us do not initially learn about sex from our parents, even though our parents may be Christian. "I looked up 'Sex' in the encyclopedia when I hit sixth grade," shared a young bride-to-be whose parents expected her to figure things out on her own. Another woman explained, "I read *The Joy of Sex*. I found the drawings highly amusing."

"I'd been introduced to sex through *Playboy* magazines placed carelessly on a neighbor's coffee table," writes Kathy Peel in *Today's Christian Woman*. "Even as an eight-year-old, I had lasting impressions of those images. They made me think women were only objects men used for their own pleasure. Then a frightening experience with a boy from junior high further scarred my most fundamental thoughts about sex. Although I wasn't actually raped, he forced me into a dark bathroom and sexually abused me. In the early years of our marriage, I found it difficult to reconcile these memories with my role as a wife. My desires to please my husband and enjoy sexual intimacy were in conflict with my feelings of anger and guilt. I asked God to renew my mind with his perspective on sex."[1]

At one end of the spectrum there are those who have learned from their parents or in church that sex is "dirty." The whole process is shrouded in shame. One of my nurses said, "My mom still insists on undressing in the dark. My dad has never seen her undress in their decades of marriage."

The daughter of Russian author Leo Tolstoy wrote in her journal of her mother's attitude about sex: "I am very happy to think that I am a virgin and have not had to undergo that fearful humiliation all married women suffer, as Mother's remarks have made so clear to me; she was so ashamed the morning after her wedding that she did not want to leave her room. She hid her face in the pillow and cried. I am proud not to have known that and I wish I may never know it!"[2]

An old *Saturday Night Live* sketch, "The Church Lady," sums up some religious attitudes toward sex: "Could it be Satan?"

Even if we are exposed to healthy attitudes about sex, most people participating in premarital sex report experiencing their first sexual encounters against a backdrop of fears about pregnancy and a need to rush to keep from getting caught. According to surveys, almost everyone has had unwanted, powerful sexual fantasies, has masturbated, or has looked at something pornographic. In addressing a Baptist youth group recently, the youth leader learned that only one member had never viewed an X-rated or NC-17 movie—the pastor's son.

About 82 percent of our young people have had sexual relations with a member of the opposite sex by age nineteen. This means fewer than one-fifth of newlyweds will be virgins. Furthermore, before they even graduate from high school, one-fifth of all students will have had at least four partners. And if current trends continue, a majority of today's high school students will live with a sex partner prior to getting married. In a large proportion of those situations, the cohabitants will never marry each other, although they will have sexual relations with each other many times before dissolving the relationship.

The human mind has an amazing ability to sometimes remember the very details we most need to forget. Fantasies, graphic movie scenes, and personal experiences follow couples into their intimate life together, usually to their detriment.

Our minds are in need of repair. We need confession and cleansing, understanding, and a reworking of our thoughts and attitudes. Having worked with couples for years as a physician and now as a pastor, I have noticed that many problems and questions follow fairly consistent patterns. So here is a representative sampling gleaned from the office and from marriage seminar participants. If a question has been asked repeatedly by women and generally not by men (or vice versa), I have indicated this by wording the question from a gender-specific point of view.

Before You Say "I Do"

Let's examine some commonly asked questions that should be settled in each person's mind prior to marrying. Some of them need to be nailed down very early on in a relationship or even before dating begins.

How far is it okay to go before marriage?

Petting, which is the fondling of breasts or genitals to arouse sexual passion, is out. Extensive and intensive "necking," which includes impassioned kissing—including neck, ears, and any erotic areas around the head and neck—can stimulate couples to desire intensely that which is reserved for marriage. This may also include French-kissing, which has been around longer than France, and which some have described as "tongue kissing," "tonsil hockey," and "swapping spit."

So what is not okay? Anything that stirs desire to sin. (That would include just about anything accompanied by moaning.) The standard is spelled out for us in 1 Thessalonians 4:3–8, which tells us not to defraud each other sexually. "Defrauding" is intentionally creating or sustaining a desire that cannot rightfully and righteously be met.

Many have defined vaginal intercourse as the only premarital no-no. Thus, many unmarried Christian couples practice oral sex, anal sex, Cybersex, phone sex, and "outercourse" (where there is intentional prolonged contact without penetration). They engage in these practices rationalizing that they have adhered to God's standard. Yet God's standard draws the line at lustful *thoughts,* requiring moment-by-moment dependence on God's power and commitment to His Word.

Rationalizing couples find themselves caught up in a cycle of obtaining sexual satisfaction in illegitimate practices, followed by conviction, guilt, and a hardening of heart against the guilt so that it becomes easier to lower the standard the next time. This is a dangerous pattern. It keeps them sliding down a slippery slope as they go further each time, continually pushing the limits. It also helps them link sexual pleasure with guilt, which can create difficulties for them later.

Our culture promotes individual dating as opposed to group dating, placing young couples who feel strongly attracted to each other in settings that increase the likelihood of their violating their own and God's standards. Group settings help take some of the pressure off of couples seeking to control their urges, while helping them develop healthy social skills. Yet ultimately, the battle gets fought in the mind.

In Song of Solomon 8:8–9, we read what the bride's brothers have to say about their sister:

> "We have a little sister,
> And she has no breasts;
> What shall we do for our sister
> On the day when she is spoken for?
> If she is a wall,
> We shall build on her a battlement of silver;
> But if she is a door,
> We shall barricade her with planks of cedar."

About the time she reached puberty, they took some responsibility for her moral actions. As Glickman explains in *A Song for Lovers,*

> They devise a simple but effective formula for success. If she is a wall they will 'build on her a battlement of silver.' That means that if she is virtuous and firm against boys' advances, they'll reward her, trying to improve on what is already good. . . . Yet if she is a door, they would enclose her with planks of cedar. In other words, if she is as open as a door to advances, they would have to be stricter with her to prevent her hurting herself for marriage. If she could handle responsibility, they would give it to her; but if not, she would be restricted.[3]

Apparently, between then and the time leading to her engagement, she grew and developed as a woman of moral purity. Here in 8:10 is her later response:

"I was a wall, and my breasts were like towers;
Then I became in his eyes as one who finds peace."

Her breasts were respected. No one touched her. As Jody Dillow wrote in *Solomon on Sex*, her breasts, though "ready for love, were inaccessible."[4] "Then" in this verse is very emphatic in the original language. It seems to imply that her purity played a factor in his attraction to her.

Is the desire to marry a virgin legitimate?

Certainly. Excluding the issues of divorce and death of a spouse, shouldn't we all want to marry virgins? Men and women both should want that. So often we have a double standard that says men should "play around" before marriage but then marry "nice girls" who didn't. Even some "nice girls" want experienced men because they grow up hearing that men should know all about sex but women should be naive. The very terms we use to describe them reflect this mentality: men are studly; women are sleazy.

"I grieved when I found out my fiancé had already had sex," shared Terry. "It's really disappointing, because I've saved myself for marriage. But he has a spirit of repentance about it. So I decided that if God has forgiven him, I can, too. I realize we may have to deal with some related difficulties in the future, but I'm willing to face that because I want him in my life."

How much importance a person places on this is an individual matter. For some, marrying a person with a "past" may not be a livable option; for others, it may be workable. When deciding on a future mate, we have to ask ourselves, "What problems am I willing to live with if my future spouse does not live up to my ideal?" (recognizing that none of us meets God's standard).

In the past I was sexually abused, and that makes it difficult for me to enjoy lovemaking. What should I do?

It's been said many times that the mind is the most important sexual organ. It's perfectly normal for significant problems to stem from past abuses. It is almost impossible to get rid of mental images from the past so that they don't interfere; this may require individual counseling.

If your partner has suffered abuse, be extremely tender. Try to discover—gently and patiently—what works best for you as a couple. You may need interesting surroundings for lovemaking that are very unlike those of the negative experience. Try leaving on dim lights to help you stay visually in touch with where you are. Look into his or her face and associate. This involves making decisions to fill your mind with the truth. If the distraction happens frequently enough, it might benefit you to find a Christian counselor who specializes in sexual abuse. As a rule, most pastors do not receive enough specialized training to handle these issues.

How do I retrain myself to realize "sex is good" and start talking openly about sex?

The church through the centuries has often been of little help here. Jerome, a great Bible translator, would not allow couples to receive communion after the "bestial" act of intercourse, and he claimed that "he who too ardently loves his wife is an adulterer." Augustine spoke of the "degrading necessity of sex," and Pope Gregory I claimed that "sexual pleasure can never be without sin."[5]

One husband explained, "I thought that if I gave my life fully to the Lord, it meant I would have to stop having a good time with my wife. It was a pleasant surprise to find out God gave sex as a gift and that it's supposed to get even better."

If you struggle with the mentality that God frowns on sex, try memorizing portions of Song of Solomon, 1 Corinthians 7, or Genesis 2:25, which reads, "The man and his wife were both naked and were not ashamed" before sin entered the world. Fill your mind with what the Bible says about sex being a gift from God. Once you are married, begin with the workbook section of this text and try to work through answers with your spouse so that you begin to become comfortable with the topic. Talk about what you agree with and disagree with, and discuss your personal preferences.

How do we handle going from "Stop! Stop!" before marriage to the mentality that we must be sex gods and goddesses once we're married?

"My fiancée and I have worked hard to keep limits on ourselves during our engagement," one man told me. "How do we go from 'sex is bad' to 'sex is great' in one day after a wedding ceremony?" His fiancée added, "How am I supposed to go from 'good girl' to 'sex kitten' overnight?"

You can begin by changing "Stop, stop" to "Not yet, not yet." The best lovemaking follows covenantal commitment between partners. A 1994 study, "Sex in America," generally considered the most accurate and complete study ever done, indicated that "intimate, exclusive relationships between spouses or committed partners provide, by far, the greatest degree of sexual satisfaction.[6] Understand that God designed marriage to provide the right context for sex. Next, get rid of messages in your mind that say sex is bad. We should not teach that sex is bad. We should teach that it is sinful *outside of marriage*. Attraction and the desire for pleasure are normal, not evil. Solomon's Song of Songs gives us some direction here. Before the couple marries, we read of their passionate feelings. Yet we also read this in 3:5 of the Amplified Bible:

> "I adjure you, O daughters of Jerusalem,
> By the gazelles or by the hinds of the field,
> That you will not arouse or awaken love
> Until it pleases."

Feelings of physical passion are good. God put them there. But as was true three thousand years ago when God inspired Solomon with these words, you don't go to bed with your dating partner or your wife-to-be. Sex has boundaries. Four times in Solomon's book we read, "Don't arouse love until it pleases." The word "arouse" means a violent awakening. Both man and woman must take responsibility for stopping. It's neither "her job" nor "his job" to apply the brakes; they're both responsible for holding the line. Yet after the wedding, Solomon records that God tells them to "drink and imbibe deeply."

In courtship, it's expected that they will wait. But once married, it is expected that they will not wait. The poet seems to be indicating that this is the voice of God Himself—the silent observer, designer, and blesser of their physical love. God pronounces His full approval on everything that has taken place, encouraging them to drink deeply of His gift. He created us—designed us—as sexual creatures. He has revealed the "rules" for our benefit and in our best interest. Sin often is a consequence of indulging a natural, normal desire in the wrong way, place, or time.

Marriage involves *developing* sexual intimacy. Developing implies a process, a progression. Through understanding, practice, applying knowledge, growing in unity, maturing in love, abounding in tenderness and kindness, your unique physical love language will develop over time. Your first encounters do not have to be your best; you will probably find yourselves fumbling and groping. Yet these experiences are precious, and they are where you begin. Song of Solomon also appears to indicate that, over time, lovers gain more boldness and deeper intimacy. During courtship, the future bride says this in 1:6 about herself:

> "Do not stare at me because I am swarthy,
> For the sun has burned me."

The highest place of beauty on a Middle Eastern woman was her skin. They wore veils in the sun to keep their skin light. So she views herself as "deficient" compared to the standard of beauty in her culture. Yet after they have been married, she says this in 2:1:

> "I am the rose of Sharon,
> The lily of the valleys."

Isn't it interesting how her view of herself has changed? Earlier, she was self-conscious: "Don't stare at me." Now her self-image has risen because she sees herself as he sees her. Through time, intimacy can grow and you will become more skilled at giving and receiving pleasure together.

One wife explained how she was able to grow in responsiveness:

"One day on our honeymoon, I (Pam) had just stepped from the shower and, looking into the mirror, I began to criticize my body. [My husband] Bill was sitting on the bed, admiring his new wife. As I would comment on an area I thought needed improving, he would counter with how beautiful it was. This went on for a few minutes until he could stand it no longer. . . . He stood up, wrapped his arms around me, and told me to look straight into his eyes.

"I complied, intrigued by the mystery of what my new husband was up to. He very seriously and lovingly said, 'I will be your mirror. My eyes will reflect your beauty. You are beautiful, Pamela. You are perfect, and if you ever doubt it, come stand before me. The mirror of my eyes will tell you the true story. You are perfect for me.'

"Over the last fourteen years, whenever self-doubt was looming on the horizon, through three pregnancies and baby blues, my mirror has never stopped telling me how perfect I am for him. Because of his continual confidence-building, I have grown more sexually adventurous. In Bill's eyes I am beautiful, and in his arms I am safe."[7]

Does sex hurt the first time?

It might. Often it is painful for women, but not always. Pain certainly is not unusual or abnormal in either gender. The man's pain is generally emotional and derives from not being nearly as "studly" or in control as he expected or hoped. For both partners, a good premarital evaluation and discussion with a physician or nurse beforehand can prevent surprises and decrease some pain. A woman can do exercises to stretch the hymen, which can significantly decrease the pain that she might experience (see appendix A). Also, nervousness and anxiety can make muscles tense. The exercises in the appendix can teach a woman to relax, which will enable the muscles to reach the appropriate diameter. The "female on top" position also can give her more control of what is comfortable.

What should I expect the first time?

Anxiety, curiosity, and anticipation. Pain and pleasure. Possible disappointment. It's highly likely you will have less of a life-changing, ecstatic experience than you may have anticipated, but you have a lifetime to perfect it. Remember, too, that the occasion truly is perfect in that the two of you are together. Don't put too much pressure on the first night; it could range anywhere from beef Wellington to McDonald's. People also bring past history and experience to the occasion. Even if you both are virgins with a biblical view of sex, you probably will not have the best love lives in the world right from the beginning. Keep a sense of humor and a heart of compassion, and you'll get off to a good start.

If you're having trouble with sex, should you go to a doctor, try new things, or go to a therapist?

When a couple has difficulty, it often is hard to discern whether the problem is founded in skill, technique, or a lack of communication. I'd recommend you begin experimenting in your lovemaking. Ask each other, "What appeals to you?" What are some things you keep wishing he or she would do? What are some of your mate's wishes? Set a time in the next few days to try to do those things. Don't keep a score card, but have a goal of *gradual* progress. Be verbal about your experiences later.

Also, keep a sense of humor and a tender heart. Hard corrective/evaluative conversations should be remote from the act of lovemaking. Hug, kiss, and say "good night," then deal with matters later, when you are not surrounded by the ambiance of nudity and a sense of failure.

Often couples find themselves in a downward spiral of frustration that leads to a hard conversation that includes crying or other release of emotions. Once the sense of relief comes they feel better, but the sense of urgency is gone. Unfortunately, with the urgency gone, the motivation to work out possible solutions to the problem sometimes disappears.

Work at keeping your motivation level high. Remember those things that you said you'd do. Next time, try to "knock his socks off" or "rock her world." Rather than acting like you're having a good time when you're only pretending, communicate what you want. Without honesty, it is extremely difficult for a couple's love life to improve. In fact, habitual deception keeps many problems that couples could otherwise deal with, beneath the surface.

If none of this works, seek medical attention. If tests reveal no medical problems, physicians can refer couples to other sources who are trained to help.

7

QUESTIONS ABOUT
VARYING LEVELS OF INTEREST

On my bed night after night I sought him whom my soul loves;
I sought him but did not find him.
—Song of Solomon 3:1

S cantily clad in captivating attire, she meets him at the door with her most seductive voice. After a busy weekend, she has plotted to make his Monday night memorable. Unfortunately, he walks past her, turns on the television, and after a quick glance tells her, "Bring me a Coke and pretzels, and I'll meet you at half-time." The same man who is so visually stimulated can become somehow visually impaired by the impending football kickoff.

As is true for most couples, levels of interest and timing are often not parallel, so some interesting problems arise as a consequence.

What should be done when he is in the mood for lovemaking and she isn't?

"The most romantic line I've ever heard came after a night of—how should we put this?—it was after a passionate interlude with my wife, a wife I had to convince to participate in the passionate interlude," Ray Romano of the TV show *Everybody Loves Raymond,* said. "Afterward she turned to me and said with a very loving tone, 'That wasn't as bad as I thought it was gonna be.' "[1]

Few men ever have a "This is gonna be bad" attitude about sex. One

husband approached his wife and handed her some aspirin for her headache. "I don't have a headache," she told him with a puzzled look. "I've
been waiting to hear you say that all week!" he replied.

Sadly, the woman's "I've got a headache" syndrome is a common
problem for several reasons. First, as we have already mentioned, men's
and women's bodies have different "timing" sexually. Also, some birth
control pills (and other medications) decrease libido. And some cultural
influences send the message that men are supposed to want sex and
women aren't.

The first question to ask is, *why* is she not "in the mood"? Is it fatigue
or illness? Where is she in her menstrual cycle? Is there an underlying
marital problem? Unless there's a major obstacle, mood often can be
generated through listening, affection, and sacrificial love.

Another question to ask would be, how much in the mood is *he?* Couples
must communicate and respond in love, both giving sacrificially of themselves. How long has it been? Is a quick romantic interlude an option? Is
there a greater problem to discuss? Is he listening to her?

A woman's lack of excitement about the prospect of making love is
understandable when you consider the amount of energy most women
expend on work, housework, and kids. They often have little energy left
for this "great experience" we've been describing. A huge factor in having a vibrant love life boils down to priorities. What takes precedence?
The immaculately clean house? Gourmet meals? Or erotic sex? What is
most important to your spouse? Most men report that sex is number one.
Most women report that their own primary needs are more closely related to having a partner who listens and converses intently. *Thus, many
a loving spouse spends the majority of time trying to demonstrate love to
his or her mate with stuff that isn't a real priority for that person.*

For the typical woman, getting aroused sometimes is more a decision
than a product of stimulation by her husband. If she has decided she is
uninterested, caressing her body will probably annoy her. If she has decided "yes," the same stimulation will usually arouse her.

First Corinthians tells us that when we marry, husbands and wives
relinquish solitary rights to their own bodies. (We explore this matter in
detail in the chapter titled "Celebrate or Celibate?") Thus we have a
responsibility to meet our husband's or wife's ongoing sexual needs.

In addition, it's important for the spouse with the lower sex drive to recognize there are other reasons to initiate sex—closeness, comfort, and love, for example—besides the body's desire for it.

What if he has no interest?

Whether husband or wife, what really matters is whether the lack of interest is an ongoing problem or a momentary blip. If he is tired or she is distracted, the situation calls for love and grace. If she is *always* distracted, if he is *always* tired, that is another matter entirely. One observation here: While women are generally unresponsive to tactile stimulation if they have not yet decided "yes" to sex, a man can more often be moved by an alluring wife who begins to fondle him. But not always. I remember one attractive patient who did all she could to get the attention of her husband, a colleague of mine. Yet he was oblivious and uninterested. She was his "trophy," not his partner.

As Paul wrote in 1 Corinthians 7, both partners have sexual needs that must be met. When those needs go unmet, the Devil is allowed a foothold. A husband who nurtures and cherishes his wife, as instructed in Ephesians 5, *must* find a way to meet that ongoing need. Lovemaking is not an optional activity for a growing believer in Christ, whether a husband or wife. The frequency and degree of involvement must be a matter of mutual consent and satisfaction.

Does he really need sex as often as he asks for it?

Fifty-four percent of men surveyed say they think about sex every day or several times a day. By contrast, 67 percent of the women say they think about it only a few times a week or a few times a month.[2] However, there's a difference between need and want. Imagine that you're on a long trip in the car. One of you has to use the bathroom and the other wants to stop for a burger. Bladder relief and hunger both qualify as needs. Yet at the moment, one is more pressing, more urgent (as in "Honey! Find a rest stop *or else!"*). So it is with sexual appetite. His need can vary in its level of urgency.

If a young man neither masturbates nor has sexual relations, he will have a nocturnal emission (ejaculation) approximately every three to six weeks. Despite pleas from lonely men and women, if anyone has ever died from lack of sex, it has never been documented in the medical literature. So it's a need, but not like the need for oxygen or food or sleep. Still, if you feel hungry and you miss breakfast, you will scope out the possibilities for food at lunch time. If you get turned down for lunch, you'll try again at dinnertime. The same is true of sex.

After about one hundred attempts by her husband, a wife might complain, "He's always after me."

"How often do you say 'yes'?"

"Never."

In your own marriage, if there are many more no's than yes's, there is a foundational problem you need to explore. This is a symptom of an underlying difficulty. If it has existed for a long time it may be harder to unravel and rebuild.

Probably the most common sexual problem of this sort is that she thinks he has a one-track mind while he thinks she is insensitive, selfish, and uninterested. Unfortunately, this can become a manipulation issue: "I'll give it to you if you mow the lawn," or ". . . if you stop watching TV sports." It becomes a means of gaining leverage. Couples must commit to each other that they will never use sex as a bargaining chip because in many households it becomes a weapon, a commodity, rather than the pleasurable, unifying gift that God intended.

The wife may ask herself, "How can I use this powerful, even irresistible, weapon to achieve a goal?" Her manipulation can lead to glorified begging on his part, which erodes the fragile framework of oneness and intimacy. The result? You'll have a man who asks 100 times in the hope of hearing an occasional "yes," married to a wife who complains to her doctor that her husband is always after her for sex.

I overheard one of my nurses counseling a young wife about this. "Every time he asks you and you're not driving down the highway, say *yes!* Take ten minutes; you'll spend longer than that arguing about it." In a healthy marriage, this is good.

To the men, I would say this: In the Old Testament the phrase "live with" often carries the idea of "have sexual intercourse with." (See Gen. 20:3; also Deut. 21:13; 22:13, 22; 24:1; and 25:5.) Peter borrows this idea when he tells husbands to live with their wives in "an understanding way," which implies acquiring knowledge and insight through a process of personal investigation. With this in mind, consider how we might read 1 Peter 3:7, "Husbands, likewise, approach sexual relations with your wives in a way that is based on insight gathered from personal investigation of her needs, not returning evil for evil, or insult for insult, but giving a blessing instead; for you were called for the very purpose that you might inherit a blessing."[3]

How do I "get creative"?

Unfortunately, many of us get a sort of butler/maid mentality. We share a bed, we share a closet, perhaps a kitchen. He has his duties of bringing home a check, taking out the garbage, and keeping the car maintained. She has her duties of all the inside home stuff, possibly in addition to a career outside the home. So start with an attitude check. Do you tend to roll your eyeballs when you see couples acting romantic? Do you think, "They'll get over it"? We should feel ashamed if we laugh. The Bible provides a model in which the love grows more intense over time. Long after they're married, Solomon says to his wife in 7:3–4:

> "Your two breasts are like two fawns,
> Twins of a gazelle.
> Your neck is like a tower of ivory,
> Your eyes like the pools in Heshbon
> By the gate of Bath-rabbim."

This is basically the same thing he told her while they were on their honeymoon.

Can you imagine a tower of ivory? No such thing has ever existed, as far as we know. It would be too expensive. He's saying no amount of money could replace her. She's so beautiful, she's a tourist attraction!

Heshbon was a busy city. And to Solomon, his wife's eyes sparkled like pools of water in a city teeming with vendors, providing for him a retreat from the life-in-the-fast-lane world. In her he found an oasis. Do you have this attitude too?

Next, ask yourself what you can do to draw the five senses into your lovemaking. Powders, scented sheets, body lotion, incense, bubble bath? *Smell is the most memory-sensitive sense.* So don't smell like two-cycle motor oil in bed. One husband reported that when he was away from his wife on a business trip, he smelled her perfume on someone in a store. He subtly followed that woman around for ten minutes, just for a "reminder whiff." In a Gallup survey, 71 percent of men and women rated smell as a very big turn-on.[4]

In addition, consider your surroundings. Where do you most frequently make love? If you are like most people, the place that comes to mind is the bedroom. (If you immediately thought of the living room couch or in a tent in the back yard, you may need less help here.) What can you do to your bedroom to express your love, rather than making it the room where all the spare stuff gets stored? One newlywed couple struggling to pay bills reported that they bought a lovely bedroom suite with their wedding money. Rather than decorating the rest of the house first, they wanted to make their bedroom the most beautiful room in the house. "Our parents thought we were being impractical," they shared, laughing. "And they were right!"

"Turning your bedroom into a no-stress zone is simple," writes Karen Scalf Linamen in *Pillow Talk*. She continues:

> The idea is to intentionally design a relaxing environment that is off-limits to many of the stresses and distractions that define your waking hours. Begin with aesthetics, making an effort to keep your bedroom neat and attractive. In other words, aim for *Southern Living* in your private quarters even if the rest of your house looks like *Mechanics Weekly*. Then begin to work on behaviors, keeping your bedroom off-limits to activities other than sleeping, relaxing, or making love. Nix the stacks of unpaid bills, piles of dirty laundry, collections of unread newspapers, and file folders from the office. By fostering this kind of space, seemingly untouched by the nitty gritty of daily life, you will have created a quiet haven where—by simply stepping inside and closing the door behind you—you can take a mini-vacation from stress. This time can then be used to pray, to relax, or to lavish your undivided romantic attentions on your husband.[5]

Ask yourself what you can do to create atmosphere. Change rooms?

Add music? Use special sheets? Add candles or special lighting? Go outside?

What you wear is also important. Tom Nelson, a pastor in Denton, Texas, has suggested, "Ladies, don't always wear the same nightgown you've been wearing since 1946. I think there's a secret that gets passed from generation to generation with women about a nightgown place in Moose Jaw, Alaska. Many women order them, and you couldn't see through one if she stood in front of a solar flare. You can feel nothing under it. *But it's comfortable.*"

Next, consider your words. As one husband has observed, "Making love with words is essential to the continuation of exciting sexual lovemaking." Notice that the couple in Song of Solomon is quite vocal in describing one another's charms and what they want in terms of creating pleasure. Get verbal. If it is difficult for you to verbalize your thoughts and feelings, perhaps you can begin by reading Song of Solomon to each other. Solomon told his wife in 4:1:

> "How beautiful you are, my darling,
> How beautiful you are!
> Your eyes are like doves behind your veil;
> Your hair is like a flock of goats
> That have descended from Mount Gilead."

On the first reading, these words may seem less than flattering. But think about Solomon as a shepherd. He looked across the hills and saw a flock of goats coming down in streams. He then saw her hair come down in tresses. This is important, because Jewish women wore their hair up. If she has let her hair down, they are at the Ritz of their day. What pet phrases flatter your spouse? Study him or her and express yourself.

What about time? You have to stop and date. Most couples when they are dating spend (at least) from 6:30 to midnight on Saturday nights. When they get married, they are fortunate to get fifteen minutes of quality time together every week. It's a matter of priority.

Here are some other suggestions from *Reclaiming Intimacy* for couples with children:

- Check into a hotel for one night every few months.
- Check into a hotel for one afternoon periodically.
- Meet for a romantic lunch at home while children are in school or are napping.
- Rent a fun video for the children to keep them entertained.
- Trade baby-sitting with another couple each Friday and Saturday night, so both couples have one romantic night a week.
- Go to work an hour late periodically, after the children have left for school.
- Hire a sitter on a special weekend night to take the children on a long walk or to a nearby playground so you can be alone.[6]

Where does oneness come in, or does it?

As one newlywed reported, "I want it to feel like 'in the moment' we are emotionally connecting. He tells me that he needs sex to feel connected to me *afterward*. I need sex *after* I feel connected to him or in response to feeling that way. Yet for him it *creates* that feeling."

Yes, everyone is different. And the reality is that orgasm is a rather self-focused event that does not direct our attention outwardly to the relationship "in the moment." God designed us that way. It's normal, even necessary to focus on your own pleasure. For example, when your sweetheart brings you Godiva chocolates, you enjoy the wonderful taste for yourself. Of course, part of the pleasure during lovemaking involves the desire to assist your spouse. But ultimately, "getting there" requires concentrating on your own pleasurable sensations. If you both want to experience orgasm, consider making it your goal to have "two shining moments" rather than one grand simultaneous one. Many textbooks on sex emphasize the orgasmic simulcast—or simultaneous orgasms. Yet as one husband shared, "For me to get the 'rhythm' right for her enjoyment, I have to sacrifice some of my own enjoyment. For us it works better to each have two separate moments of intense pleasure—one when we focus on our own sensations and one when we enjoy the fact that we are bringing pleasure to the other."

Where does God come into the experience itself?

Some teachers have suggested that sexual functioning should be a "spiritual experience that is focused on God." However, nowhere in the biblical literature do we find that a couple should be thinking about God or spiritual concepts during lovemaking. In Proverbs 5:18–19 we read this:

> Let your fountain be blessed,
> And rejoice in the wife of your youth.
> As a lovely hind and a graceful doe,
> Let her breasts satisfy you at all times;
> Be exhilarated always with her love.

God encourages his children to express physical love, and certainly couples derive at least some benefit in knowing they have God's approval. Sex within marriage glorifies God. He created our sexuality, and when expressed in accordance with His will within marriage, our pleasure is within His plan and purpose. As Colossians instructs us, we should do all for the glory of God.

Although sex for you may be an experience like "the end of the world as we now know it," this is probably not the time to ponder your theology of end times or any other thoughts that take away from focusing on your beloved.

Couples experiencing difficulties have often found it healing to pray before and after their times together, and we certainly recommend this. One wife shared, "We were having some trouble, and it was painful emotionally for both of us. So beforehand we prayed asking God to help us. It's wonderful to think that God cares about this area of our lives and we can ask for His help together. It brought peace out of anxiety."

Both our love lives and our prayer lives reveal how we handle intimate relationships; the two are linked. Sexuality is a huge part of the spiritual journey. Many who consider themselves spiritually mature act immature in their approach to lovemaking. They're selfish, impatient, demanding, even manipulative. Or they ignore the commands to meet the other partner's needs because they feel little sex drive themselves. It's vitally important, considering how much God has to say and how much He cares about our physical bodies, that we demonstrate godly love and seek His help in this as in all other areas.

Why can't my husband be physically affectionate without making a sexual move?

He can. But God has "wired" him in such a way that physical affection often brings arousal, which makes him want sex. "I feel like we have a third person in our relationship—my husband, me, and sex," Dennae shared. "Sex is this presence that always looms. He is so easily stimulated that anything remotely sensual makes him 'head down that path.' "

Express to him how important it is to you to be cuddled without it having to "go somewhere." And remind him continually. He may need these reminders, not because he is insensitive to your needs but because what comes naturally for him appears to be different from what comes naturally for you. Remember, he has approximately fifteen times more testosterone running through his veins than you do. Many women do not realize that God made most men in such a way that they desire a sexual release quite frequently under normal circumstances.

Unfortunately, some men selfishly show affection in words and gestures only when they want sex. Yet the desire for cuddling without sex is legitimate. It's important for a wife to know that her husband loves her mind, heart, and interests as much as he loves her body.

Sarah struggled with a strong dislike of sex. When she mentioned to her therapist that she just wanted to be snuggled by her husband without sex having to follow, the counselor replied that she had this need because her parents didn't cuddle her enough when she was a child. A man who wanted nonsexual cuddling justified his feelings by explaining, "I was not breast fed as an infant." But *everyone* needs nonsexual intimacy, not just those who had a difficult childhood! This pleasurable side of intimacy should be cultivated by every couple interested in developing a deeper, more meaningful relationship.

Every time my husband sets up a special night out, I feel like he's manipulating me to get sex.

One couple recounted this conversation:

Him: "Let's go out Saturday night."
Her: "Sounds great."

Him: "What do you want to do?"

Her: "I don't know. I thought you might have something in mind."

Him: "No, not really. A movie? Dinner? What would you like?"

Her: "How about both?"

Him: "Okay. And when we get home?"

Her: "We'll see . . ."

Him: "What do you mean by that?"

He thinks, *She never wants to make love. I get my hopes up, and pow. Maybe later, maybe not. Makes me think she doesn't even like sex. Why do I feel guilty for wanting sex with my wife?* She thinks, *He always thinks of sex first. I feel like a prostitute: How about a movie and dinner in exchange for sex? Does there always have to be a sexual motivation to spend time with me?*

Some couples report solving this problem by having two different "nights out." At least in their early, childless days of marriage, they have communication night and date night. He has one night when he can "count on it"; she has one night in which she can decide spontaneously, with no pressure, whether or not she wants to make love. However, more importantly, there is the need for this couple to dicuss why one feels manipulated and why they have unparallel levels of interest.

My husband told me he gets aroused several times during the day when he sees women other than me. Should I be worried?

Probably not. It depends on how far he allows his mind and actions to go. Wives sometimes feel dismayed over their husbands' ability to become sexually aroused by other women. However, this is a normal male response. Arousal doesn't mean much to a man. It certainly does not have to mean he desires a *relationship* with that woman. In fact, sometimes he experiences arousal when he doesn't want to. It is possible to feel the physical sensation of arousal without even engaging in an actual specific sexual thought, although a thought or visual stimulus usually triggers it. Sometimes it occurs spontaneously without a trigger (as it does the *entire year* following puberty for boys!). Women are often physically aroused by men other than their husbands yet may remain unaware of their own responses.

Is it okay to fantasize?

That depends on what you mean. There's a difference between fantasy and lust. If you mean thinking of an adulterous relationship to help you get or stay excited, no, it's not okay. But if you're thinking about your spouse, it may be okay. Why do you need to fantasize? Are you unsatisfied in some way? Is there something you and your sweetheart need to discuss?

A fantasy involving someone other than your spouse may be an expression of resentment toward your spouse. If so, talking about the actual source of your resentment would be the loving thing to do.

Sexual fantasies are designed to meet some need. A women's magazine ran an article on how to "get more interested." The author suggested watching an X-rated film, reading a trashy novel, masturbating, fantasizing about extramarital affairs, and watching soap operas. These are all wrong because they encourage sin in "fantasy worlds."[7] But the author went for the right strategy in starting with the mind. In Philippians 4, Paul tells us to let our minds dwell on *good* things. So think romantic thoughts. Concentrate on remembering intimate times together, what you love about him, and what is right with your marriage instead of wrong. Move from there to plot ways to be creative in your lovemaking.

In terms of fantasizing while making love, one man wrote, "I never fantasize that I'm with someone else, but I may fantasize that my wife has a smaller waist. I may fantasize that she has long hair instead of short hair. Those images help me get aroused and make orgasm that much better." However, changing your spouse, even if only for the purpose of arousal, seems potentially dangerous in that you are expressing your love to that which is not real. In this context, the desire to fantasize may signal a need to talk together.

Some couples report enjoying the process of "going on a fantasy together." If you're comfortable with it, talk to each other during sex: "Imagine we're on a beach in Hawaii. . . ." Most people do fantasize during sex.

Who decides when to have sex? The man or the woman?

Some have the idea that the man always has to initiate. Psychiatrists have observed that in a maturing marriage, the wife feels the necessary freedom to initiate lovemaking more frequently as the marriage relationship grows. Either partner should feel free to initiate when desire develops and "the heat is on." You can give many verbal and nonverbal signals. The wife taking a bath at night when she normally showers in the morning could be a "clue." A husband shaving at 10:30 P.M. (why else would a man shave at 10:30?) or offering, "I'll put the kids to bed if you want to slip into something *less* comfortable" might be his way of declaring interest.

How do I satisfy my husband?

Ask him! Communicate. Find out what his desires are, and as far as you are comfortable, fulfill them. Find out what he likes and doesn't like. What is his favorite environment? What time is best? Is place important? What sort of visual stimulus works best? Get specific about actual activities. This goes for husbands asking wives, too. Don't try to read your partner's mind. Have him tell you or write a "wish list," and you do the same.

Communicate, but not necessarily "during the act." As we've said, timing of conversation is important. *How* you do so is also important. Often adults communicate about sex by pouting, moping, withholding, acting petty, and generally behaving like children. Others have discovered that once they stopped resisting a sense of adventure, their partners realized that rug burns were less comfortable than mattresses with nice sheets after all.

However, it is not your duty to satisfy him any more than it is his duty to satisfy you. Your spouse has no control over your concentration and level of participation. If you feel anger, fatigue, or distraction, it may be impossible for even the most attentive spouse to "satisfy" you. Ultimately, you satisfy each other by being satisfied, rather than by merely tolerating the act of regularly lending your bodies to each other.

What are the most common sexual difficulties?

Talking about sex. Sex is the *number one thing* couples have trouble discussing. Some studies reveal that half of all American marriages are troubled by some form of sexual distress ranging from lack of interest and boredom to outright sexual dysfunction. The sexual problems people tell about most frequently have to do with inhibitions and guilt, performance anxiety, erotic boredom, and blind acceptance of sexual misinformation or myths. In fact, these four problems collectively account for more than 80 percent of the sexual dissatisfactions in modern America.[8] Probably the most common physical problem for men is premature ejaculation (which we'll discuss in the next chapter). Some of the most common *relational* issues that damage sexual love are selfishness, fear of vulnerability, treating your spouse as a sex object, unloving expressions of anger, and desire for control or dominance.

We often see a wife who is unenthusiastic, content with a rather regimented routine. The husband generally wants more adventure. One wife shared, "I didn't realize my husband thought we were stuck in a rut. But I asked him if he was happy, and he told me nicely that he was rather bored. I was surprised because I was thinking we had a great love life. I asked him to get specific about what he wanted, and then I tried to meet his desires. After many years together, we are both finding renewed passion."

8

QUESTIONS ABOUT ORGASM

Let his left hand be under my head
And his right hand embrace me.
—Song of Solomon 2:6

What is an orgasm supposed to feel like?

That's a little like asking, "What does the color green look like?" or "What does a banana taste like?" The best we can offer is a general description. It's probably safe to say it is supposed to feel good, though the sensations of pain and pleasure are so closely related in our bodies that a few people have trouble distinguishing between the two. In fact, judging by your partner's facial expressions and sounds, you may wonder whether he or she is in agony or ecstasy.

Both men and women report a broad spectrum of sensations, including pelvic muscle spasms, "loss of control," and a mellow "glow" afterward that is brought about by a release of chemical substances called endorphins. But there are many variables here. If you ranked every experience from one to ten depending on many factors, most would fall short of absolute perfection, especially if we used TV and movie experiences as the standard.

A woman may have an orgasm but wonder, "Is *that* what that was? I'm not sure." A husband may describe his own orgasm in such incredible terms ("Oh, wow, honey, it was the ultimate!") that his wife can't help but think, *But that's not exactly my experience.* Dana shared, "I read that on average, a man usually rates his marriage four points higher than his wife does. I'm guessing the same may be true of their sexual experiences."

Several factors can contribute to the degree of intensity experienced from one orgasm to the next. For example, many men who wait more than several days between "encounters" tend to experience a higher degree of physical sensation. Also, an extended amount of foreplay can add to the amount of pleasure. Age can be a negative contributor, as the intensity of sensation and force of ejaculation decreases gradually over time.

Ultimately, orgasm is meant to be extremely pleasurable. God created us to enjoy intense physical pleasure. He designed the system, the muscles, the endorphins—the entire sexual response is a gift we can enjoy immensely, in the proper context.

Him: What am I doing wrong? My wife is not experiencing orgasm. Her: Why am I unable to reach orgasm? What do you suggest?

There can be a variety of reasons for this. Not all women even want to achieve orgasm. It involves a degree of "loss of control" or surrender that many would rather not experience, particularly if the relationship is shaky. Yielding can be scary. It also takes more energy and concentration than some women feel like expending.

However, if she is trying but having difficulty, she can begin by asking if anything is distracting her or is unpleasant to her. Is something breaking the rhythm of physical sensation, such as an abrupt move from manual stimulation to vaginal intercourse at the last moment? (This is where constantly striving for the goal of simultaneous orgasm can damage an otherwise great sexual experience.) Is her husband ejaculating before she is ready? The two must talk about the right rhythm and pressure. No guessing!

Anatomical problems, fear, past negative sexual experiences, guilt over illicit relationships, and negative teaching about sex can all contribute to problems here. However, in the absence of these difficulties, given the right stimulation and sufficient time, it will probably happen. If the anatomy is normal, the appropriate stimulation over a sufficient amount of time will generally succeed. Some report that spraying warm water on the clitoris helps to relax muscles and can aid in pleasurable sensations.

Vibrators, which are readily available through mail order and on the Internet, may help, too (more on the ethics of this later). It's probably better to use natural stimulation, as the intense, unique sensation of a vibrator cannot be matched by the sensations of normal intercourse. Some people report becoming dependent upon vibrators. However, if the wife finds she cannot experience orgasm without one, a couple might opt to use it until she becomes familiar with the sensations leading to orgasm.

You might try changing positions to one that allows more direct clitoral stimulation. For example, usually the wife receives no such stimulation when her husband enters her from behind. Often she receives more stimulation of her clitoris if she sits astride him during intercourse. If she is on top, she may want him to shift his body slightly toward her feet or more toward her head to give sufficient clitoral stimulation for climax. For the wife who finds any direct stimulation uncomfortable, it may help to initially straddle her husband's leg so she can control the level of pressure without direct stimulation. She may later proceed to lay on him with the penis between her legs but not in her vagina, allowing it to stimulate her clitoris rhythmically. Another suggestion is that she try altering her body position by placing a pillow under her buttocks. In addition, couples can try positions that free the hands, allowing manual stimulation during intercourse.

Remember to be sure she is getting stimulation for a long enough period. Three to five minutes is generally not enough. As we said earlier, most women need an average of ten to fifteen minutes, or even more, of uninterrupted clitoral stimulation to reach orgasm.

Manual and oral stimulation are also options for many couples. Discover what works best through trial and retrial. Keep trying, but don't force the issue. If you tell yourselves, "This has to be the night," you will probably set yourselves up for failure.

How do I communicate, "I don't like that; please try something else"?

Guiding your partner's hand to the right spot is easier than employing the verbal instructions—"move to the left; no, no down; now up a little"—we might use when getting a back rub. For more detailed help, most partners prefer a straightforward discussion later. Conversations about sexual technique often are less threatening outside of the context of the moment. A statement such as, "You're doing it wrong!" made while engaged in the act itself will no doubt abruptly short-circuit any energy and enjoyment present in the encounter. I believe it's better to evaluate what happened an hour or two later: "I liked this. I didn't like that. This was too hard, too soft, too fast." Most couples have great difficulty discussing these things openly, but it is very important to get the words out.

Of course the extreme here is saying, "Honey, you are a lousy lover; try pretending I'm actually here and alive." Men and women are fairly unanimous in expressing that they want "corrective" information to be delivered in a gentle way. "When he told me I didn't know how to do oral sex, I never did it again," one wife shared. Anything that seems like criticism can so destroy confidence that it inhibits the relationship. Consider Walter Wangerin's thoughts on this subject:

> Talk truthfully, without a hint of guilt or criticism, even about sexual difficulties. Where there is fault, there can be forgiveness, and forgiveness permits a beginning again. Where there is no fault (sex can fail for reasons perfectly blameless), there can be helpful, open, and constructive talk. Be sure you know the difference between fault (the indifferent selfishness of one of you, perhaps) and no-fault (a true physical problem). How often our personal frustration makes us take things personally—when in fact there was no sin done against us at all.[1]

If you feel you simply cannot talk about it, and you are uncomfortable writing, you might begin by looking up Bible verses about sex and discussing them. But *somehow*, you must break the ice.

My *wife doesn't get very lubricated. Does this mean she isn't enjoying lovemaking much?*

No. Lubrication is not necessarily an indication of her level of enjoyment. Other factors besides her degree of excitement may play a role here, including individual anatomy, hormones, age, and even medication. If you would like more lubrication, consider using products such as K-Y Jelly, Maxilube, Sensilube, or Replens.

One husband wrote, "If she isn't wet enough, it can be painful for her and I don't get as much sensation. Then again, too much lubrication—usually from, say, a lot of K-Y Jelly—cuts down on sensation as well. So I'm careful not to use extra lubricant unless I have to. It's like cooking. You can always add more spices, but once they're in there . . ."

Do I *have to achieve an orgasm*?

No man has ever asked me this. But some women really don't find reaching climax worth the effort required—at least not always. Others may be unable to do so due to anatomic reasons, or they may have reached it at times but feel content with sex without orgasm. Some have husbands who pressure them to climax. At this point it's time to reveal an important principle: *Whether or not she wants to achieve an orgasm is her decision.* He must let her decide for herself when she is satisfied.

Unfortunately, some have labeled women who don't have orgasms as "preorgasmic," implying that they'll get there if they keep trying. That's fine if they want to. But consider the dogmatism of this statement: "The wife who never has experienced orgasm is being cheated out of normal sexual intercourse and needs to ask God for a wise counselor to help find the reason."[2] This attitude simply adds pressure to an already sensitive situation.

Another person writes, "The husband is responsible to meet his wife's sexual needs. He must regularly and lovingly arouse her to a complete sexual experience, climax (or orgasm). Likewise, the wife must meet her husband's sexual needs. She must regularly and lovingly arouse him to a sexual experience, climax (or orgasm)."[3]

"Responsible to meet"? "Must . . . arouse"? These are strong words. We need to depressurize this situation, allowing more freedom for partners to express affection the way they want to. While it's important to satisfy your partner, your partner has the privilege and joy of determining when his or her own satisfaction is achieved. Not every intimate encounter must by necessity end with an orgasm. In fact, only 20 percent of women experience orgasm more than half the number of times they make love. Add to that the pressure to achieve multiple orgasms and/or simultaneous orgasm, and we have set up a standard of success that guarantees frustration and failure for most people most of the time.

Imagine that you have cooked your wife a nine-course meal. What if she is full after the fourth course? Must she force herself to "gorge" merely because you have prepared it? For whose pleasure have you prepared it, then?

One counselor has observed that, in his practice, women with an abundance of energy usually choose to climax whenever they make love. Low-energy women or those who feel exhausted at the end of a hard day may choose not to. Yet men almost always choose to, probably because it requires so little additional time and effort.

In a giving sexual relationship, both partners will take these differences into account. The kind husband will not put pressure on his wife to climax, because it may be more enjoyable for her not to have one. However, if she would like to, he should provide the additional time and effort required.

Again, statistics are only numbers. You are you. Learn what works best for the two of *you* and enjoy the journey of sharing life together.

Where is the G-spot and what is it?

The G-spot is named after gynecologist Ernst Grafenberg (1881–1957), who first put forth a theory concerning this. His theory was that a particularly sexually sensitive area exists within the vagina about halfway between the pubic bone and the cervix at the rear of the urethra. (Others have described its location as being "in the upper interior of the vagina, just beyond the PC muscle." Still another says, "In order to find it, one has to stimulate it; and to do just that, one has to find it!") Sometimes arousal and orgasm triggered in this way are accompanied by ejaculation of fluid through the urethra. This is called a "flooding response," or female ejaculation.

A small percentage of women do find this general area highly responsive to stimulation, reporting a deep, intense orgasm that occurs when it receives stimulation. Leading scientific papers still do not publish any related research, considering the whole concept "unscientific." So while it may be true that no scientifically verifiable G-spot exists, a particularly sensitive area *may* exist, and the release of fluid in some women is possible.

Several years ago at the Masters and Johnson Institute, a physician catheterized women with this response so that their urinary bladders were empty. The husbands then stimulated their wives to orgasmic response. When the doctors examined the fluid, it was not urine in chemical composition nor in appearance, even though it came from the urinary bladder.[4]

One husband described the technique that works best for him and his wife: "I insert two fingers into her vagina and rotate them from side to side very fast. Quite tiring, but it has the desired effect."

Just as there are a variety of responses to other "standard" erogenous zones, not every woman is particularly sensitive in this area. Yet some people go so far as to claim that "every woman has a G-spot." The proof may not be as important as private perception and preference.

Is it better for my wife to achieve orgasm while my penis is in her vagina or while I'm stimulating her clitoris more directly?

The inability to have orgasm during intercourse is the second most common complaint of women. Some studies report that as many as 70 percent of women need direct clitoral stimulation to respond with an orgasm. In other words, they find themselves unable to achieve orgasm during sexual intercourse from penetration and thrusting alone. Yet many couples believe that "real" orgasms have to happen during sexual intercourse. The result is that women who could be experiencing orgasm are not because they reach a certain point in their excitement level, their husbands enter them, and the needed direct stimulation ceases. The nerve endings in the clitoris are located such a distance from the vagina that, for many women, intercourse in the "man on top" position won't do much.

Some suggest varying positions if vaginal intercourse does not result in orgasm. You can try that, but if you need clitoral stimulation, changing who's on top during intercourse probably won't help. Some counsel that the man should stimulate the woman externally until she is "almost there," and then quickly move to intercourse. This not only upsets the rhythm, it wrongly suggests that vaginal intercourse is "better," or "the right way" to experience orgasm.

Should we make simultaneous orgasms our goal?

As if the pressure to have vaginal orgasms were not enough, there is additional pressure to have simultaneous orgasms. What are the chances of simultaneous orgasm? Ten percent would be a generous estimate. Yet we found this information in a Christian sex manual: "[The plateau] phase should last long enough to bring you both to orgasm, usually simultaneously." Others suggested that within a few weeks of "trying hard," a majority of couples could "master this skill." Suggesting that couples should master any skill that requires controlling an involuntary response sets them up for frustration.

Jack Mayhall said it well in *Marriage Takes More Than Love:*

> Many manuals . . . hold that the epitome of the sex relationship is to have a climax together. This can be like a carrot held out to a bunch of racing rabbits—always just out of reach. As long as both are enjoying the physical relationship and both are usually *reaching* a climax, it just isn't that important to reach it together. The enjoyment is the primary concern. And the climax will not be the same every time. I have talked to people who think that unless they have the greatest, most exciting feeling in their lives each time, they are disappointed.[5]

One couple, who in their fifteen years together have experienced simultaneous orgasm three times, shared that each time it happened, they said, "Let's write to the people who wrote that sex manual telling us this would be the norm to tell them 'We finally got it.' "

If it happens, great; but don't lose energy and enjoyment in striving for it. In fact, the waiting and waiting to get the timing perfect will generally produce a less-than-optimal orgasm for one or both because concentration is lost.

Is it always going to be better for him?

While men rarely struggle with orgasmic response, women may have difficulty. Men more often have problems related to the "when" of their response, while more women struggle with the "if." Men seem to be fairly similar in their orgasmic responses, while women's responses may differ both from woman to woman and also in the same woman from one experience to the next. Women have the potential for multiple or sequential orgasms, but the actual orgasmic experience can vary from three to five contractions in a mild orgasm to eight to twelve in a more intense one. Also, whereas going a long time without sex will intensify the pleasure for most men, it often has a retarding effect on their wives, for whom an orgasm may happen more easily if she has recently had one. As some sex experts have observed, this tendency to go in opposite directions may be one more indication of the reality that we were created to be together, and to experience sexual release on a regular basis.[6]

The differences have prompted some men to wonder, *If my wife knows how good it feels, why doesn't she crave it again?* A woman will *rarely* be as "driven" due to hormonal differences. A man who has been in the "coma" stage for about twenty minutes is perhaps in the best position to understand what it's often like for his wife. He knows orgasm feels good, but in the absence of a strong hormonal drive to move him in that direction, he probably will not desire sex without some coaxing.

It's difficult to compare the intensity of pleasurable sensations. Sex can be wonderful for both partners. If it's unsatisfactory for you, don't just accept it until you have exhausted all possibilities. Search for causes and solutions. There are many simple means of evaluating and improving. Different does not mean better or worse. And your love life is worth trying to improve even when you're eighty or older!

Is it possible to have multiple orgasms?

If you mean more than one in a lifetime, certainly! If you mean in one evening, probably—if you both desire it and you're patient. Men and women differ in their orgasmic potential.[7] Men generally need "recharging" time between encounters—an average of twenty to thirty minutes. Women differ here in that it is possible for them to have more than one orgasm within several minutes (though it usually takes ten to twenty minutes to achieve the first one). A woman can have an extended orgasm with additional contractions (which some have termed "multiple") without a refractory period, or she can have a slight plateau of several minutes and then achieve orgasm again (called "sequential"). Gearing up for a second or third orgasm, however, may postpone her enjoyment of her endorphin release because of the concentration and focus required. Additional orgasms are not necessary and many do not desire them, but it is helpful for some to know the potential exists.

How do I keep from ejaculating if she's not ready for me to do it?

As one woman shared, "He wants me to be more 'into it' but premature ejaculation is a problem. I know that if I get more 'crazy,' he'll 'lose it' faster. Then I'm left unsatisfied. What should I do?"

Experiencing orgasm before they want to is the most common sexual problem men face. The fear of "Oh, no; it's going to happen again" can become a self-fulfilling prophecy for some. Holding back requires a combination of physical sensation and mental focus. You can develop some control. The first few times you have sex you'll probably find you have little control, and that can be discouraging if it's unanticipated. But you can develop a pace, tempo, or position that is less overwhelming in terms of sexual stimulation.

One frustrated wife stated, "The only thing making it better is to do it more often, and that makes me feel more pressure."

I would like to offer a suggestion that should remove some of the pressure. Consider planning to have sex twice in the same night. Make the first time the faster of the two. During the second encounter, take the slow road. This means starting earlier in the evening (as in 8:30, not the typical 11:30) and allowing about a thirty-minute window for the second erection. Once you've had some positive experiences, the confidence you gain will become self-reinforcing. The first time could focus on him and the second could focus on her. Couples can find ways to satisfy both. After the first time, he will have virtually no interest for a little while because of the nature of the refractory period. During this time he may be tempted to say, "Never mind. We've had enough for one night." That's why you need about thirty minutes before trying again.

Some recommend the "squeeze technique" (this technique is included in the workbook section for those who are interested). Others suggest the man find a distraction—such as thinking a sad thought or mentally rehearsing multiplication tables to "slow him down." I don't recommend this. In particular I don't like the idea of interjecting negative thoughts and/or sensations right before a man is ready to orgasm. What kind of associations will result?

As one frustrated wife shared in response to these techniques, "The whole thing about premature ejaculation is that it's not that simple to just follow some instructions in a book. It's a very long process of working together at finding a satisfying solution." While this is true, it's well worth the time and effort expended.

How do I deal with impotence?

Therapist Helen Kaplan asserts that ". . . approximately half of all males experience occasional times when they lose an erection or cannot even become erect for intercourse." When we were looking into building a home, a contractor my wife and I consulted was apparently suffering from erectile dysfunction when he told me, "Doctor, if you can help me 'raise a stake,' I'll build your house for free." It took awhile for me to figure out what he was talking about but eventually it dawned on me. Erectile dysfunction can be devastating because, generally, a man's sexual functioning is a rather fragile and ego-defining thing.

The first step is medical evaluation, which may include urological examination. There is much debate about what percentage of erectile difficulty is psychological and what percentage is biological. The best evidence now is that many erectile dysfunctions are more biological than psychological in origin. Alcoholism prevents many men from attaining erections. High stress or illness may drive down testosterone levels, thereby reducing erectile ability. Many medications, especially heart medications, reduce sexual function somewhat. Long-term and uncontrolled diabetes may also cause erectile problems.[8] So we often find a medical cause.

One step you can take in self-diagnosis is to observe whether you ever wake up with an erection, which demonstrates that it *can* happen. Physically healthy men have an erection for ten minutes or so about every ninety minutes all night long.[9] If you are not having nighttime erections and you are not becoming somewhat sexually aroused by attractive stimuli, it is possible that you have a physical problem. Psychological causes also factor in. For example, feeling intense guilt over an affair can cause erectile dysfunction.[10]

Childbirth can also cause difficulty, in that "the parts don't fit as snugly as before." There's also a psychological side to childbirth. Some men who have witnessed the delivery room scene find themselves repelled, having seen the blood, stretching, and tearing that happen as a normal part of the birth process.

In addition, much of sexual functioning is dependent upon ambiance. Does your partner take care of herself? Does she exercise good hygiene? Has she had a recent vaginal infection? I suggest allowing sufficient time, creating an inviting atmosphere, and incorporating all five senses (e.g., clothing, lighting, music, scents, and oils) into your lovemaking to help focus on positives.

Although diagnosis may sometimes be easy, treatment is always more difficult. For example, if medication is causing the difficulty, you can't always just stop taking it. In these cases, find alternative ways to give and receive pleasure together.

Researchers are engaged in active investigation of ways to help couples coping with erectile dysfunction. Some solutions involve replaceable/ removable therapies including pellets of medication that, when inserted down into the male urethra (this is not painful) will usually produce an erection. This developing method may replace some penile injections and adds another alternative to surgical implants and prosthetic devices that enable erection and penetration.

My husband has a sensitive ego when it comes to lovemaking. How should I respond when he has a premature ejaculation or temporary erectile dysfunction?

Be as gentle as possible. Do all you can to keep from turning the temporary embarrassment into a lifelong dysfunction or source of grief or damaged self-esteem. For most men sexuality is a central issue of pride or ego. We men seem to think we must be able to perform any time, anywhere, and could (theoretically) satisfy anybody. Men who have difficulties sexually often end up struggling with low self-esteem. However, if there's a medical diagnosis, this tends to be less of a problem. He can tell himself, "It's not my fault; it's not really *my* problem." But there is still often a sense that "If I am unable to satisfy her, then I'm no man." Your husband needs you to take the attitude "This is normal—we can work it out!" And he needs continual reminding that he is, in fact, "The World's Greatest Lover."

Solomon's bride told him, "The maidens love you." It's a wise woman who begins early in her relationship with her husband to say, "Any woman would give anything to be your wife, but I got you!"

What is a "quickie"?

It's a rapid, intense romantic encounter that skips significant foreplay and goes directly into intercourse. A steady diet of this type of sex is not good for a relationship. It usually does not allow the woman to experience orgasm, and as a rule it satisfies only the man's desire. She might be "attending to" him so she can get back to what she feels she needs to be doing. If she's not that interested (she's menstrual or premenstrual, pregnant, tired, bored, or busy, for example) and he has a need, this is a valid, even loving sexual encounter, as long as he meets her needs when she wants "all the bells and whistles." It is one possible solution to "He's always asking, and I'm always saying no."

The goal of a "quickie" is sexual release. Often circumstances are such that the time available makes the "nine course meal" impossible, or even unappealing. When you're seeking quick satisfaction, usually for the male, this can be perfectly reasonable. Some nights when the kids have soccer practice, you go to a drive-through restaurant instead of sitting down to dinner together. It's a reasonable option. However, it's not great for your health to have a steady diet of only fast food and french fries. So be flexible; ride the ebb and flow of life events, making intimacy a priority.

When God says "Imbibe *deeply*," He is referring to a "meal" to be shared throughout years of developing intimacy, communication, and oneness. This is not a life of "quickies." Talk to couples who are still in love after several decades and they will often tell you, "It's so much better years later. The embers burn more deeply."

Is it okay to have manual sex (bringing each other to climax with your hands)?

Certainly. This is an option, particularly if one partner has an active herpes lesion or other medical condition preventing intercourse. Couples should find many ways to please each other, and they can use the whole arsenal when the time is right. Some have argued that this does not measure up to the "one flesh" ideal. However, the one flesh relationship is a far greater picture than merely that of sexual intercourse. When two are one, they want to satisfy each other and meet each other's needs as well as possible.

Is it okay to use devices such as vibrators to enhance pleasure?

This is a question the Bible nowhere addresses directly. The potential danger is that these create such intense sensations that it's difficult to match them with "normal" activities. Thus, if used extensively they can make regular sex unsatisfying. Also, any "sex toys" used to enhance stimulation or to spice up a couple's love life should be used only by mutual desire.

9

OTHER QUESTIONS
COUPLES ASK

What kind of beloved is your beloved?
—Song of Solomon 5:9

My partner wants to do things that make me uncomfortable.
Is oral sex even biblical?

Couples frequently ask some variation of this question: "Which behaviors and frequencies are okay for the conservative heterosexual Christian?" A wide range of behaviors fall within biblical parameters. However,
each of us has a feel for what we consider normal or weird or sinful.
Some people have a strongly negative response to the practice of oral
sex. Others draw the line at anal sex. It's important to understand how
your spouse thinks and feels in these delicate areas. Also, physical restrictions may factor into his or her feelings.

The Roman Catholic church teaches that procreation must always be
a possibility in any romantic encounter. Therefore they rule out oral,
anal, and manual sex. However, the Bible suggests no such limitations.
The church bases its teaching on an erroneous interpretation of a text
about a man named Onan. He "wasted his seed on the ground, in order
not to give offspring to his brother." In this Genesis 38 story, God condemned Onan because he disobeyed a clear command to give his de-
ceased brother a heritage so that his name would be remembered.

This passage is used as a "proof text" to condemn masturbation, and birth control as well. (We explain this passage more fully in the chapter on contraception.) The Roman Catholic church forbids any practice that "wastes seed" that could have been used for procreation. Yet normal intercourse "wastes seed" when the wife uses the bathroom after relations; nocturnal emissions "waste seed," too.

Lacking specific biblical prohibitions we must then ask, "What is loving?" and "What is satisfying between husband and wife?" Within the clear biblical limitations, anything is acceptable. Some individuals and even entire cultures reject practices that go beyond such restrictions as these: only in bed; only on Saturday night; only with the lights out; only in the "missionary position." If you or your partner grew up thinking "Yuck! That's the *worst!*" about a particular sexual practice, respect those feelings. Don't pressure anyone to do something that exploits him or her.

During one of my premarriage talks, a lady sitting in the front row blurted out, "Why do all men love oral sex so much?" Actually, not all do. But some who do explain that it's an entirely passive sexual experience—you can focus only on receiving pleasure for a time without also worrying about whether you need to shift your weight, what to do about your arms getting tired, being out of breath, and so on. Ninety percent of couples engage in some sort of oral/genital foreplay on occasion, so it is common. Also, it's important to communicate what is actually desired here. One wife said she spent years hating oral *foreplay* because she thought her husband wanted oral *sex* (i.e., ejaculation).

In Song of Solomon 2:3 (italics mine) there may be an implicit reference to the oral pleasures of sexual love:

> "Like an apple tree among the trees of the forest,
> So is my beloved among the young men.
> In his shade I took great delight and sat down,
> *And his fruit was sweet to my taste.*"

The apple tree is a frequently used symbol in the Near East for sexual love (perhaps similar to what we think when we hear "mistletoe"). In extrabiblical literature, "fruit" is sometimes equated with the male genitals or with semen, so it is possible that here we have a delicate reference to an oral genital caress, which she is initiating. Later she says this in 7:13:

> "The mandrakes have given forth fragrance;
> And over our doors are all choice fruits,
> Both new and old,
> Which I have saved up for you, my beloved."

On first reading, this may not seem very romantic. But the original Jewish audience probably would have said, "Ooooh, I cannot believe you *said* that!" Mandrakes are called *man*drakes because they resemble a human body. In that culture they were eaten to create desire and fertility.[1] What do you do with mandrakes and fruit? You put them in your mouth. This is very provocative language.

Notice, too, that she says she has *something old and something new* for him. Variety is good. Be inventive. As we said earlier, it's easy to get in a rut. You and your husband or wife will have different views on what's weird, sinful, risqué, fun, or great. But within your comfort zones, seek to explore new avenues of expression rather than the "same old same old" all the time.

Medically, such practices are not generally harmful, although patients sometimes get infections from having anal sex followed by vaginal sex. Also, I have seen cases in which foreign objects (bottles in particular) have become caught in the vagina and the suction created has done considerable damage when couples forcibly extracted the object. Here's another principle: *Use common sense.*

A final word here: Submitting to each other means sacrificing our own desires for the good of the other. If your spouse is genuinely uncomfortable, find other ways of expressing your love. Either partner needs to know he or she can gently say "no" at any time. Both must feel safe to remain in their "comfort zones."

Are there any sexual practices that are biblically not okay?

Yes. For starters God forbids sex with animals and dead people (most people have little trouble adhering to this standard). From there He also prohibits engaging in premarital, extramarital, or group sex, both actually and mentally. (The mental part is what catches most of us.) Oral and anal sex are not mentioned in any list of prohibitions. Some states have laws against anal intercourse, but as far as we know, no married person has ever been prosecuted.

The general placement of nerve endings (they are densely concentrated around the anus) would indicate that anal sex could potentially bring a high degree of pleasure. However, in my years of practicing medicine, I have never met a woman who engaged in anal sex because she thought it was "the best thing going." Most were doing it because their partners were pressuring them. Thus, it's imperative that the partner wishing to engage in this practice consider and defer to the preferences and/or conscience of the one who has misgivings. The fact that anal sex is not specifically listed among the biblical prohibitions, in addition to what we know about how God placed the nerve endings, causes me to conclude that we should exercise caution in declaring this to be "big time sin" between consenting, married partners. However, that being said, if couples wish to engage in this practice, they should know that at first it can be somewhat painful, cleanliness is important, anal contact followed by vaginal contact can cause infection, and anal sex carries with it the potential for damage to the sphincter.

Why does he/she have to be reminded 100 times about what I like?

People have short memories, and we are all wired differently. The general placement of nerve endings, media influences, and wishful thinking all combine to create specific desires and expectations. We have to be retold because we cannot read minds. What the other person wants does not come instinctively to us. One bride shared, "I have to remind myself that he is not being thoughtless. One time we were getting into it, and he did something I had just told him I didn't like. I stopped him and asked, 'Don't you remember?' He covered his face and said, 'Oops. Sorry. Let me leave the room and come back in and start over.' "

A husband observed, "I tend to think it will intoxicate her with passion for me to move fast, because that's what I find exciting. To me, bold is beautiful. But the opposite is true for her." His wife confided, "Yes, after years of telling him, 'Start subtle, be subtle; that's what works for me,' I still have to remind him sometimes that I want him to slow down."

I miss kissing. Why doesn't my husband kiss me anymore?

Make sure you've used mouthwash and remind him that kissing "lights your fire." Most partners will give what's desired once the desire is expressed. However, you may have to provide gentle reminders.

Why do I sneeze after sex?

Some people do. Along with other areas that congest, the nasal passages can congest during intercourse, so the "person on the bottom" may have a sneeze or two following a romantic interlude. Fascinating creatures, aren't we? God has created us with such diversity and complexity!

My husband is working on a graduate degree, and he always has to study late into the night. We both desire sex but I'm not a night owl, so we never seem to connect anymore. Suggestions?

The wife of a graduate school student reported that her husband would work all week, then he would spend his evenings and weekends studying and working with youth. She began to feel isolated and starved for his affection. He said he missed her, too. Fortunately, when he took a marriage-and-family class, a wise professor urged those in attendance always to go to bed with their spouses. "If you need to get up at 4:00 A.M. while she's still sleeping, fine, but don't let her go to bed by herself night after night," he told them. For the remainder of his years in school, this husband made sure his wife never went to sleep alone.

What is the normal sexual frequency for couples? How often do most people have sex?

One person asked, "How often is okay?" I responded, "How often is it okay to grocery shop?" You decide what works for you.

I hesitate to define "normal," as I explained earlier. I had one patient who, after thirty years of marriage, reported that she and her husband had sex every day of their marriage except when she was hospitalized for surgery or giving birth. She thought that was normal and delightful. Another patient shared that in their three years of marriage, she and her husband had sex three times a day. We would certainly hate to discourage couples if this is what they desire. On the opposite end of the spectrum, you will find couples who do not have sex or only do it on holidays.

If you want to know the statistical averages as reported, they might be summed up as progressing from "tri-weekly" to "try weekly" to "try weakly." Couples aged twenty to twenty-nine generally have sex three to four times a week. Couples aged thirty to thirty-nine have sex an average of two to three times a week. People from forty to fifty average one to two times a week, while couples over fifty make love less than once a week. (We'll talk about the sexual habits of older couples later.) However, it's important to note here that many have admitted to me that they lied (both in saying they did it "more often" and "less often") on all sorts of reports of frequency. Thus, it's hard to know what is true. But at least this gives us some general ranges.

A woman wrote to Ann Landers:

> It has never been determined how much sex is "normal." Furthermore, no one knows exactly why some people have a stronger sex drive than others. I refuse to believe something is wrong with me because I don't want my husband hot and wild all the time. I know that sex is important to a marriage, but if that's all there is, the marriage is doomed.

Ann responded, "When the first flames of passion die down, if there is nothing of substance to keep the embers glowing, the fire goes out. Good sex is like the frosting on the cake; but it's the meat and potatoes that provide the nourishment."

What are the meat and potatoes for you? For your spouse? In his book *His Needs, Her Needs*, author Willard Harley identifies a man's top marital needs in order of importance (as consistently expressed by his clients). They are (1) sexual fulfillment, (2) recreational companionship, (3) having an attractive spouse, (4) receiving domestic support, and (5) admiration. Women have identified their top five needs as being quite different: (1) affection, (2) conversation, (3) honesty and openness, (4) financial support, and (5) family commitment.[2] Notice what does not even make the list for most women.

Several newlywed women, in adjusting to marriage with normal, healthy husbands, have told me how surprised they were that their men had such active interest in sex. Perhaps the "normal frequency" figures can help them to see that their men may not have a problem with sex after all.

By the way, there's no prize at the end of life for the couple who made love the most times!

Is masturbation okay within marriage?

Not as the sole means of sexual experience, but perhaps as an occasional adjunct. Mutual masturbation (manually bringing each other to orgasm without sexual intercourse) may be a good option at times, particularly in the late stages of pregnancy. If your spouse has extended illness or fatigue, or you must endure a lengthy separation, this may be an acceptable option. There is no biblical prohibition, but Christians will want to consider broader issues as well.

Solo masturbation, while quite common among Christians, according to the best available information, can be addictive and detract from true marital intimacy. The fantasy life and images required for the continual practice of masturbation certainly pose a potential danger. Even if you are thinking about your spouse, it's easy to imagine practices that can make the "real thing" rather dull by comparison. Also, with self-gratification you don't have to communicate to someone else what you want. For most people these do not turn into major issues, but for some they can become a problem.

Masturbation is not just a "male thing." One husband shared that his wife lay tense and motionless when they had sex, but then she would get up and masturbate. She apparently experienced no pleasure when she was with him, but experienced intense pleasure from self-stimulation. This pattern proved very damaging in their relationship, which eventually ended in divorce.

Both husbands and wives are instructed to fulfill their duty to each other in 1 Corinthians 7. One wife, who had been wanting sex for weeks, found her husband masturbating and felt deeply wounded that he had not allowed her to share his body. Thus, it would seem that masturbation is very damaging when used as a regular means of sexual gratification within marriage in place of intercourse.

Does sex always have to be spontaneous?

No. In fact, spontaneous sex may be *impossible* with children and certain living arrangements. (It's hard to engage in spontaneous lovemaking on the floor of the den with teenagers around or mom-in-law breezing through for a midnight snack.)

Some couples bristle against the idea of planned sex because they hate to feel regimented. But it's unrealistic to think we can be spontaneous all the time. One author we read explained it well:

> By advocating planning, I don't want to discredit the value of spontaneity. It's just that, in our busy lives, spur-of-the-moment opportunities to create lasting memories together are rare and golden. Planning ahead assures that these moments won't be overlooked entirely in the hustle and bustle of our daily lives. Planning ahead also lets your spouse know how much you value your times together.[3]

Planning demonstrates interest, and it can provide opportunities to create the environments that can fulfill each other's desires. Even if you actually *are* able to pull off multiple spontaneous encounters, you can count on having to accommodate interruptions—someone calling or knocking on your door. Keep your sense of humor and flexibility.

What does sex mean to him? To her?

Ideally, ask your spouse this question. Is it the ultimate expression of intimacy? Is it the thrill of knowing you have given pleasure to the other? Is it both and more? Is it the expression of intense loving feelings? Is it primarily about pleasure for you?

In general, men consider sex very important. They certainly find it satisfying and unifying. It is the ultimate expression of *pleasure*. While it has relational implications, that's not the central focus. A wise wife will not underestimate its significance to her man. It has been suggested that perhaps it's as important to him as "being listened to and sharing your heart" is to her (something that, unfortunately, is often considered an "extra" by men).

What does it mean to her? In general, at its best it is the deepest expression of loving *feelings*—communicating through the fingertips what the mind cannot articulate because even the best words cannot find utterance for its depth. Good sex for her is the crowning relational moment. When she is in love and the relationship is good, having sex is really about loving with her *whole* being. For her, "full meal" sex (as opposed to the "fast food" quickie) is a deeply loving experience, the most intimate expression of herself.

As one writer theorized,

> Wives view sex in the context of the entire relationship. Women link their sexuality with where they are at emotionally and relationally. If a woman is lonely for communication, romance and nonsexual intimacy, she'll feel emotionally disconnected from her husband. And she won't be all that interested in sex. Men are more fragmented in their experience of sexuality. They are quickly stirred up. If a guy gets the urge, he's ready for sex— even if he and his wife just had an argument.[4]

Can marital sex match the "excitement" associated with forbidden relationships?

Yes and no. Most surveys show statistically that monogamous people are the hottest Valentines over the long term. However, the very nature of sin is that it entices for a season but then it brings consequences. Some of the attraction in forbidden relationships may have its source in the rationalization that "I can be perfect" or "That person can be ideal for me" because the two people in the illicit relationship don't know each other like married partners do. The fantasy—complete with white knight or fair maiden—becomes reality temporarily. The illusion remains unchallenged by dirty socks on the floor or globs of toothpaste left in the sink.

Yet sin over the long term does not deeply satisfy. Often men who selfishly pursue women with whom they have no personal interest have an "It's over; I'm outta here" attitude immediately after sex. For example, someone with a sexual perversion that drives him to seek out a prostitute will often leave immediately after he ejaculates—the moment of "conquest." The thrill is usually followed by guilt and negative feelings. We see this in the Bible story of David's son Amnon, who "fell in love" with his half-sister, Tamar. He longed for her until he raped her. Afterward, "Amnon hated her with a very great hatred; for the hatred with which he hated her was greater than the love with which he had loved her. And Amnon said to her, 'Get up, go away!' " (2 Sam. 13:15).

Regina learned the pitfalls of a forbidden relationship the hard way:

> God's Word is a map through a mine field, designed to enhance rather than take away fun. I dated a guy named Chad in college. We were both believers who actively participated in the campus outreach for Christians, but we slept together regularly. Amazingly, I never got pregnant. About a year later we broke up. Five years after that, I married my husband. Now more than ever, I have so many regrets—the greatest being that Chad was a better lover than my husband.
>
> Actually, I wonder if that's true. Stolen cookies taste better. There's a sense in which there's more excitement in sneaking. True, the relationship was less secure and there was guilt, which took away from what we had, in one sense. But in the pure physical pleasure of it all, Chad was more exciting. It's hard to get him out of the bedroom every time my husband and I are together. I have to decide *every time;* it never gets easier. I wonder if my memory presents the past in accurate terms. Have I idealized what actually happened? I wonder if God is punishing me. Sexually speaking, ignorance would have been bliss. The short-term pleasure is definitely not worth the long-term pain.

Sadly, many patients have echoed Regina's words when they have told about past lovers who were "better" sexually than their spouses.

However, it is interesting to note that some very credible researchers have discovered that people who engage in extramarital affairs in general report that they are more gratified sexually by their spouses than by their lovers. To add insult to injury, these people also have sex less often than those faithfully married. It has been suggested that part of the reason for the decreased level of gratification stems from the practical torments we generally do not think about, that weigh on the minds of those engaging in extramarital sex: Will he (she) like it? Will she (he) have an orgasm? Is my body attractive? Do I smell badly? Can I keep going long enough? Will he (she) *really* like me? Am I better than he (she) has had before? Am I being too rough? Not rough enough? Too responsive? Not responsive enough? And on and on.[5]

Can't sex become an addiction if I engage in it regularly?

In 1 Corinthians 7 we read that God *intends* for couples to "engage regularly." In fact, he warns against not doing so. When discussing addiction, therapists often ask, "What is your favorite defense against emotional pain?" In the context of sex, is it an increasing indulgence in pleasure to the point of ultimately caring only for your own desires and not for your partner's needs?

Some define "addiction" as a preoccupation that interferes with a normal sexual relationship with one's spouse. This can be anything from thoughts, obsessions, and compulsions through addictions in which you don't care who the partner is. The activity does not necessarily require physical involvement; it may be mental. One movie—*The Truth About Cats and Dogs*—had a scene with a couple engaging in "phone sex," in which they talked through the act while they masturbated. With the introduction of the Internet to many homes, people are connecting with perfect strangers and having intense sexual "conversations." If you are seeking only self-gratification, you're driving down the wrong road.

What are your suggestions for sex during pregnancy?

Many a husband finds his pregnant wife cute, if not downright sexy. Her breasts swell, which is often a source of pleasure for both partners (although the breasts can be too tender to touch for a while). But others find pregnancy distracting and distasteful.

Many pregnant women are especially interested in sex because their estrogen climbs to high levels during this time. Yet during the later stages of pregnancy, sex is difficult, even impossible. So it's important to keep a good sense of humor, a spirit of adventure, and mutual understanding.

The uterus contracts with orgasm. For this reason, with some pregnancies sex may be a bad idea because it can start the contraction process, resulting in premature delivery. But don't give up on intimacy. Even if the best you can do is a back rub or a neck rub, find a way to express love through the sense of touch (more on this subject in a moment).

"Now that I'm pregnant, I'm a lot more tired," a young wife confided. "I need to have hope that just because I'm pregnant, it doesn't mean I will have to wait another eighteen years to have a love life again." There is hope!

What about after delivery? What should I expect?

When a woman is nursing, her hormonal environment is such that she has less estrogen, less lubrication and elasticity, less desire, and more discomfort or even pain. Some normal women have *no* interest for months. Also, it may take three to six months or more before her body begins to return to its prepregnancy state. This is generally not a happy time sexually, and couples should recognize that this is normal. They will need to make the extra effort to express their care and support for each other.

So what about those times in a marriage when sex is impossible for whatever reason?

I am reminded of a single friend who said, "I heard on the radio that the average person needs twelve physical touches a day to feel loved. I'm down by about 240." Let's face it, touch is important.

Dr. Paul Brand, a noted leprosy specialist, was treating a bright young man in India. In the course of the examination Brand laid his hand on the patient's shoulder and informed him through a translator of the treatment that lay ahead. To his surprise the man began to shake with muffled sobs. The translator asked why he was crying, and then reported to the doctor, "He says he is crying because you put your hand around his shoulder."

Even when sex is impossible, God has created us with a deep need for touch. Partners must make time to mutually meet these needs. For some it is more important than for others: "People have different 'love languages,' " writes Gary Chapman, author of *The Five Love Languages*. "We know that physical touch is a way of communicating love. Holding hands, kissing, and embracing are all ways of communicating emotional love to one's spouse. For some individuals, physical touch is their primary love language. Without it they feel unloved."[6]

"A pat on the shoulder, a warm hug, or a tender kiss on the cheek often generates a strong sense of caring and concern which is important for a best friendship in marriage," write Robert and Debra Bruce, authors of *Reclaiming Intimacy in Your Marriage*.[7]

Dr. Harold Falk at the Menninger Foundation says, "Hugging can lift depression, enabling the body's immune system to become tuned up. Hugging breathes fresh life into tired bodies and makes you feel younger and more vibrant. In the home, hugging can strengthen relationships and significantly reduce tensions."

In our culture, different touches mean increasing levels of intimacy. Even when sex is impossible, we suggest that you use them all. Physical intimacy generally progresses according to this pattern:

hand to hand
hand to shoulder
hand to waist
hand to face
hand to head
mouth to face
mouth to mouth
hand to body
mouth to body
body to body

Especially when your spouse is unable to engage in full intercourse, a tender pat on the shoulder, a warm hug, a gentle caress, an unexpected kiss, sensual words, and sensual strokes generate a strong sense of caring. Touching breaks down barriers and says, "I love and care about you."[8]

It's also vitally important for the spouse who is sexually impaired to communicate continuously, "My current inability is not because you are unattractive or unlovable."

What effect does aging have on a couple's sex life?

Sex drives change some with age, as we mentioned earlier, but often couples report an increase in pleasure. While drives may decrease, fear of pregnancy is gone, and they may find they have less disparity in interest levels.[9] Hopefully, after years of godly marriage, your love for each other will run deep and strong.

One man wrote this observation about his decreased interest in sex: "I'm thankful for my less powerful sex drive. I used to battle with lusting after women I could hardly stand. It bothered me that my sexual urges were so out of line with my feelings. That's different now, and what a relief."

A gradual increase in the time needed to reach orgasm has certain benefits, enabling older men to prolong the pleasure for themselves and their partner. While textbooks might tell us men reach their sexual peak in adolescence, with women reaching theirs shortly thereafter, they are actually focusing only on genital responsiveness. They measure, for example, the quickness with which a man will have an erection, his speed in getting a second erection, and the strength of his ejaculations. Yet speed can actually hinder sexual fulfillment for wives, so the aging process can equalize a couple's timing.

In addition, "If you want intimacy with your sexuality—which has a huge psychophysiological impact—then there isn't a seventeen-year-old who can keep up with a healthy fifty-year-old," writes David Schnarch, Ph.D., in *Psychology Today*. He continues, "As people get older, their capacity for self-validated intimacy—and intimate sex—increase. . . . In terms of sex at profound intensity or emotional depth, most of us are virgins. . . . If we teach teens that they won't reach their sexual potential for another thirty years or so, they can relax (and parents can too)."[10]

Kathy Peel wrote this about sex and aging:

> After twenty-four years of marriage, our "lust" has grown into a deeply rooted love. We know we can't have all our own needs met. . . . Maybe it's hormones, maybe it's the kids getting older, maybe it's being comfortable with who [I am], but the "lust" I felt before we married seems pale in light of my feelings today. I don't know if I've caught up with my husband's sex drive or if he's adjusted to mine, but it seems that all of the long, sometimes painful conversations, the hard work, the prayers, and the years of patience are paying off in a wonderful way. . . . As our

bodies age, the need for deep relationships is even more important. [In the future] we'll do what we did before—talk, pray, and
work our way through it. . . . Prayer and sex are rarely mentioned in the same sentence, but they should be.[11]

As couples reach their elder years, sex often remains important because it is such an integral part of maintaining self-esteem and expressing love for one other. Many older people maintain active sexual
relationships.

Often, senior men have difficulties with erectile dysfunction. However,
they can still enjoy providing pleasure to their wives through manual
stimulation. All evidence documents that clitoral sensation remains
throughout life, so older women can retain the capacity for orgasm.

The following information about seniors' love lives, taken from a poll
done for *Parade* magazine, reveals some interesting statistics:

- On average, of the last ten times they had sex, men sixty-five and
  over reported reaching orgasm eight times, women five times. Almost half reached orgasm every time.
- The percentage of sexually active seniors declines with age: 55
  percent of those between sixty-five and sixty-nine are sexually active; 48 percent between seventy and seventy-four; 28 percent between seventy-five to seventy-nine; 21 percent between eighty to
  eighty-four; and 13 percent of those eighty-five and older.
- Seniors reported having orgasms an average of seven of the last ten
  times they had sex, compared with eight in ten for younger lovers.
- Seniors reach orgasm sooner—in an average of 12.4 minutes, as
  opposed to 17.3 minutes for the younger sample. (Perhaps years of
  practice pay off.)
- 4 percent of senior women who are sexually active had never experienced orgasm.[12]

What about those who become physically disabled? They can often
express themselves sexually using a wide range of pleasure-enhancing
techniques, from stroking the face to oral-genital sex. Many disabled
individuals are still able to provide sexual pleasure for their spouses.

Even if a person is unable to experience orgasm, it is tremendously rewarding and stimulating to be able to give an orgasm to one's spouse.

How will menopause or hysterectomy affect our love life?

Physical intimacy need not end following surgical procedures such as hysterectomy or after the normal "change of life"—menopause. It may require some change and creativity but a satisfying sexual relationship can result for most.

Hysterectomy and other surgical procedures performed on the female reproductive tract (ovaries, tubes) may bring with them certain freedoms. Pregnancy is virtually impossible following hysterectomy, removing one of the major fears inhibiting sexual enjoyment. Surgeons reconstruct the vagina in such a way during surgery that following the normal post-operative recovery period, most find intercourse quite comfortable. In women for whom endometriosis, symptomatic fibroids, or excessive bleeding prompted the surgery, intercourse may become far more enjoyable, with decreased pain and reduced difficulty with flow and cramps.

The ovaries excrete small amounts of testosterone until a woman is into her eighties. Disease or a family history of ovarian cancer may necessitate ovarian removal separately or at the time of hysterectomy. Since testosterone stimulates sexual desire, her drive may decrease noticeably once the ovaries are removed. If this becomes a problem— that is, if she notices a difference—estrogen tablets that also contain testosterone can be prescribed. So this matter is easily addressed.

Menopause and the several years preceding the ultimate cessation of menses *(perimenopause)* are particularly critical times in the life of a woman. The regular, predictable release of female hormones eventually decreases in all women, upsetting the emotional environment for many and physically bringing to an end the childbearing years. During the perimenopause, which may last several years, cycles and moods may be irregular, with unpredictable fertility and distressing hot flashes. Many women are candidates for estrogen replacement therapy during this time but this is a complex decision requiring in-depth consultation with your physician.

Most women make this passage without too much difficulty, but the emotional and physical changes can disrupt normal patterns of intimacy.

One patient described a hot flash "like being dipped in hell. I wanted to tear off my clothes and jump out the window." One wonders how her befuddled husband processed this episode.

The majority of women complete menopause and, with estrogen replacement or good lubricants and otherwise healthy lifestyles, return to enjoying an active and satisfying sex life. Another patient said her sex life and her husband's sex life were better than ever—no "bleeding," no worries about pregnancy, and "We've finally figured out what we like!"

10

WHAT IS MARRIAGE?

Beneath the apple tree I awakened you,
—Song of Solomon 8:5

I magine exercising only half of the body. Kind of illogical, right? In the same way, when discussing marital intimacy, the "how-to's" about sex constitute a mere fraction of the whole. We've started with the physical description, but what about the spiritual and emotional sides? A couple can understand all about anatomy and function, but without a foundation for relating as God desires, their sexual relationship will suffer.

First of all, sex is no surprise to God. He made it. It is not, as some suggest, the product of male lust. At one extreme we get the idea that "spiritual Christians can't have good sex." At the other end of the spectrum, we've seen disgraced televangelists who communicate the notion that some Christians put no limits on sex. Karl Barth observed that human sexuality has been a vacillation between evil eroticism on the one hand and an evil absence of eroticism on the other.

God created us to be sexual beings, and as our Creator, He invites us to fully enjoy sexual pleasure—within the boundaries of marriage. Yet consider some "Revised Standard" views of marriage:

- "I will be devoted to my spouse as long as the love shall last."
- "When you run out of romance, you run out of the marriage."
- "A marriage license is just a piece of paper."
- "We have a prenuptial agreement."

Where did marriage originate? What does it mean? Where does intimacy fit into marriage? When I teach a premarriage seminar, I ask engaged couples these questions. Often they give me blank stares. They're about to enter into this relationship, but they can't even explain what the goal is.

Marriage involves making a legal contract. When you stand there together, whether before a justice of the peace, a pastor, or a rabbi, if you exclude all the religious trappings, the fancy clothes, and the music, you commit yourselves to each other legally. Anyone who has tried to escape that legal relationship realizes how difficult and costly it can be. But marriage ultimately is a covenant, a binding agreement, made before God; and it is *God* who joins husband and wife together.

Marriage is unlike a business partnership, although some people think of it as that sort of arrangement; if it doesn't work out, they feel they can always sign off as they would with a failed business relationship. Yet God involves Himself in this covenant we make before Him. And He is the one who seals it—which makes marriage different from all other relationships and is the reason why efforts to "undo" marriage create enormous problems and evoke profound pain.

Marriage isn't society's idea; it's God's. It began in the Garden of Eden. We read in Genesis 2:18, "The LORD God said, 'It is not good for the man to be alone. I will make him a helper suitable for him.' " God had spoken all of creation into being except for humans. God personally formed Adam from the dust. Finally, He fashioned Eve from Adam's rib.

We also read in the second chapter of Genesis that marriage began at God's initiative. Note that God instituted marriage before the temptation and sin of Adam and Eve. Although humanity had fallen into sin, Jesus later blessed and validated marriage at the wedding in Cana by His first miracle. So sin did not erase God's blessing of and plan for marriage.

According to God's description, marriage involves two things: (1) leaving father and mother, and (2) cleaving to each other. Leaving and cleaving involve decisions to leave home and join each other for a lifetime, establishing a new family and a new priority. Why is that important?

Going back to the beginning, when God made Adam, He created him alone. Then He declared that it was *not good* for man to be alone. After we have read numerous times in the Genesis account that God made something and declared it "good," we have a contrast. He said it was *not* good for man to be alone. As Adam named the animals, exercising his God-given authority, he no doubt quickly realized that male horses have female horses, and male monkeys have female monkeys, yet he himself had no counterpart. God created in Adam a sense of need. Then He met that need by creating—in a spectacular way—his wife. We read what Adam said when he first viewed her, "This is now bone of my bones. . . ." In the Hebrew, Adam's "This is now" statement carries considerable enthusiasm, like saying "Yahooooo! Finally!"

Parents whose children marry would be wise to note that God describes "leaving and cleaving" as the natural order of events when couples marry. Their new relationship takes priority over even the parent-child relationship. I hear about parents who tell their children on their wedding days, "If your spouse ever treats you badly, if you are ever unhappy, you can always come home."

They would do better to advise, "When you say 'I do,' keep your commitment in sickness and health. We're renting out your room tomorrow. Drop by sometime—for a visit!"

What does it mean to "leave"? Many marriages crash and burn on the rocks of a partner's refusal to "leave" mom and dad. Dan and Carla had struggled with in-law problems throughout their entire ten-year marriage. One day Carla and her mother-in-law, Mary, disagreed over how to spend leisure time. Mary felt Carla should cook meals when the family vacationed together; Carla, who worked full-time and rarely got a break, wanted to order pizza. Dan sided with his mother because she was his "blood" relative. Within the year Dan and Carla had divorced over vacation cuisine. "Leaving" does not necessarily mean moving physically, although this might be wise. Rather, it means choosing to nurture the new relationship over those with one's blood relatives.

What does it mean to "cleave"? It means to cling together, to be joined together. The new relationship *takes priority* over the parent-child relationship. God joins you together.

In Deuteronomy 24:5, we read that God told husbands to stay home from war their first year of marriage so they could "give happiness" to their wives. It's important to spend extra time in those first, foundational days of being "joined," so the two of you can adjust to being married.

During this time you will need to work out who will do what, figure out your unique styles of communicating, and develop sexual intimacy. We throw couples together for a "weekend honeymoon" and expect them to return knowing how to live as one!

There is no "leaving and cleaving" involved in premarital sex or adultery. God says clearly that sexual intimacy outside the marital union is sin, not "instant marriage." Michael, a single man, was serving as an associate pastor when he met Pam. They started dating, and he found himself fascinated by her. Even though he saw many indications in her life that she had a half-hearted commitment to the Lord, his attraction to her caused him to ignore them. Before long their physical relationship had progressed further than it should have. Soon after that they began having sex. Michael would repent, but then a week later, the same thing would happen. In his mind they had become "married in God's eyes," yet this union did not come with God's blessing. Guilt overwhelmed him. So he tried to "make it right" by proposing to her. Within two months they married. And they have been miserable together ever since. Some believe, as Michael did, that if you have a sexual relationship with someone, God considers the two of you married. That is untrue; it's not what Scripture teaches. You are engaging in sin, not marriage. Marriage is a leaving, cleaving, lifelong commitment before God.

What else do we learn about marriage? The Creator's design for marriage is spiritual, emotional, and physical oneness. God makes a couple "one flesh." He's an integral part of each marital union. What about people who don't even believe in God? Marriage is God's institution, and it is meant to operate according to His plan, whether or not those involved acknowledge Him.

Adam and Eve were naked and unashamed. Only sin brought the awareness of shame. The body is beautifully crafted by God in His own image—it is complex, intricate, amazing in its ability to function. We learn in 1 Corinthians 6 that the body of the believer belongs to God, and He indwells this "temple" with His Holy Spirit. We are instructed, therefore, to glorify God in our bodies. Adam and Eve felt comfortable together. They received each other visually and appreciated and enjoyed each other.

Marriage is a serious commitment. It isn't the sappy emotional bond we may connect with the saying, "Sugar is sweet and so are you"; it's a decision of the will: "I take this woman [this man] for better or worse; for richer, for poorer; in sickness, in health, till death do us part." In Matthew 19, we read what Jesus taught about marriage. He said, "What therefore God has joined together, let no one separate" (verse 6). God puts husbands and wives together in a unique one-flesh union and no one should tamper with it. Now, as it turns out, divorce happens, but God allows it by concession. It is an exception because some people have such hardened hearts, hearts so closed to God, that they deal treacherously with those they've pledged to love; their spouses cannot live with them in this sinful world.

We see it on television and we read about it in the newspaper: Spousal verbal abuse is on the rise. Partners commit acts of physical violence against each other that sometimes even lead to death; this is not the intent of the vow, "Till death do us part." Yet even more unsettling than all the lawyers and custody battles are the emotional divorces. If surveys and studies included those, we would find a large, lonely group of "unhappily married people." What are emotional divorces? These are the relationships of couples who live under the same roof but say no more to each other than, "What's for dinner?" "Have a nice day," and "Did we get any mail?"

Someone has estimated that of a dozen couples, four divorce and six stay together without love or joy for the sake of their children (or for continued access to them) or due to their religious beliefs or careers. Tragically, only two couples enjoy an intimate and happy marriage.[1]

For the many survivors of divorce, regardless of who was at fault, remember this: divorce is not the unpardonable sin. Earlier in Matthew 5, Jesus said divorce does not automatically reflect sin on the part of the divorced person. Even if you were at fault in a divorce and have since wrongly married again, you did so either out of ignorance or out of rebellion. Confess this decision to the Lord. Find His forgiveness and focus on making your current marriage what He wants it to be.

Does remarriage constitute an ongoing adulterous relationship? No. In Deuteronomy 24 we read about instructions for a woman who has divorced and remarried. Her new spouse is called her "husband," not her "adulterous relationship." When Jesus met the woman at the well, He said she'd had five husbands—not one husband and four adulterous relationships. So apparently, in God's eyes remarriage exists, and the marital relationship in which you currently find yourself is where you should remain and grow.

Yet is marriage forever? No. Each of us has a spirit that will live eternally—believers will dwell in the presence of God and unbelievers will be separated from God's loving presence. If we were spiritually "married," or united, even death would not end the marriage, and the remaining partner would not be free to marry. But we read that in heaven there will be no marriage (Mark 12:24–25), and the bereaved spouse left on earth is no longer bound to his or her departed spouse (Rom. 7:1–2).

The disciples said in response to Jesus' words about divorce, "If this is so, it's better not to marry!" (Matt. 19:10). Jesus basically replies with, "You're on the right track; it is better not to marry than to marry wrongly." So don't marry unless it is to another believer and you are committed to that one for a lifetime. If you are willing to give yourself to that person by choice of the will—in sickness or in health, for richer or poorer, and until death separates the two of you—knowing there will assuredly be tough times, marriage can be life's greatest blessing. Understand that one of God's purposes for marriage is to present, through your relationship, a picture to the world of how Christ and the church relate to each other.

It's so important that believers marry only other believers. The Bible warns us to avoid becoming "unequally yoked" (2 Cor. 6:14). This metaphor springs from the fact that two oxen plowing a field together cannot accomplish anything if they are going in different directions. In context, the passage is talking about a business relationship, but how much more important is the marriage relationship? Believers who marry unbelievers are asking for trouble. They don't live in the same kingdom; they don't worship the same Lord; they're not headed in the same direction.

When I teach a premarriage conference, I use Play Dough—a lump of blue and a lump of yellow. When you take the man and woman—represented by the blue and yellow dough—and mix them together, signifying life's trials and triumphs, a change takes place; you get green Play Dough. No matter how hard you try, you can't get the yellow and the blue back. You can split the combined lump up into two lumps again, but some changes are irreversible. The two "colors" have become one new color, one new entity. So it is with marriage. Those who have been through a divorce or the death of a spouse realize how dramatically marriage changes you internally and "in essence." You become part of another person and that person becomes part of you. It goes beyond the physical picture.

As I (Dr. Bill) look at my own marriage, I see that in some mysterious way God has joined me to my wife—through the years of quiet evenings when we've "connected"; through surgeries, kids' accomplishments, parenting challenges, and loss of family members; through sweet stolen moments, family vacations, and failures; through times we have ministered together, the threat of malpractice suits, and through personal accomplishments, hers and mine. The sorrows have been easier to bear, the joys heightened. As life has pounded us, "mixed" us together, our synergy—the "together we are stronger than as two individuals"—has made us resilient because we've had each other.

Maybe sometimes we tend to hold a low view of marriage partly because we see the world's standards displayed in our TV sitcoms and movies. But marriage is of God's origination, not Hollywood's. He sets the rules and we ought to know them and walk in them. Obviously, starry-eyed nearly-weds need little encouragement here, but physical intimacy cannot develop in the absence of spiritual harmony. I'm not saying folks can't have enjoyable sex for a time; they just cannot experience the fullness of marital intimacy that God intended apart from relationship with Christ.

Love that endures is much more than just erotic attraction. Marriage is not merely something to be endured. Many say, "But we just don't love each other anymore." When questioned about how much effort they had put into restoring their marriages, most say they tried but got tired and frustrated. They have confused the emotion of love with the commitment to love unconditionally. There is still hope. If Christ can be trusted for eternity, surely we can trust Him in day-to-day difficulties.

Someone asked a wife celebrating her fiftieth anniversary, "What is your secret to remaining happily married as long as you have?" She answered, "When we married, I made a list of ten faults—ten flaws—that, for the sake of our marriage, I would overlook in his life." She never actually wrote them down, but whenever a difficulty or argument arose, she would say to him, "You're lucky that was on the list." This wife demonstrated the kind of forgiveness and acceptance necessary to make a marriage work. So often we demand our own rights, and in the process we miss out on the joy God intended. Practically, marriage works when we willingly sacrifice ourselves and our rights for the sake of the beloved:

"My beloved is mine, and I am his." (Song of Solomon 2:16)

Marriage, as designed and ordained by God, provides a picture of God's heart to a world in darkness, a world in desperate need of reconciliation in its most intimate relationships. During His earthly sojourn, Jesus demonstrated complete submission to the will of His heavenly Father. Jesus walked in humility and compassion, the perfect servant leader. Jesus Christ embodies the faithful "lover" of all who respond in faith to the sacrificial offer of His pure life for theirs. In earthly, God-centered marriages, such faithfulness, gentleness, and steadfast love should reflect the sweet relationship God desires with His people. Thus, marriage not only fulfills us as created beings, it also gives testimony to a needy world of God's marvelous provision and His passionate desire for abiding fellowship with his children, who are created in His image.

The Scriptures call this one-flesh picture a "mystery," but not the same sort of mystery as an Agatha Christy murder mystery. It's something we would never have guessed had God not chosen to disclose it. Yet he did reveal it. He tells us that the marriage of one man to one woman for a lifetime pictures Jesus Christ and His bride, the church. Throughout Scripture we find that Christ considers His relationship with us to be personal and intimate, as groom and bride. He loves us as individuals, and He wants to relate, to fellowship, and to commune with us. Jesus leads with humility and total sacrifice. He shows this in the deepest, most personal relationship we as men and women can experience—a godly marriage.

11

A WORD TO HUSBANDS

Like an apple tree among the trees of the forest,
so is my beloved among the young men.
—Song of Solomon 2:3

When Ron and Cindy married, Cindy was the picture of perfect health. A fine athlete, she enjoyed a weekly round of tennis and played on the church softball team. However, after she began to experience numbness in her legs, she sought medical diagnosis. The report came back with bad news—Cindy had a debilitating disease. Today she can barely move most of her muscles, and she constantly fights depression because she must rely on her family to continually serve her. "I have the mind and motivations of an athlete," she shared. "Yet my body will not cooperate. It's so frustrating! I can only cope with each day by God's grace, taking one day at a time. Sometimes I would like to take *two* days at a time!"

This was not what Ron expected to happen when he married a vibrant, healthy young woman. Together they have grieved the loss of Cindy's health, and it has been a constant battle to remain optimistic. However, Ron shared, "Our communication is at its deepest level ever." Ron has taken seriously his vows to love his wife "in sickness and in health." By God's strength he continually—day in and day out—models God's picture of a self-sacrificing, loving husband, and she a godly, supportive wife, to the best of her ability.

After addressing wives in Ephesians 5, Paul shifts gears and instructs husbands. He records detailed guidelines for men, no doubt because we need it! Under the Holy Spirit's guidance, Paul wrote:

> Husbands, love your wives, just as Christ also loved the church and gave Himself up for her; that He might sanctify her, having cleansed her by the washing of water by the word, that He might present to Himself the church in all her glory, having no spot or wrinkle or any such thing; yes, but that she should be holy and blameless.
>
> So husbands ought also to love their own wives as their own bodies. He who loves his own wife loves himself; for no one ever hated his own flesh, but nourishes and cherishes it, just as Christ also does the church, because we are members of His body. For this cause a man shall leave his father and mother, and shall cleave to his wife; and the two shall become one flesh. This mystery is great; but I am speaking with reference to Christ and the church. Nevertheless let each individual among you also love his own wife even as himself; and let the wife see to it that she respect her husband. (Eph. 5:25–33)

Paul tells husbands to model Christ's love, which is *sacrificial, sanctifying,* and *satisfying* for the beloved.

Sacrificial love. God calls Christian husbands to a life of sacrifice. He sets a high standard for us. The word translated "love" is *agape*, a selfless, sacrificial love. It's what Paul describes in 1 Corinthians 13:5 as love that does not seek its own way. This love is primarily "other centered." A lot of men like to regard submission as subjection, thinking of the husband as commander-in-chief with his troops. But the reality of the biblical picture reveals that the husband never gives orders. Rather, he acts in love. When we insist on having our own way, our expression of love is clearly not of God.

Reject the whole military picture. There is to be no marching about, screaming orders, nor should men expect to be saluted like General Patton or Baron Von Trapp in *The Sound of Music* (Von Trapp even used a separate whistle tone to summon each of his children). Instead, picture Christ washing the disciples' dirty feet. If you bark commands, if you make demands, if you expect your wife to wait upon you, you violate the imperative to love in the biblical sense. Authentic Christian manhood in the home models sacrificial love, bringing order, not chaos. It involves men giving of themselves—not giving commands, not laying down the law, not expecting maid service. Men are to lay down their own wills, yielding the desire to have things their own way—to the point they would give up their very lives.

Are you willing to pay the price? Are you willing to give yourself up for your wife? No commands or demands, but servanthood by choice, setting an example by following Christ? To make this choice as a husband is to truly act in obedience to Christ.

Sanctifying love. A husband's love is to sanctify his wife. "Sanctify" means to set apart or to make holy. When a couple marries, God sets them apart, and they forsake all others in the most intimate sense. Saying "yes" to one means saying "no" to everyone else.

When we say the husband must have "sanctifying love," we can give the wrong impression. A lot of people think that this means the husband has to possess more spiritual information than his wife does. Yet because in our culture many churches offer women's Bible studies and because women can often tune in to excellent Christian television and radio programs, wives may actually have more exposure to spiritual truth than their husbands do. A wise husband provides an environment in which his wife feels free to pursue and express her interaction with God's truth without worrying that this is a threat to him. They can grow together in grace and truth as they discuss each other's spiritual insights.

A godly husband does not *have* to hold a formal "instructional" time for his family, as many have suggested. The Bible doesn't say, "Every Tuesday night you will lead family devotions." This is a wonderful model, but not the *only* model. Godliness is first a matter of character over activity and may be expressed differently in different homes.

Consider Diane, whose husband feels uncomfortable leading a formal devotional time with her. She wanted to know what a couple's spiritual life should look like. Eugene Peterson, author of the best-selling, paraphrased version of the Bible known as *The Message*, responded to her question as follows:

I don't think there's any picture. At a pastor's conference I told [the audience] that at noon on Mondays, our Sabbath/hiking day, [my wife] Jan prayed for lunch. In fact, I think I said, "I pray all day Sunday. I'm tired of it. She can do it on Monday." There was one woman there who was really irate. She said I should be praying; Jan should not be praying because I'm the priest in the family and she's not the priest. That's silliness. You are brother, sister, man, wife, friends in Christ. You work out the kind of relationship before the Lord that is intimate. And no, I don't think there's any kind of picture you have to fit into, that you have to produce. That's oppressive, isn't it? After all, this is freedom in the Lord.

A godly husband loves the Lord with all his heart, soul, and might. And he teaches God's Word to his children (if he has any). He talks of it in his house and when he walks and when he lies down and when he rises up (see Deut. 6). In the 1990s, we could say he initiates spiritual conversation while he's driving his kids to softball practice or taking his wife to dinner. He models a godly example, initiates setting a Christ-centered tone, responds sensitively to spiritual truth, and encourages and affirms his family members in their efforts to pursue their individual relationships with God.

Jesus Christ is the ultimate example of sanctifying love. He gave Himself for us in such a way that He purifies His bride, the Church—male and female. So a husband must love his wife in a way that purifies her. His love should challenge and encourage her to grow in holiness.

In turn, Christian marriages reflect this picture of purity and holiness to the world. We must make it our priority to spend time with God personally because we can get going so fast that we fail to recharge spiritually. Then in turn, our marriages suffer. We have to be growing spiritually on an individual basis to be able to create a home environment where spiritual truth is affirmed. We also need God's supernatural power to enable us to "lay down our lives."

With Christ indwelling both husband and wife, each should make it a priority to have individual times of prayer and Bible study. Then together they seek His will, submitting themselves to Him. Husbands should model a life of devotion and submission to God, but that too will vary in appearance. Godly friends and solid church-family relationships contribute significantly to maturing in the Christian faith. Do you as a husband make fellowship with other believers a priority? Does she need you to offer to take the kids to the park or vacuum the hall so she can spend a few quiet moments with the Lord? This may be the model for you.

Satisfying love. Additionally, we men must demonstrate satisfying love. Paul says husbands must "nourish" their wives as their own bodies. This doesn't mean to obsess over making the body an irresistible hunk of manhood—a "babe magnet," as it were. This is not to suggest that we should totally blow off our own physical condition, appearance, or hygiene either! Yet the focus is on the wife. In the same way we care for our bodies by giving them proper rest and nutrition, we should care for our wives. When I care for my wife, Jane, I am caring for myself at the same time. Not in a selfish, self-serving way, but I'm honoring the woman whom God has entrusted to me. An investment in your wife is really an investment in yourself, because the two of you have become "one." To nourish implies the provision and protection of careful tending. A farmer who "nourishes" his garden by weeding, watering, and watching over it with care anticipates a bountiful yield, trusting God to provide rain and sun.

Many men feel comfortable with the "nourishes" part. We often say, "I'm working long hours and putting food on the table, so I must be doing all right." Yet, if during our own childhood we had experienced only this kind of provision, we would have reached adulthood as emotionally deprived people (which, unfortunately, is true for many of us). God created us to need so much more than that.

Do you nourish your wife's physical needs? Do you nourish her intellectual needs? Her spiritual needs? Her emotional needs? Do you encourage her to share her heart freely with you, and do you confide your deepest thoughts and dreams?

Then there's the "cherish" part of how we men are to relate to our wives—that's even more challenging. It reminds me of the story of a wife who had been married twenty years. She asked her husband, "Do you still love me?"

"I said I did when we got married," he answered. "If that changes, I'll let you know." When was the last time you said "I love you" with meaning? God instructs husbands to cherish their wives. "Cherish" is a very tender word. It carries the idea of being full of compassion and sentiment. The closest description of this that comes to mind might be something like "cuddling" or "lavishing with tender affection." As Proverbs 19:22 states, "What is desirable in a man is his kindness." God paints a picture of a hopelessly head-over-heels-in-love romantic wooing his bride of however many years (unlike many men today who think romantic foreplay is shouting, "Ready or not, here I come. . . ." or "Brace yourself"). Do you cherish your wife? Does she receive from you the comfort, compassion, and tenderness that God made her to need?

We all have different needs—intellectual, emotional, physical, and spiritual. You cannot begin to meet your spouse's every need. Yet you can play an integral role in fulfilling those needs, particularly if she spends all day with toddlers or is dealing with moody teenagers! Can you put down the paper so you can talk together? Do the dishes so she can talk with a friend on the phone? Feed and bathe the kids while she takes a night class?

Think of her intellectual needs. She may have watched sixteen straight hours of *The Lion King* or had a frustrating afternoon trying to grocery shop with a toddler. She may not have heard a sentence with more than two words in it for an entire day. When you're home, she would like to hear words arranged in sentences and paragraphs with questions and answers. Or she may simply need you to listen. Our quiet, attentive presence is often the best support we can provide.

Our wives do not necessarily need us to play Mr. Fix-It when they share their problems. They may merely need our "ministry of presence" in times of grief, in times of joy, and through the sheer monotony of daily living.

And what about emotional needs? We all need to know we are significant, that we are important, that others value us as individuals. Do you help meet those needs for your wife? Sometimes "being strong for her" is not the solution. We may have to demonstrate our emotional sensitivity and vulnerability so our wives can see how much they mean to us.

Then there are physical, sexual needs. The Scriptures speak boldly and clearly about these. To pretend they don't exist is foolish. The marriage relationship can meet physical needs in a wonderful, glorious way. The world may do all it can to distort, pervert, and twist our views about sexuality, but God designed sex as a beautiful expression of joy between a husband and wife and of His love and feelings of intimacy toward us.

To summarize the Ephesians passage, a husband must love in a way that's sacrificial, sanctifying, and satisfying. As a result, his wife will have an ideal environment for growing in godliness. There's no contingency or "escape clause." Love honors God.

Notice that the text doesn't say, "Love her sacrificially if she submits to you." A husband cannot demand or even expect submission. In obedience to God, he loves his wife and entrusts her to the Lord. I think of a friend who faithfully visits his wife, an Alzheimer's patient. He loves her; he feeds her; he walks with her. Yet she does not know him. Sometimes she yells statements that humiliate him. He expects nothing of her, and daily he fully gives of his love without any hint of hope that she will respond. That is the kind of love to which God calls us, and it is possible by His supernatural grace.

Another husband, Bobby, is married to a woman who battles mental illness. She frequently spends all day in bed and feels threatened and angry if he tries to do housework; she struggles against bouts of depression that keep her inside the bedroom for days at a time. It has been years since they had any sort of physical relationship. "I would gladly trade places with someone whose wife is physically limited," he shares. But Bobby chooses daily to show sacrificial love to his wife while his needs remain unmet.

God calls men to love sacrificially, even if they find themselves in a less than ideal situation. Are you willing to display this kind of love even if you go years without having any of your needs met, perhaps waiting on the Lord to soften her heart? Many marriages fail because we are unwilling to pay the price of self-sacrifice or we've never considered the biblical guidelines for marriage. We let our own desires take precedence over our created purpose, which is to worship and obey God.

When two sinners marry each other, you can bet they will have moments of unhappiness ahead. At some point, your spouse will treat you badly. All marriages face stress and trials. Our bodies fail us. Our job security falls through. Life happens. Yet it's the total, unswerving, God-centered commitment to one another and to the marriage that provides the glue that holds a couple together.

Husband, study your wife. When couples come to me for counseling, I ask a seemingly simple question: Name three things that your spouse likes. The women can usually rattle them off. In fact, most could rattle off ten of them. But the men may ask, "Me? Are you talking to *me?* Three things she *likes?* Okay, me, myself, and I." But if I ask the men to list their wives' favorite hobbies, their favorite places to go, what snack foods they really like, and so on, some of them who have been married for decades sit there dumbfounded and without a clue. We must communicate better, more frequently, and more deeply to understand the precious gift God has given us in our wives.

I read one study that said husbands and wives communicate an average of thirty-seven minutes a week. That's five and a half minutes a day. Communication does not mean reading the paper while you pretend to listen with, "Uh-huh. Yeah. Yeah. Uh-huh." It doesn't include flipping the channels and saying, "Honey, can I have a Coke?" "Honey, what's for dinner?" "Honey, the kids are making noise." You score no "communication points" at all for these utterances. To get points we have to set down the paper, physically turn to face her, and communicate with body language, "I'm listening and interested." Good communication doesn't require agreement, but you must hear and understand what is said.

Now let's see what Peter says to husbands. He provides some brief but powerful instructions: ". . . live with your wives in an understanding way, as with a weaker vessel" (1 Peter 3:7). Now, we may read "live with" or "tabernacle with" or "share the tent with" and assume that as long as we provide the place to live, we are fulfilling this Scripture. Wrong! As alluded to in Ephesians, the Bible directs us to share our time and lives and hearts. To live with a wife in an understanding way, or according to knowledge, means you actually have to know something about this woman with whom you live. Ignorance is dangerous! The phrase "live with" has sexual connotations, too. In addition, understanding our wives requires conversation, communication, the ability to sense and recognize needs, share joys, and bear sorrows.

Peter tells husbands to live with their wives "as with a weaker vessel."

This does not mean weaker intellectually; it does not mean weaker spiritually; and it does not mean weaker emotionally. It is a comparative term that suggests weaker in a physical sense. Think of the difference as like that between the tin of an army mess kit and fine china; or the difference between a mason jar and fine crystal. Peter says the wife is precious, a jewel. So "handle with care."

A wife is a treasure in God's sight, female by divine design. She is a woman, crafted by God in His image. God says to grant her honor as a fellow heir of the grace of life. She's a co-heir and co-equal in essence and value. Both husbands and wives submit to the Lord. One does so by respecting her husband; the other does so by treating his wife as a precious treasure, to be continually enjoyed.

How do you talk to her? Do you speak of her as a wonderful companion, a helper for whom you are grateful to God? Are you willing to give up your life for her? Or do you speak of her with sarcasm and disrespect in front of others? Do you whine at her requests with, "Yes, dear!" or worse yet, treat her as if she weren't there? Do you act as though she were your personal slave and attempt to justify your actions by saying that's your biblical role?

While sex is the number one expressed need for most men, the corresponding need for most women is relational interaction that includes talking, affirmation, and affection from their husbands. If you feel frustrated that your wife is not "giving" you sex often enough, ask yourself, "Am I giving her my interested, undivided attention as often as she desires it?"

To live in an understanding way means you have to listen well, to talk and ask questions. One member of my church said, "Our marriage works great; I find out what she wants to do and I do it." While he said this "tongue in cheek," I suspect many marriages operate under the "Don't rock the boat" philosophy: Pretend all is well—don't ask, don't tell—and keep peace at any cost. That's not what Scripture says men should do. Husbands need to strive for unity with their wives, but they should also retain their individuality and initiative, seeking ultimately to do what God wants them to do.

Peter pictures husbands consistently granting their wives honor, respecting them, treating them as precious treasures. Thus, Scripture is clear on this—there is *never* an excuse for physical, verbal, or emotional abuse. If unresolved anger remains between you and your wife—if you have not settled your differences to the fullest extent that you are able— you are out of fellowship with God, and Peter writes that your prayers will be "hindered." Scripture says my relationship with my wife impacts my relationship with God. Are your prayers being answered or hindered?

Our marriages affect our prayer lives. If you have a problem with anger, bitterness, or slander, you are not allowing the Spirit to control your life. Praying, except to seek forgiveness and reconciliation, is wasted breath.

So in Peter's passage, too, we see a call for husbands to love self-lessly. That could mean laying down your life, but it could also mean something that may be, for you, even more difficult: It could mean laying down the remote. It might mean giving up the bigger bowl of ice cream . . . or the Rose Bowl game on New Year's Day!

I grew up dreaming what it would be like to have a family. Back then I imagined that when I married, I would be a great husband who treated my wife like a queen. But royal families historically have little to commend them. I came to realize I'd better find some better models. A healthy dose of a book penned by a different king—Solomon's Song of Solomon—shows us that Christians have the potential to have the best romances in the universe. Husbands, do others who observe you comment about how much you love your wife? In Song of Solomon 2:4, the bride says this:

> "He has brought me to his banquet hall,
> And his banner over me is love."

In Solomon's time, when the troops needed to regroup, their leaders raised a wide banner so that all could see where to go. It was like a gigantic traveling billboard for the company whose insignia it bore. Solomon's love for his bride was like this banner. It was public and easily seen by anyone observing. Rather than being ashamed of her, he openly delighted in her.

Think of times when you have seen a man treating his wife tenderly in a public place. Maybe he opened her car door, took her hand, and said kind words to her. Maybe he leaned forward over dinner to whisper something sweet. You probably said to yourself, "That guy really loves his wife."

Much of the lasting joy in a marriage comes from little things—the small courtesies, the day-to-day doing of the stuff that you might consider insignificant. We may think that if we pull it together for Christmas and anniversaries and maybe even Valentine's Day, we are "Husband of the Year" material. Yet we cannot erect a magnificent monument on a poor foundation. Those one-time "big deals" do not compensate for a lack of daily kindnesses.

When I practiced obstetrics/gynecology, I frequently asked women about their homes and their husbands. I learned that wives generally are unimpressed with the many hours their husbands put in at work. They actually prefer more time with their men at home. When we get to the end of our lives and stand before the Father, I doubt He will assign "mansion space" according to the number of hours worked. However, God will hold us accountable for whether or not each of us loved his wife sacrificially.

The flip side, which is equally destructive, is the husband who refuses to work or insists on keeping a failing business afloat, declining to provide adequately for his family's material well-being. This does not honor the Lord.

Work-related difficulties are not the only environmental hazards that can erode relationships. Factor in hobbies and sports. I know guys who play softball five nights a week, bowl four nights a week, and have nights out with the guys two nights a week. That's more nights than there are in a week! So I'm guessing they're not home a lot. Now, none of these activities is inherently bad, but we've got to keep them in balance. How do you know if you're overdoing it? Ask your wife. If you come in and say, "Hi, honey!" and she asks you to show some photo identification or state your full name, you've probably been out too much.

Just ask, "Do you feel like I spend enough time with you?" If the answer is "No," do something about it without delay.

You can improve your marriage. No matter how good it is, it can always be better. So start where you are and make a commitment now to cultivate the relationship, to think creatively of ways to bring more joy to your wife. Of course, if you've been as romantic as Jabba the Hut for a long time and start to love your wife sacrificially, she may have a heart attack. But go for it anyway—at least she will be a happy woman as you rush her to the hospital. Communicate love that is tender, compassionate, and sacrificial.

When I went on vacation with my wife one year, I learned that she collected thimbles. So now whenever I travel, I try to find thimbles. To my surprise, I later learned that she also likes collecting onyx turtles. I search for those now, too.

Marriage is full of adventure, and change is a significant part of that journey. We grow; we learn more; actions that were great yesterday may not be so great today. You may do something caring and compassionate one day, and she appreciates it; yet you try it again and it falls flat. That keeps life interesting.

One evening my friend Danny picked up a damp bath towel and, oblivious to the implications, exclaimed, "Ummmmm! Charlotte, this smells like you!" His wife of many years replied, "Ooooooooooh, Danny, that's the most romantic thing you've ever said!" Though not grasping exactly how his recognition of the scent of her body lotion on the towel constituted a romantic remark, Danny seized the moment. A wonderful, romantic evening followed.

Almost gleeful about his incredible discovery—the key to his beloved wife's inner fire—Danny could hardly wait until the following night. Once again, armed with passion unquenchable, he declared, "Charlotte, this towel smells like you!" His remark was met with silence. He repeated in the most seductive voice he could generate, "Charlotte, this smells like you." She dashed the hope in his heart with her response: "Yes, I just used that to dry off." No romance, no passionate embrace. Just a matter-of-fact reply. An educated man with a doctoral degree, Danny concluded, "Women: a mystery." Few would argue with his astute assessment or with the ageless truth that the key to unlocking the heart's passion remains elusive.

Each marriage is unique, but all marriages experience growth and change. People resist nothing more than change. Sometimes change may mean, as in Ron and Cindy's case, adapting to the shocking revelation that your marriage is going to require a lot more work than you anticipated. Circumstances that stretch us to the limit of our ability to give sometimes develop, requiring us to rely more on God's all-sufficient grace. We don't like to change; we resist it. But together we honor God as we rely on His strength to live our lives as godly husbands, and in the process we create a beautiful living, breathing portrait of the love of Christ for His church.

12

A WORD TO WIVES

I am the rose of Sharon,
the lily of the valleys.
—Song of Solomon 2:1

J ust for fun one night, my (Sandi's) married sister, Mary, and her single
friend, Angie, spent an evening doing an Internet search of Christian
dating services. They both groaned when they read one advertisement
that read, "Christian male looking for buxom woman with biblical view
of submission."

In the same way that a "Christian beefcake with a biblical view of
self-sacrificing love" would be less than the whole picture of God's ideal
man, a Barbie look-alike with a servant heart is less than the sum total of
God's ideal woman.

What does the Bible say about what a good woman looks like? God
has a lot to say. It all starts in the Garden of Eden. God created Adam's
wife as a helper, but to understand exactly what that means, consider
what type of help we see in these nonmarriage examples:

- A daughter asks her mom for some *help* with math. The mother
  understands algebra and can explain and guide her daughter through
  working the formulas.
- One friend *helps* another by showing her how to use the computer
  so that she has the necessary skills to change jobs.
- An obstetrician involved with a complicated delivery calls out for
  his partner to *help*. He wants someone who knows what needs to
  be done without having to be told what to do.

In each of these cases, the helpers have strengths they use to aid the ones needing help. Unlike an apprentice who helps from an untrained or unskilled position, these "helpers" give assistance from a position of ability. Now consider Genesis 2:18:

> The LORD God said, "It is not good for the man to be alone; I will make him a helper suitable for him."

In the past, many have suggested this word "help" involves subordination, indicating that woman is lesser than man. Frankly, at first glance this word is a little less than exciting if we link it with common uses of the term—such as Hamburger Helper or "plumber's helper." Yet when we consider how biblical writers used this word, we see that it carries a strongly positive meaning linked to words like "aid" and "support." It frequently was used in reference to God helping his people in the face of enemies. In fact, no fewer than fourteen times we read that God helps humans.

To demean the woman's God-intended task of helping her husband by insinuating (or outright declaring) that hers is a somehow less important "role" ignores the biblical use of the word elsewhere. As helper to the man, the woman meets his insufficiencies with her own sufficiencies. Perhaps this is why opposites tend to attract. Together you reflect the image of God as your strengths and weaknesses complement each other. Author and speaker Zig Ziglar cites an example: "I travel a great deal and sometimes I leave town short of cash. Often without being asked, my wife checks my money and if I'm short, she gets it for me."[1]

Genesis also describes Eve as "suitable." This means "like opposite him" or "according to what corresponds to him—equal and adequate to himself." Thus, the woman is an aid equal to and corresponding to the man, a helper who will enable him to achieve the blessings of God that he cannot fully achieve on his own. Her presence in creation was the only addition needed before God could pronounce his creation "very good."

You might ask, "How can I help my husband?" Begin by figuring out his strengths and weaknesses and then weighing them against your own. During a marriage conference someone asked, "Who should balance the checkbook?" The answer: Whoever the two of you decide can best handle it.

Contrary to what has been taught in many churches and seminars, the husband does not have to "buffer his wife from the stress of finances" by handling all of the money matters. Consider Paula, a CPA, who is married to a man who asked, "So I actually have to have income before I can deduct expenses?" If this man handled their money, he would not buffer her from stress; they would be *in* the buff, because they'd have no money to buy clothing.

Another asked, "Who washes the dishes?" Again, that depends. Are you both working outside the home all day? Do you need to divide the domestic tasks so you'll have time together? Or is one of you working in the home or unemployed, and thus available to do a greater percentage of the domestic tasks?

Nowhere in the Bible does it say, "The man earns the money, takes out the trash, and handles the lawn and cars; the woman changes all the diapers, provides all the parental instruction, does all the shopping, washes the dishes, and keeps the laundry done." Some believe this is the biblical division of labor. Does your husband love to cook? We see biblical examples where Jacob made stew, Stephen and a small group of men served food to widows, and Jesus prepared fish for his disciples.

Questions about division of household labor are some of the greatest struggles couples encounter in their first years together. However, as we mentioned earlier, another marital frustration is that men generally rank sex as their number-one need; women generally rate sex below their top five. Many women focus most of their energy on food preparation, running the kids to sports practice and other activities, and keeping the laundry done. A wife often invests so much time and emotional energy in the kids and housekeeping that her husband wonders, "Where do *I* fit into this deal?" Yes, children are demanding, and some wives have to remind their husbands that fathers are not baby-sitting when they watch the kids; they are parenting. Yes, housework is a never-ending job. But the priority relationship in the home is that of the husband and wife—and that relationship needs to be nurtured.

Statistically, the average couple who has children will spend more than half their lives without kids. Why are divorce rates so high between ages forty-five and fifty-five? Because people "run out" of children. They've hung together because at least they could argue about the kids:

"You're not doing that right!" or "You should be teaching that kid some manners." It ties them together. But that's not what makes a marriage.

Other men wish their wives would keep pace intellectually. Or a husband may struggle with his wife's cavalier attitude about her appearance: "What will an extra fifty pounds hurt?"

What does he consider his greatest needs? *How can your priorities reflect your acknowledgment of what's important to him?*

Now that we've visited the Garden of Eden, let's move to Proverbs (31:10–31 NIV) for another glance at God's ideal for wives:

> A wife of noble character who can find?
> > She is worth far more than rubies.
> Her husband has full confidence in her and lacks nothing of
> > value.
> She brings him good, not harm, all the days of her life.
> She selects wool and flax and works with eager hands.
> She is like the merchant ships, bringing her food from afar.
> She gets up while it is still dark;
> > she provides food for her family and portions for her
> > servant girls.
> She considers a field and buys it;
> > out of her earnings she plants a vineyard.
> She sets about her work vigorously;
> > her arms are strong for her tasks.
> She sees that her trading is profitable,
> > and her lamp does not go out at night.
> In her hand she holds the distaff and grasps the spindle
> > with her fingers.
> She opens her arms to the poor and extends her hands to the
> > needy.
> When it snows, she has no fear for her household;
> > for all of them are clothed in scarlet.
> She makes coverings for her bed;
> > she is clothed in fine linen and purple.
> Her husband is respected at the city gate,
> > where he takes his seat among the elders of the land.

She makes linen garments and sells them, and supplies the
merchants with sashes.
She is clothed with strength and dignity;
she can laugh at the days to come.
She speaks with wisdom, and faithful instruction is on her
tongue.
She watches over the affairs of her household
and does not eat the bread of idleness.
Her children arise and call her blessed;
her husband also, and he praises her:
"Many women do noble things, but you surpass them all."
Charm is deceptive, and beauty is fleeting;
but a woman who fears the LORD is to be praised.
Give her the reward she has earned,
and let her works bring her praise at the city gate.

One woman insisted, "I can't stand that Proverbs 31 lady. I feel tired just thinking about her." This woman is so competent, so intelligent, so industrious and strong that she certainly challenges any view that might suggest that the "little wife" has no independent thoughts, that she is less intelligent than any man, or that godly women must be passive, timid, dainty, or fearful.

Perhaps it would help you to know that a king named Lemuel wrote this passage of Scripture in Hebrew. It forms an acrostic poem, with a line for each letter of the Hebrew alphabet. The contemporary English equivalent might be something like, "An Excellent Wife—from A to Z." It has also been suggested that this is not a snapshot of one day in this woman's life. Only the Bionic Woman could in one twenty-four-hour period find and purchase exotic foods, make a real estate purchase, plant a vineyard, operate the spinning wheel, make and sell clothing, help the poor, and so on. The mere reading of it is enough to cause heatstroke.

Rather than a snapshot, this is more like a movie of the phases of this woman's life. At the end of her days her children rise up and call her blessed. After her youth is gone and wrinkles line her face, she still is a woman to be praised because she has the qualities that outlast physical beauty.

The word translated "noble character" could also be rendered "excellence" or "strength." It's used in other places to describe both physical strength and strength of character—so this woman is virtuous, noble, or possessing valor. This is no helpless waif who depends on her husband to make every decision. Within a context of mutual trust characterizing this woman's relationship with her husband, she possesses so much competence that she can go buy a field on her own. She completes him, taking all her abilities and developing them to the fullest.

She is also a woman of relationships. Her servants, the needy, her children, and her husband all depend on her strength and character. Yet her key relationship is her vertical one—with the Lord.

So a godly wife is a helper and a woman of strength. Now let's look at one more word that describes God's model—*submission.*

Submission? Whoa! The "s" word! Mention it and people think of slave girls who nod "Yes, Master," enabling domestic violence, "doormats," even "Christian" Internet ads.

Yet "submit" is a biblical word. Husbands usually are instructed to love their wives and wives usually are instructed to submit. There are places where wives are told to love their husbands (Titus 2:4) and husbands are directed to honor their wives (1 Peter 3:7), but the emphasis usually is the other way around. Four times God instructs wives to submit:

- "Submit to one another out of reverence for Christ. Wives, submit to your own husbands, as to the Lord. For the husband is the head of the wife as Christ is the head of the church, his body, of which he is the Savior. Now as the church submits to Christ, so also wives should submit to their husbands in everything" (Eph. 5:21–24 NIV).
- "Wives, submit to your husbands" (Col. 3:18 NIV).
- "Likewise, teach the older women to be reverent in the way they live, not to be slanderers or addicted to much wine, but to teach what is good. Then they can train the younger women to love their husbands and children, to be self-controlled and pure, to be busy at home, to be kind, and to be subject to their husbands, so that no one will malign the word of God" (Titus 2:3–5 NIV).

We'll look at another Scripture passage, 1 Peter 3, a little later.

First of all, I have heard it said that the wife's "role" is to submit. However, submission is not a role. Being a wife is a role. Submission is an attitude and an action. When God gives his development plan for intimacy, he tells wives to submit, but he usually does so within the larger context of sharing lives together in fellowship with the Spirit of God.

Because the word "submit" carries so much "baggage," perhaps it would help to begin by clarifying what submission does not mean.

Submission is not . . .

- the idea that a wife should give up all efforts to influence her husband, giving in to his every demand.

- letting him think he's better at something than you are when he isn't. Here's an example of faulty thinking along this line: "In a restaurant, let your mate or date do the ordering. You may know more about vintage wine than the wine steward but if you are smart you'll let your man do the choosing and be ecstatic over his selection even if it tastes like shampoo."[2]

- instruction that wives must wait on their husbands hand and foot. (The woman in Proverbs 31 *has* servants; she is not herself a slave.)

- obedience. Submission is a different word from "obey," which is given as instruction to children and slaves.

- the belief that the husband makes all the final decisions.

- tolerating abuse. (Submission *never* means tolerating abuse. The best way to be a "helper" to an abuser is to expose him.)

- going along with your husband even if he wants you to sin (as Sapphira did in Acts 5), or if he endangers your life (as in the case of Abigail, described in 1 Sam. 25).

Finally, submission is not the sum total of what a wife is to be. It is one aspect of biblical instruction for her. She is a helper, an able woman full of character, and within that context she needs to respect her man. Most often God tells husbands to demonstrate sacrificial love and He tells wives to submit. These are two sides of the same coin.

Jesus Christ demonstrated submission perfectly. As a result, Paul exhorts us in Philippians 2:5–8 (NIV):

> Your attitude should be the same as that of Christ Jesus: Who, being in very nature God, did not consider equality with God something to be grasped, but made himself nothing, taking the very nature of a servant, being made in human likeness. And being found in appearance as a man, he humbled himself and became obedient to death—even death on a cross!

Jesus demonstrated that submission is not to be feared or avoided but embraced. Submission involves "emptying ourselves." Imagine the Philippians 2 passage restated from the wife's perspective: "Even though you are equal with your husband, do not consider equality with him something to be held on to, but empty yourself. . . ." It involves having the same kind of attitude Jesus demonstrated toward the Father in the Garden of Gethsemane: ". . . Not my will, but yours be done" (Luke 22:42).

So what is submission? Submission is . . .

- being willing and ready to renounce our own will and way for that of another.

- the opposite of striving, rebellion, self-assertion; and of loud, pushy, obnoxious, or boisterous opposition toward another. It involves deference and surrender, inner stillness, and peace.

- *willingly* yielding our rights.

- a *voluntary* attitude of respect and cooperation.

- restricted to a woman's actions toward her own husband (as opposed to the belief of some that all women should submit to all men).

- an act of worship. It demonstrates our love for the Lord. One wife whose husband insisted that she make lunches for him every morning shared, "The only way I could motivate myself to do that tedious little task was by deciding I was doing it for the Lord, not for my husband. I told myself, *I need to get up to make lunch for Jesus.*"

- entered into with a gentle, quiet spirit. This does not necessarily mean silence, although sometimes silence may be necessary to demonstrate a kind and gracious attitude that radiates peace.

As the Bible teaches over and over, "the way up is down." The way to be great is to serve. The submission wives are to demonstrate is a voluntary attitude of cooperation, of assuming responsibilities.

Though evidence may seem to prove your husband is less than ideal, your responsibility as a godly woman in obedience to God requires submission. You may say, "Submit to him? He's a jerk; you don't know him." True. In fact, perhaps submission is a greater part of a wife's responsibility when her husband is the kind of man who spends their vacation money on a satellite dish and then sits belching as he channel surfs, yelling, "Hey, woman! Bring me a beer!" If he is thoughtful, she can focus more of her energy on helping and supporting him with her strengths; if he is difficult, she must expend more energy working at demonstrating respect when she wants to lash out with, "Would you like that beer with strychnine in it?"

We are given these instructions in 1 Peter 3:1–6 (NKJV):

Likewise you wives, be submissive to your own husbands, that even if some do not obey the word, they, without a word, may be won by the conduct of their wives, when they observe your chaste conduct accompanied by fear. Do not let your beauty be that outward adorning of arranging the hair, wearing gold, or of putting on fine apparel; but let it be the hidden person of the heart, with the incorruptible ornament of a gentle and quiet spirit, which is very precious in the sight of God. For in this manner, in former times, the holy women who trusted in God also adorned themselves, being submissive to their own husbands, as Sarah obeyed

Abraham, calling him lord, whose daughters you are if you do
good and are not afraid with any terror.

We have to understand the culture of the day. When Peter wrote this
letter, he wrote it to Christians living in a pagan culture. Members of
false religions went to a temple where they expressed worship by engaging in sex with temple prostitutes. In those times the wife assumed her
husband's religion; to do otherwise was considered unfaithfulness. So
Peter wrote to Christian women, wives who had come to know the Lord
yet remained married to spiritually lost men. Can you imagine what that
would be like?

It came as a real shock for these men when their wives became Christians. They would arrive home from worship at the temple of Aphrodite
(or that city's equivalent) only to find that their wives had become believers in Jesus Christ and were trying to live godly, pure, reverent lives.
These wives might then take exception to their husbands excursions of
"worship," creating major conflict. Of course, when these wives came to
know the Lord, the first thing they wanted to do was tell everyone else
about salvation in Christ.

Missy, a modern-day new believer, shared that she wants to exclaim
to her husband, "I can live again; my life is full and complete because
the Spirit of God now indwells me!" Yet because she is married to a man
who does not know the Lord, she knows this sort of enthusiastic talk
would alienate him from the gospel. Scripture says the way to win a
"lost" husband is to demonstrate chaste, pure, reverent behavior—and
to do so without uttering a word of correction. What you do is more
important than what you say. In ongoing intimate relationships, quiet
actions communicate truth best.

Peter goes on to write about external appearance: "Do not let your
beauty be [merely] outward adorning. . . ." Avoid making yourself attractive only on the outside—by braiding your hair, wearing gold jew-
elry, and wearing pretty dresses. (However, neither should your adornment
always amount to wearing baggy gray sweats and pink curlers.) Concentrate on the inner person, the hidden person of the heart, working to
develop the imperishable quality of a gentle and quiet spirit, which is

precious in the sight of God. This does not mean a wife can't have an extroverted personality; it means she has a quiet *spirit*.

You as a wife are your husband's peer, his equal in value to God. You glorify God by complementing your husband. You can create, imagine, emote, reason, and process information. You can buy, sell, diagnose, build, design, philosophize, and write epics. Together you share life as equals, as joint heirs of the grace of life.

This is God's ideal. Yet we do not live in an ideal world. So we ask, "How can I submit, especially if he's not loving me?" The only way we can do *any* of this is by God's grace. Lemuel gives us a hint of this at the end of Proverbs 31, where we read, "A woman who fears the LORD shall be praised." Jesus said, "Apart from Me you can do nothing" (John 15:5). Living this way requires supernatural enabling. It means having a moment-by-moment walk with the Lord in which you draw on His power to be all He intends you to be. The greatest thing you can do for your partner is to be controlled by the Spirit.

A woman who reflects godly qualities—she is a helper, a woman of strength, a wife who willingly "empties herself" and demonstrates respect for her husband, and above all else she fears the Lord—has "worth that is far above rubies." She will influence more than her husband and family. In the larger community, people will often sit up and notice. A first-century, non-Christian Roman who opposed the gospel still wrote enviously: "What women these Christians have!"[3]

13

CELEBRATE OR CELIBATE?

I adjure you, O daughters of Jerusalem,
By the gazelles or by the hinds of the field,
That you will not arouse or awaken my love,
Until she pleases.
—Song of Solomon 2:7

An unmarried couple goes "too far" and she winds up pregnant. She has the baby, but conceals the father's identity to protect his reputation. A scenario from *Baywatch?* From *Melrose Place?* No, it was the plot of Nathaniel Hawthorne's book *The Scarlet Letter,* written almost 150 years ago.

I spoke at a pastor's conference overseas, and the spiritual leaders of that nation expressed amazement over the sexual problems currently facing their Christian singles—a trend toward immorality running about twenty years behind the emergence of a similar trend in America. Sexual immorality is public and prominent today, but sexual issues have probably plagued every culture, just as they did Corinth nearly two thousand years ago. (You may want to read 1 Corinthians, particularly chapters five through seven.)

God's Word remains as relevant to us today as it was to the Corinthians then. We have sexual desires that God created, and the Scriptures assume that if we are married, we will meet each other's needs. If unmarried, we are to stay celibate—that is, remain sexually inactive. That's not what we are going to see on TV and in the movies, read in magazines, or pick up from other worldly sources. Yet it is clearly what God desires and has determined to be best for our well-being.

God speaks boldly about sexuality. He created us male and female, so our sexuality is no surprise to Him. And He made us with sexual needs.

It all starts at conception, when God determines whether we will be male or female. Biology demonstrates that maleness or femaleness begins in the chromosomes at the very moment our DNA lines up. The Bible reveals the same thing in Psalm 139: "For you created my inmost being; you knit me together in my mother's womb. . . . All the days ordained for me were written in your book before one of them came to be" (vv. 13, 16 NIV). God knows us as individuals while we are nothing more than composite masses of molecules in the physical realm.

Soon, a young child grows and reaches that dreaded time called puberty, when a hormonal storm hits; hormones can overwhelm young people. At puberty the body starts to change, and the child's maleness or femaleness becomes more pronounced. This is a difficult, confusing time, a period of great transition. During puberty a person has a full range of feelings, including sexual drives and impulses. This is not wrong. Our sensuality, our feelings based in our sexuality, is from God. The fact that men are attracted to women and women are attracted to men does not shock or surprise Him. This time of raging hormones can bring confusion about exactly what or whom a young person is attracted to. It's a delicate time. (That's why we as mature, Spirit-filled adults must point our kids to what's right while communicating to them that it's okay to have some strong desires and feelings. Otherwise, they're going to get plenty of distorted instruction from the world.)

Most of us survive puberty and make it to adulthood. We find that we still have feelings—strong feelings—as adults. We tend to underestimate the power of hormones, the power of visual stimulation, and how smart the media is. They sell everything from cars to cosmetics using sexual imagery because it works. As a society, we fall for the idea that if a pretty girl or a studly guy drinks a certain brand of soft drink or drives a particular type of car, we need one, too. Madison Avenue knows our susceptibility, and they sell us their products by taking advantage of it.

We tend to go to extremes. If we don't lean toward overindulgence in sex, we view it as did Count Leo Tolstoy, a married man and professing Christian who wrote the classic *War and Peace*. He advised husbands and wives to sleep in separate rooms. The Shakers, an American sect, preached the abolition of sexual relations. After reading some of their literature, Tolstoy wrote to a friend: "I shall not overcome this problem in a hurry, because I am a dirty, libidinous old man!" What a tragedy that he considered his God-created desires dirty. His biographer wrote,

> For him the enemy was woman; and the reason was that he was too strongly sensual not to be continually led into temptation. In physical pleasure he abandoned some part of himself; when the act was over he hated the woman who had gained that moment of power over him and he scurried back into his shell, determined not to come out of it again.[1]

Tolstoy considered marriage nothing more than legalized prostitution. Either extreme about sex—the view that it is legalized prostitution or the belief that "anything goes"—is wrong.

In his first letter to the church at Corinth, chapter seven, Paul began to answer specific questions the church had sent to him, including a discussion of sexuality and celibacy. He was not writing an unabridged manual on the subject; he wrote specifically to one set of issues. For this reason it is important that we not limit our understanding of God's teaching on marriage and singleness to this one portion of Scripture. Still, it's important to consider what Paul said here.

Corinth stood at the center of a religious system that fostered sexual immorality. "Religious" men regularly went to the temple and had sex with temple priestesses as part of their worship experience. Because immorality ran rampant in their city, the Corinthian Christians asked Paul, "Isn't it better just to totally forget about sex? Wouldn't it be smarter, even as married Christians, to abstain from that stuff?" These early Christians were willing to embrace this extreme position because they had been strongly influenced by the Greek thinkers of their day, who commonly believed there was something inherently sinful in the flesh. The Corinthian Christians adopted the Greek idea that "the flesh is lower and dangerous, and must be forsworn for true holiness."

In response, Paul wrote this: "Now concerning the things about which you wrote, it is good for a man not to touch a woman" (1 Cor. 7:1). "Touch" in this context is a euphemism meaning sexual intercourse; it's used here in the same way we use "sleep with" to refer to sex. It's like saying you want a "bite to eat" when you mean you want a whole sandwich. He goes on to say, ". . . but because of immoralities, let each man have his own wife, and let each woman have her own husband" (7:2). Paul was advocating gender equality, a ground-breaking concept in his culture, which imposed upon women the status of property with no rights.

"Let the husband fulfill his duty to his wife, and likewise the wife to her husband," he continued. "The wife does not have authority over her own body, but the husband does; and likewise also the husband does not have authority over his own body, but the wife does. Stop depriving one another" (7:3–5). Although Paul uses the word "duty" here, keep in mind that this "duty" also includes a sense of sensual pleasure. Recall that God told Abraham Sarah would conceive Isaac. She asked, "Shall I have *pleasure,* my lord being old also?" (Gen. 18:12).

Paul's next statement, the idea that marriage partners have authority over each other's body, represents one of the least popular sections of Scripture for some. These people want to believe, "I have my rights. I can do what I want with my own body." But if you have chosen to marry, you have yielded that right.

When I (Bill) practiced medicine, I used to teach a "soon-to-be-married" class at church several times a year. I taught them about sex. Many churches and most Sunday school teachers don't want to talk about sex. Uneasiness and insecurity brought many invitations for the "doctor" to address this issue. Each time I did so, I would hand out cards so they could write questions, because nobody would actually raise their hands and ask, "Do you have to have sex when you're upset or 'not in the mood'?" or "Do I have to give it to him every time he asks?" Yet at least one person has asked these questions at every conference. (The questions they submitted are the basis for the Q & A chapters of this book.)

Apparently we've ignored a key distinctive of marriage. The Scriptures say the marital union is a relationship in which we no longer have final say about our own bodies. When we marry, we voluntarily relinquish those rights, giving that authority to our wife or husband. We take what God has entrusted to us—the temple of His Spirit—and in turn entrust it to our husband or wife. One counselor we know recommended that a client deprive her husband of the sexual relationship for months, until she decided she "wanted it." This counselor reasoned that it would be damaging to have sex just to meet her husband's needs.

Paul suggests otherwise. He tells us not to deprive each other. The word "deprive," like the word "defraud," was commonly used in relation to debt. His idea is that when you marry, you owe a debt to your partner. You obligate yourself to meet his or her physical needs. To deprive that person, to defraud him or her, fails to keep that promise; it amounts to defaulting on a debt.

As we study Scripture, we see that Paul gave only one reason for allowing physical needs within marriage to go unmet. That one exception was when a couple agreed together that, for a short time, they would abstain to devote themselves to prayer. But it is only "for a time" and "by agreement," according to Scripture. This clearly counters the erroneous view that God created sexual pleasure solely for the purpose of procreation.

The Corinthians wondered if real, spiritual Christians truly need physical sexual interaction. They thought that perhaps celibacy, even within marriage, was a much higher moral good. But Paul argued, in essence, "No, that's dangerous thinking. You start depriving one another and Satan will get a foothold." That's what he is saying when he writes, ". . . lest Satan tempt you because of your lack of self-control" (7:5). We live in a day when this may be the most popular of Satan's footholds. Of all the areas in which he can attack us, our morality seems most vulnerable. *Before* marriage the great temptation is to engage in immorality together, and *after* marriage Satan tempts us to deny each other sexual relations.

God designed sex to help build marriages; He didn't intend it to be a weapon for use in interpersonal warfare, nor is it intended to be used as a bargaining chip. He designed it to be a means of intimate communication between a man and a woman who have committed themselves to each other for life. In any other context, the purpose of sex gets twisted, bringing negative consequences.

God says marriage is a good thing; but marriage isn't the only thing. In the larger context of life, our obedient service to God is more important, and we can do that as single people. Paul goes on to address singles: "Yet I wish that all men were even as I myself am. However, each man has his own gift from God, one in this manner, and another in that. But I say to the unmarried and to widows that it is good for them if they re-main even as I" (7:7–8). He brings up at this point the topic of celibacy, and he uses the word "gift," which in Greek is *charisma*. It's the same word he uses in later chapters to describe the spiritual gifts with which we serve the church.

"Without a partner" does not necessarily mean "without a ministry." Clearly God uses single people. Jesus never married; John the Baptist never married; Paul was probably married at one time but was single at the time he wrote this epistle. (Paul was a rabbi and perhaps a member of the Sanhedrin, which required its members to be married. The leaders may have made an exception for Paul, but it's more likely either that his wife died or she left Paul when he became a Christian.) So when Paul wrote this, he was single. He said, referring to his single status, "I wish you were even as I." He goes on to explain why singleness is of great value, using the word *charisma*, or "grace gift." Celibacy is a gift from God. That gift means God so fulfills an individual that a partner is unes-sential for a satisfying life and ministry. In addition, he or she can go about doing God's business unhindered by family responsibilities.

Paul had more to say on the subject: "But I want you to be free from concern. One who is unmarried is concerned about things of the Lord, how he may please the Lord; but one who is married is concerned about things of the world, how he may please his wife" (vv. 32–33). It's very practical. Paul was saying that, in the day and time in which they lived— in a distorted and confused culture—it was easier to devote oneself to ministry as a single, focusing on God's will without worrying about events at home. Why? Because, as he told us, a marriage is precious, and mar-ried people have a responsibility first to God and then to the family. Ministry for married partners comes *after* family responsibilities. It's as though Paul was giving orders to the troops before they went out to combat, and he said, "You can fight the fight better if you don't have your mind and heart at home." To be unmarried is no tragedy; in fact, it can often be quite useful for the Lord's work.

An unmarried person must consider how God wants to use him or her. In Matthew 19, Jesus teaches that some are born eunuchs, some are made eunuchs by man, and some are eunuchs by choice. Jesus was say-ing that some people by birth are unable to marry and bear children.

Some become that way through surgical procedures, or as a consequence of weapons or warfare. But some, for the sake of God's kingdom, choose celibacy to more fully devote their lives to God through giving up what is good.

While that is true, single people still have sexual needs. We should encourage deeply affectionate but nongenital relationships among singles. They can express their sexuality through warm, satisfying friendships, and the church can help here by providing a context for these friendships to develop. Even though they should abstain from sex, singles need the sense of touch. In fact, they probably need it more than many married people do.

Marriage is the norm for most people; yet celibacy is good. Singleness by choice is fine, but what if you find yourself single and you don't have the gift of celibacy? You feel consumed with the idea of finding a partner—your heart longs for that soul mate. Pray for God to provide that special one. Pour out your heart to God, and "seek first His kingdom and His righteousness."

Perhaps you are at an "in between" stage. You are single, but you are involved in a romantic relationship that may result in marriage. How can you reflect your sexuality within that relationship?

First, recognize that God has designed us with sensual appetites but He has also given us the commands and the ability to control them. He says to walk in the Spirit and you won't commit the deeds of the flesh (see Gal. 5). Jesus as Savior has delivered us from the power of sin, though not yet from sin's presence. He has sent the Holy Spirit to indwell us, counsel us, comfort us, and convict us of wrongdoing. The Spirit also enables us to live a holy life, pleasing to God.

If you don't know Christ, if you haven't yet trusted Him as your Savior, then you don't have the power to live a holy life. We live in a fallen world that has surrounded us with sensuality and temptation. But God offers a way to access His power. He also offers us forgiveness and cleansing when we fail Him. Receiving Him as Lord involves praying and acknowledging our inability to save ourselves, accepting our need for cleansing from sin, and placing our faith in Christ's work on the cross as being sufficient to save us. Only after placing our faith in Him in this way will we have the supernatural power to overcome evil.

According to the Bible, sexual relations are to be engaged in regularly but only by those with lifelong marriage commitments to each other. Yet today, premarital and extramarital sex are common, even between couples who have no intention of committing their lives to each other. Sex distorts these relationships, detracting from what God would have them to be. It stunts spiritual growth, alienates the sexual partners from God, and erects a barrier to true intimacy in the future.

If you've failed here, remember that God provides a way of spiritual reconciliation. Confess your sin to Him and receive the forgiveness He promises. Change your thinking, make a new start, and recognize that we cannot dabble in immorality and walk away untouched or unchanged. It leaves its mark. It has consequences. It does things in our minds and in our spirits, because God didn't create us to have multiple partners.

The believer who wants to remain pure must date only other believers who are committed to maintaining the biblical standards that limit physical expressions of intimacy. Keep in mind that lust produces superficial, momentary pleasure that falls well short of the full experience of marital sex because it denies relationship. Lust turns the other person into an object, a thing, a nonperson. Jesus condemned lust because it cheapened sex, making sex less than God created it to be. One non-Christian man who actively engages in multiple sexual encounters wrote, "I am wondering—will sex be better when I am actually in love?"[2]

Next, find someone outside of the relationship to whom you can be accountable. One of my (Sandi's) single friends wrote this to me:

> We broke our rule about doing nothing intense while lying down. Except for the fact that we broke our own rule, we did not do anything morally wrong, so don't worry. We are very aware that it will be easier next time to want to bend the rules again. That was Saturday night, on our date—which was a picnic in the woods, with a fire and everything. So you could probably call that a compromising situation as well. Boy, I'm not doing too well here, am I?

Just knowing she would have to later give account for her actions helped to keep this young woman from "going further."

"Long distance relationships help," laughed Tara, a single woman. She went on to add more seriously, "I think integrity and respect for the other person as a creation of God are strong incentives against violating him or her. You have to learn to focus on their good, and not personal selfishness, or what feels good for *you*. Also, you have to keep the long-term goal in view. Women need to realize that they do things that cause guys to want more, and that guys do things to cause women to want more. *Both* have to take responsibility in restraining the physical relationship."

John, who is currently engaged, said, "We set some rules: Nothing below the neck, under a blanket, or lying down. It's just too hard otherwise." Another single suggested, "We never get into the car together unless we've decided ahead of time where we're going. That helps us avoid the temptation to cruise around and end up at the lake in the back seat. We know that if we demonstrate selfless love in our physical relationship before marriage, we are more likely to demonstrate that same kind of love to each other after we are married."

We know of Christian parents who believe their sons will have sex before marriage but not their daughters, because "guys do." This is wrong! Both men and women are fully responsible for their own actions; *both* must take full responsibility for "slowing down."

One single woman shared, "It's sometimes beneficial to know and communicate when the other person is hitting hot buttons and to stop at that point, instead of going to the 'point of no return.'" She laughed and went on, "I like the 'beep, beep, beep' warning approach myself. It lets the other person know that he is going in the wrong direction, yet does it in an amusing way." She continued, "It's easy for us women to think we owe men for the dates and food and the stuff they buy us. A lot of women don't think enough of themselves to say, 'I should be pursued for *me* alone and not what I can give with my body. I'm worth getting to know, *period*.' I've had trouble with this."

Another suggestion is to keep the engagement period short. By the time a couple reaches engagement, they are entering levels of intimacy that should not be sustained for long without expression in sexual inter-course. As Paul advised, "It is better to marry than to burn."

Today, wise people follow God's directives to relinquish bodily rights within marriage and abstain from sexual relations outside of marriage. Fortunately, when couples engage in sexual immorality these days, no one has to wear a scarlet *A* for "adultery." However, what we do with God's gift of sex leaves its mark internally. Whether that mark is a scar or a blessing is up to us.

14

PROTECTING YOUR SEXUALITY

I was a wall, and my breasts were like towers;
Then I became in his eyes as one who finds peace.
—Song of Solomon 8:10

Imagine waking up every morning, looking out over the pyramids, and eating leeks and onions. Your family has sold you into slavery, so you have gone from having your own servants to serving as a slave. Your boss, Potifer, is in charge of the pharaoh's bodyguards. The brightest, most educated, most powerful, most articulate, most attractive people surround you, yet you have nothing. Then your boss's wife, a beautiful woman, makes it her life goal to seduce you. In fact, she tries daily. Finally one day, she throws herself at you, and you have to literally run out of the room.

Taken right out of Genesis 39, this is Joseph's story.

A group of Christian wives who were employed in various businesses met for a weekly Bible study. As they worked their way through the Bible, they focused on its great and not-so-great women. During the session in which the women studied Joseph and Potifer's wife, each of them confessed that she had struggled with moral temptation. Each had met a man other than her husband to whom she felt strongly attracted. For them, the struggle had not begun with physical lust as much as the sense of "falling in love" and a strong desire to pursue a wrong relationship. In every case, those wives said that they were happily married and that it was not because their husbands had failed to meet their needs.

In his book *Torn Asunder: Recovering from Extramarital Affairs*, Dave

Carder identifies three kinds of adulterous relationships. He labels them as follows: (1) The one-night stand. An otherwise faithful husband or wife meets someone at a movie matinee and they end up sleeping together. It has never happened before and it never happens again; (2) the entangled affair. A woman and man who work together for a long time grow into a deeply intimate relationship that leads to regular sex; and (3) the sexual addict. A man or woman has a pattern of engaging in sexual acts outside of the context of any relationship.

Carder labels the second as the most problematic and one of the most difficult to rehabilitate due to the extensive emotional involvement: "In the entangled affair, the man and woman have a relationship—often akin to the marriage relationship."[1] In addition, the "innocent spouse" has a harder time dealing with this type of sin on many levels. "A prostitute shows a woman there's something wrong with her husband; an affair suggests that maybe something's wrong with [the wife] herself," explained the wife of Dick Morris, who left the Clinton Administration after a tabloid exposed his adultery.[2]

Many of the books and magazines we found tended to blame the marriage for failing to meet needs. While this may certainly be a factor, it ignores the fact that marriage, by its very nature—with its cornerstone covenant of committed love and security—will not offer the mystery, the conquest, the rush of "live for the moment" that some seek out in illicit relationships. They've seen in movies, or have experienced but can't match within the confines of marriage, the thrill of the chase and the added excitement that comes from fear of exposure. Unfaithfulness has strong elements of selfishness and ego satisfaction. And the third party can offer a thoughtful listening ear and sexual variety. Or as a *Newsweek* writer described it, they can provide "the kind of respect and admiration that wives find it hard to give their husbands after watching them fall asleep in front of reruns . . . for the last twenty years."[3]

How widespread is adultery? A 1994 survey found that 21.2 percent of men and 11 percent of women admitted being unfaithful to their spouses at least once in their lives. (The key word here is "admitted." In addition, if we factored in "mental adultery," we would find it to be the societal norm.) Within the last twelve months, 3.6 percent of men and 1.3 percent of women reported infidelity. Those who attended church were roughly half as likely to cheat.[4] However, we should probably note that those who attend church are also less likely to admit they have committed adultery. All things considered, nearly 100 percent of all married people will find themselves tempted at some time in their lives.

In premarital counseling, some couples are incensed that I (Bill) would caution them in this area. Yet making the assumption that we are going to be tempted at some point keeps us from thinking "I am immune" or "I am never going to fall." Countless women have confessed to me their moral failures, explaining, "I never thought it would happen."

The Bible has plenty to say on the subject. We have Joseph's example of literally running away. We read Paul's exhortation to Timothy to "flee youthful lusts." We know Jimmy Carter endured ridicule for alluding to Jesus Christ's statement, "You have heard it said 'you shall not commit adultery,' but I say to you that anyone who lusts after a woman has committed adultery with her in his heart." We also find a father's warning to his sons in Proverbs 5:3–5:

> For the lips of an adulteress drip honey,
> And smoother than oil is her speech;
> But in the end she is bitter as wormwood,
> Sharp as a two-edged sword.
> Her feet go down to death,
> Her steps lay hold of Sheol.

If adultery is such a common problem, what can we do about it? First, let's look at how we think about this issue.

Myth #1: A little fantasy never hurt anybody.

Consider how it hurt Jeanette:

> As a believing wife and mother who had an affair several years ago, I want to warn others that if they first yield to mental adultery, it could easily take them the whole way down the wrong road. If there is time to be alone with the other man, the two of you will most likely confess your struggles to each other. After allowing wrong thoughts, this is the most dangerous step to take. If he is a fellow believer, you will say you must conquer this

thing together in prayer. You will feel such a tenderness toward each other that you will need to express your affection with warm embraces and "holy kisses." It is a short road from there to the point where you allow yourself the pleasure of more and more sensual temptations. Finally, you quit trying to resist.

If you are truly a believer who is used to enjoying fellowship with God, you are in for a lot of misery. You will long to go back to the time when you could sing, "I Love You, Lord" and mean it. You will cry over songs like "He Is Lord," knowing that now He is not Lord of your life. You will become unable to give testimonies or share with other believers on anything but a surface level. You will be unable to concentrate on anything else. Then, to cover your sin, you will lie.

At the same time, you will be involved in a passionate, romantic relationship. You will feel beautiful and part of life will seem wonderful. While you know it is sinful, you will find yourself helplessly in love and enjoying part of it.

Eventually the two of you will talk of ways to end the relationship. You may even take some very painful steps. You will feel like you're going through a divorce without being able to tell anyone. The pain is so strong, and the pull is so strong, that these steps will not last long. The longer it all goes on, the more a part of each other's lives you become, and the more you will have stored in your memory. You will realize how much easier it would have been to stop it all at the "thoughts" stage. You would give anything to go back and do it all over differently.

You will have lost your relationship with the Lord. And you will realize you have also lost your relationship with your husband. Either you will go through the rest of your life keeping something from him or you will eventually confess it to him and destroy him in the process.

Your memories will be your worst enemies. You will both cherish them and hate them. You will long for the days when your husband's lovemaking was the only way you knew, when certain scents, songs, clothes, places, and words did not stab you with reminders. In the strongest way I can say it, *you will be sorry, sorry, sorry.* Yielding to the excitement will never be worth what you have to reap.

I am not suggesting that a person who has had an affair must live in bondage and condemnation forever. Yes, God can bring spiritual and marital healing, even of the painful memories. But it will be very hard.

If you have already yielded and know it must stop, take the risk of praying, "Lord, do whatever you have to do to make me willing to stop." Then be prepared for what He brings. In my case, it was an unplanned pregnancy. I had to confess to my husband. Years later, we are still working through it.

All of this did not start or end overnight. It was gradual. It starts with thoughts. And those wrong thoughts should be avoided at all cost.

Another woman, Kathy, shared how she had to change jobs and move to another city to get away from a wrong relationship. "It all started with what I thought were some harmless thoughts. It ended with me praying and praying that God would take away my feelings for this man. I became angry with Him that He didn't. It took me a long time to realize that you can't always ask God to bail you out of a situation you lived yourself into."

More people are staying together after unfaithfulness these days. At one time people generally considered the offended spouse "weak" if he or she reconciled; but fortunately, it is becoming more socially acceptable to "work it out." Some do it for the kids; others do it for the sake of constant *access* to the kids. They also don't want to be single again, as one person put it, "out there with germs and creeps." Sexual betrayal is painful, but so is divorce.

Myth #2: I can have a little liaison without consequences.

Ever since the 1960s and 1970s, we've lived in a society of "free love" in which indiscriminate sex has become the premarital norm. We consider monogamy mundane, and we've discarded biblical standards. Yet our divorce rates rise. Premarital sexual involvement places couples at higher risk in the future: If you can't hold to God's code of conduct before marriage, it gets harder to draw the line later.

Both premarital and extramarital sexual involvement is wrong, though acceptable in our society. Just because you may not have AIDS, sexually transmitted diseases, unwanted pregnancy, or embarrassing discoveries doesn't mean you don't endure consequences. As Billy Graham has explained it, "Your soul is marked."[5]

Before King David sinned with Bathsheba, he experienced nothing but blessings from God; after his sin, he suffered consequences for the rest of his life. In the short term, he lost an infant. Long term, his sin had far-reaching effects, including in his family relationships—his children followed his example and engaged in immorality. Apparently what is true today was also true several millennia ago: If parents are unfaithful, they place their children at a higher risk for infidelity.[6]

Later, David lost respect in the eyes of the nation, and he had nothing but political trouble from that time forward. Even though God forgave David, he never again experienced the relative tranquillity he had enjoyed. Years later, his son, Solomon, the wisest of all men, wrote this in Proverbs 6:25–29:

> Do not desire her beauty in your heart,
> Nor let her catch you with her eyelids.
> For on account of a harlot one is reduced to a loaf of bread,
> And an adulteress hunts for the precious life.
> Can a man take fire in his bosom,
> And his clothes not be burned?
> Or can a man walk on hot coals,
> And his feet not be scorched?
> So is the one who goes in to his neighbor's wife;
> Whoever touches her will not go unpunished.

Many who have been scorched would attest to this.

Myth #3: *Marriage will cure lust.*

During my senior year at college, I (Sandi) remember how stunned I was to hear one of my professors say he battled lust more since his marriage. "Now that I have a more 'informed' view of what goes on behind closed doors, I lust more specifically," he explained. In 1 Corinthians, Paul seems to indicate that a failure to mutually meet each other's sexual needs can lead to escalating levels of temptation.

Yet a healthy love life in marriage is not a cure-all. Marriage does not cure lust any more than regularly eating healthy meals cures cravings for chocolate cheesecake, particularly if such a "sweet tooth" was cultivated before marriage. If you are craving pepperoni pizza, no amount of quiche will do.

"During a period of my life when I was battling sexual temptation, I came across an article that referred me to a thin book, *What I Believe*, by the French Catholic writer Francois Mauriac," wrote Philip Yancey in *The Jesus I Never Knew*. Mauriac dismissed most of the arguments in favor of sexual purity that he had been taught in his Catholic upbringing:

> "With self-discipline you can master lust": Mauriac found that sexual desire is like a tidal wave powerful enough to bear away all the best intentions.
>
> "True fulfillment can only be found in monogamy": This may be true, but it certainly does not *seem* true to someone who finds no slackening of sexual urges even in monogamy. . . .
>
> Mauriac concluded that self-discipline, repression, and rational argument are inadequate weapons to use in fighting the impulse toward impurity. In the end, he could find only one reason to be pure, and that is what Jesus presented in the Beatitudes: "Blessed are the pure in heart, for they will see God." In Mauriac's words, "Impurity separates us from God. . . . Purity is the condition for a higher love—for a possession superior to all possessions: that is of God. . . . That is the motive to stay pure. By harboring lust, I limit my own intimacy with God. The pure in heart are truly blessed, for they will see God. It is as simple, and as difficult as that."[7]

We never permanently "quench" our sin nature by substituting holy activities. By God's grace we conquer it on a moment-by-moment basis as we love Him, walk with Him, and desire to see His face above all others.

Myth #4: If I fall into sin, it's because my spouse has somehow failed to meet my needs.

This is the best of all cop-outs. Don't believe it. Even if there were some truth in it, this would not be acceptable biblically.

After twelve years of a strong marriage, Sue and Dick wondered what had happened to them. Dick had begun taking medication for a medical condition, and they didn't realize one of its side effects was depression. It was nearly a year before they determined the cause. In the meantime, they struggled with how to deal with Dick's altered personality. They still had a loving, supportive relationship with an active love life, and they experienced no additional conflicts, but they both felt sad a lot, and they found it difficult to cope with Dick's negative outlook. Though their marriage was "happy," it was at risk.

During that time, Sue began to feel attracted to a man in her office. Finally she sat down with Dick and told him, "I don't want to add to your depression, but I think we need some counseling. I don't know how to deal with your pain. And I'm finding other men—one in particular— a lot more attractive than before."

Confiding her secret feelings relieved some of the pressure for Sue. And Dick immediately found a counselor for them to begin seeing. Even though the depression had a physical cause, they both needed help in dealing with the emotional fallout.

My friend Kelley asked me (Sandi) one time, "Do you remember where you were standing when Kennedy was shot?" I told her I did. She laughed and teased that she was too young to remember. But then her mood changed. She said soberly, "In the same way you can recall where you were when Kennedy was shot, I remember where I was when I heard that Gordon MacDonald had an affair."

MacDonald, a widely respected Christian pastor, speaker, and author of *Ordering Your Private World,* put it this way: "I am a broken-world person because a few years ago I betrayed the covenants of my marriage. For the rest of my life I will have to live with the knowledge that I brought deep sorrow to my wife, to my children, and to friends and others who have trusted me for many years."[8]

MacDonald relates a conversation that happened several years earlier:

I gave a speech at a college commencement. Before the festivities began, a member of that school's board sat with me in the president's office. We'd never met before, and we were asking questions of each other that might help us get better acquainted. Suddenly my new friend asked a strange question. I've thought about it many times since then. "If Satan were to blow you out of the water," he asked, "how do you think he would do it?"

"I'm not sure I know," I answered. "All sorts of ways, I suppose; but I know there's one way he wouldn't get me."

"What's that?"

"He'd never get me in the area of my personal relationships. That's one place where I have no doubt that I'm as strong as you can get."[9]

MacDonald now warns, "An unguarded strength and an unprepared heart are double weakness."[10]

"The heart is more deceitful than all else and is desperately sick; Who can understand it?" we read in Jeremiah 17:9. The Bible tells us that even the best of humans are masters at deceiving themselves and others. No one is immune, and if we think we are, we are that much more vulnerable. Put another way, "Let him who thinks he stands take heed lest he fall." If David, a man after God's own heart, can fall, we can, too.

The reality here is that even happily married people are at risk. There is no way to absolutely "affair proof" a marriage for a lifetime; a day-to-day, minute-by-minute decision to remain faithful to one's spouse is required. Nor is there a way to so totally satisfy your mate that he or she will never stray because even the best feeling of satisfaction is short-lived. Yet neither is it hopeless. In the next chapter we will talk about some safeguards and ways to minimize risk.

Myth #5: If I spend time with God every day, I will not be "at risk."

It's true that your relationship with God is the strongest factor in maintaining moral purity. But it has to be a moment-by-moment relationship. If we purify our hearts daily through a quiet time of confession, repentance, and redirection, we've taken a big step. Do spend time with Him daily. But don't assume that because you spend time with God each day, you can relax. Consider a Bible college professor who had an adulterous affair and left his wife and ministry, but reported, "I ride my bike ten miles daily, attend church, and have a scheduled Bible study time." One man involved in an adulterous relationship resolved never to "cheat" on Sunday—and he kept his promise.

On the other hand, if you are neglecting daily time with God, you are at *far* greater risk of falling into sexual sin.

Angela felt a strong attraction to a man with whom she was working on a multimillion-dollar business project. So in addition to her time with the Lord, she would sing—and pledge within her heart to be responsive to—the words of the hymn "I Surrender All" during her thirty-minute drive to and from work. Then she would think through the specifics of how she expected to be tempted and pray through them. She'd commit to avoiding "extra" trips to his desk and decide she would not make unnecessary phone calls to him; she would think through and do the right thing that day in every specific way she could anticipate. "You have to make many decisions throughout the day," she confided. "It's not something you just decide once and for all and never have to face again. Fortunately, after two years the project ended, and though I felt really sad, I knew God knew what He was doing to take me out of that situation."

15

DEVELOPING A LOYAL HEART

Put me like a seal over your heart . . .
For love is as strong as death.
—Song of Solomon 8:6

I (Sandi) was sitting in a Bible class one afternoon as we were discussing David and Bathsheba. A student raised his hand and asked the teacher, "How can we make sure this doesn't happen? I read that 30 percent of evangelical pastors have moral failures. I don't want to be in that statistic. But I think I would be naive to think it couldn't happen. You've been married for four decades. How have you managed to remain faithful to your wife?"

Perhaps for the sake of simplicity, the instructor answered, "You do three things. You tell your wife every day that you love her; you never touch your secretary; and you never go to lunch with another woman."

In one way he was right, but on another level he was wrong. Secretaries are not the only danger; neither are male/female lunches unpardonable sins. Yet he was right in encouraging us to invest our affections and energies in the right relationship, as Proverbs 5:15–19 encourages:

> Drink water from your own cistern,
> And fresh water from your own well.
> Should your springs be dispersed abroad,
> Streams of water in the streets?
> Let them be yours alone,
> And not for strangers with you.

Let your fountain be blessed,
And rejoice in the wife of your youth.
As a loving hind and a graceful doe,
Let her breasts satisfy you at all times;
Be exhilarated always with her love.

God gave us biological desires, and here He encourages the expression of sexual love within marriage. His Spirit enables us to channel our drives responsibly. Proverbs 5:20–23 continues:

For why should you, my son, be exhilarated with an
    adulteress,
And embrace the bosom of a foreigner?
For the ways of a man are before the eyes of the LORD,
And he watches all his paths.
His own iniquities will capture the wicked,
And he will be held with the cords of his sin.
He will die for lack of instruction,
And in the greatness of his folly he will go astray.

This is important advice.

Our instructor left out an important encouragement: *We can win the battle where it starts, in our thoughts.* What begins as legitimate appreciation of physical beauty or character frequently turns into selfish desire. James wrote, "Let no one say when he is tempted, 'I am being tempted by God'; for God cannot be tempted by evil, and He Himself does not tempt anyone. But each one is tempted when he is carried away and enticed by his own lust. Then when lust has conceived, it gives birth to sin; and when sin is accomplished, it brings forth death" (James 1:13–15).

In her book *The Quest for Love*, Elisabeth Elliot wrote, "The battleground is the mind. To pray, 'Deliver us from evil,' lays on us the responsibility to struggle against the evil in our minds, for that is where trouble begins and where it must be conquered."

When Janice, a single woman, worked in the media department at a

Fortune 500 company, she often helped with video editing. This involved sitting with the door shut in a darkened room with the video editor, who in this case happened to be a married man. Janice and Ed spent hours looking at the screen, throwing around creative ideas, and developing projects together. Sometimes they would walk down to the corporate cafeteria and continue talking about the project over food. Having lunch together, which some might label as "dangerous," was actually the safest time of day for them because of its public setting. When the mind is right, location is not a great worry. When Ed's parents died, Janice hugged him. "To do otherwise would have seemed inhuman," she explained.

There were moments in their relationship when they'd be working together and Janice would realize, " 'Whoa. This is a member of the opposite sex. This is not a girlfriend I'm hanging out with.' He has many wonderful qualities. The fact is, just about every Christian (and most non-Christians) of the opposite sex have qualities that, if you got to know them well enough, you would find attractive and unique." But, she added, "It was okay, because I had made a choice to think and feel as I was supposed to. I handled it at the level of my thoughts, continually checking my context, my motivation, and my attitude. We worked together for more than a decade before moving on to other careers. Today we remain good friends."

Liz, a university student, was asked to intern for a male professor. She spent the year sitting across from him in his private office, joining him at his appointments, going to meetings with him, attending his off-campus lectures, and sometimes even heading down to the campus food service building with him to grab a bite to eat.

"He's a wonderful man, and I love him as a dear friend," Liz shared. "He has many appealing qualities, including the fact that he is unashamed to be my friend. Yet I don't remember ever having one wrong thought about him that entire year. It's not that I couldn't have been tempted. But I had made a decision, and by God's grace I stuck to it—I wasn't going to let my mind go that direction."

In the past twenty years an increasing number of women have entered the work force, so we need guidelines that encompass the changing situations in which we find ourselves. For example, Shanelle had always said, "I will never get into a car alone with a man who is not my husband."

But one night her husband needed to stay at church to counsel someone, and she needed to get home to do some work. One of the guys in their college department—someone with whom she felt no particular "chemistry"—offered to drive her home. At that point, she realized that declining his offer would be ridiculous. So she had an uneventful ride home with him. She later shared, "I had made rules to safeguard myself in situations that were not dangerous. I needed to make them closer to the heart: I would never ride in the car alone with a man I was *dying* to be alone with, and I would never have lunch with somebody who made me feel like I was with Tom Cruise."

External rules alone can prevent a few problems, but many people have "fallen" without ever compromising their external rules. It is possible to love your spouse, never go to lunch with a member of the opposite sex, and never touch your subordinates, yet still become embroiled in an adulterous relationship. Besides, some guidelines can make us rigid where we need to show flexibility, as was the case with Shanelle. Externals are easy to "get around," but if we set righteous *internal* guidelines, if we continually reject all wrong thoughts and feelings, we cannot "get around the rules."

Dr. Frank Pittman, the author of a book on infidelity, says unfaithfulness is a sin of the heart as much as or even more than the body. Most affairs are conducted primarily on the telephone: "The essence of an affair is in establishing a secret intimacy with someone"—a secret that necessarily must be defended with dishonesty. Infidelity, he says, is not *just* about "whom you lie with. It's whom you lie to."[1]

Frances was working with the associate pastor of her church on a project for the church youth. It didn't take long for them to realize they worked well as a team. They enjoyed working together, and the time flew by when they met to throw around ideas and make decisions. Before long this pastor, Ronnie, was calling her at work for her help with incidental decisions. She began faxing him Garfield cartoons that she knew he would enjoy. Then he began confiding that he was unhappy in his marriage. Frances, being a compassionate person by nature, felt deep sympathy for Ronnie and wanted to help. Before long, she realized she was involved in a mental affair. She begged God to take the feelings away, but He didn't. She found herself leaving out parts of conversations when recounting them to her husband, knowing he would be upset if she told him the whole truth.

Finally, recognizing that in her own strength she stood powerless against her feelings, Frances met with a friend and confessed that she needed some accountability. Her confession helped to break the obsession. Together they worked out the steps Frances needed to take to unravel the tangled web of the relationship she had built in her mind. Eventually she decided that, because she was "in so deep," she had only one option: to remove herself from all situations where she had contact with him.

Cindy and Patrick had been married for ten years when they began working with Bob and Glenda at a drug rehabilitation center for juveniles. They were best friends, working together and supporting each other in a difficult ministry. After several years, Cindy began to feel herself drawn to Bob, and she was fairly sure he felt the same way. Soon they were exchanging notes, running errands together, and looking for each other in crowds.

The relationship began to intensify, and Cindy took a bold step. She confided in her husband that she needed his help in keeping Bob at a safe distance. Patrick ignored the warning, even sending his wife on more errands with Bob. This made her feel that her husband did not cherish her enough to help her stay faithful, so she rationalized that her temptation was his fault. It wasn't long before she and Bob became physically involved. The affair went on for months before someone caught them.

Patrick was bewildered. "I thought it was wrong to be jealous!" he insisted. Both couples resigned from their jobs and tried to rebuild their marriages. Several months later, Cindy called Bob. He told her that he wanted to rebuild his relationship with his wife and that he didn't want to hear from her again.

Elements of these scenarios are all-too-common. In his book *His Needs, Her Needs*, Willard Harley describes a typical affair as consisting of two people combining sexual lovemaking with feelings of deep love.

> The relationship that combines sex (usually very passionate sex) and very real love threatens the marriage to its core, because the

lovers experience real intimacy, and it meets at least one need of the spouse outside the exclusive marital relationship. . . . An affair usually begins as a friendship. Frequently your spouse knows your lover; not uncommonly the third party is the husband or wife in a couple you both know and consider "best friends." In another common pattern the outside lover comes from your spouse's family—a sister or brother. Or you may have met your lover at work.

[Often] the attraction is not necessarily physical, but emotional. What really turns you on is not your new partner, but the fantasy. . . . The longer it goes on, the more difficult you will find breaking it off. In some cases the above process may take only a few months; in other cases it will take many years.[2]

Many warn that because of the danger of cross-gender friendships, men and women should never be friends. Movies such as *When Harry Met Sally* hint that male-female friendships will always develop into something more. Comedians joke that men have no female friends— they just have women they haven't yet slept with. And they say women have no male friends—they merely have men they keep around "just in case."

While we would agree that inappropriate affection should be handled with extreme measures, the solution is not to avoid relationships with members of the opposite sex. Often there is little we can do to keep friendships from happening anyway. Meetings, projects, and ministries throw us together. Besides, God made men and women in His image, so both genders working together, using their unique gifts, bring a balance to any project.

Consider some examples of male-female relationships in Scripture. Paul called two women in Philippi his "co-laborers"; he also sent greetings to women named Lydia and Priscilla. Jesus entered a house occupied by two unmarried women and talked with them on a below-the-surface level about spiritual things. He showed utter disregard for custom in doing so. He showed the same intimacy and esteem toward Mary and Martha. He praised Mary over Martha for sitting at His feet engaged in deep communication. He touched women, and He received touch from them—such as the time He received Mary's worship when she anointed Him with costly perfume.

"We must be human; we need intimacy, touch, meaningful conversation, and much more outside the marriage bonds," writes Richard Foster in *The Disciplined Life*. "Otherwise we will be asking the marriage to carry more than is reasonable for even the healthiest relationship."[3]

During an interview with Eugene Peterson, I (Sandi) asked this man who had pastored successfully for thirty years, "For a long time it seems that believers have discouraged male-female friendships. How do you handle friendships with women?"

"Is sex a contagious disease?" he asked. "Sex is a danger, but money is a danger, too. Do you refuse to take a salary because money is a danger? I've not lived cautiously. I have friendships with women. They are my friends. Touch is a human thing, not just a sexual thing. It is dehumanizing to deny touch. I am convinced that the so-called failures in ministry are not motivated sexually. For both men and women, they're motivated by arrogance, pride, power, and a hunger for intimacy. It doesn't happen overnight. They have long histories before them. The failures don't happen because you touch somebody; they have to do with character development—part of learning to be a man and learning to be a woman. It's part of spiritual maturity and spiritual formation. If you pour all your energies into trying to avoid sexual sin, you will fail in another area. There are other failures that are terrible, too. Life is messy."

So how do you tell the difference between friendship and romance? Your thoughts and motives give you away. We read in Proverbs, "Watch over your heart with all diligence, For from it flow the springs of life" (Prov. 4:23). Here are some questions to help us identify misguided affections:

- Do you make special trips past her desk or his house?
- Do you manipulate situations so you can be alone in secluded, private settings?
- Have you started taking special care of your dress and overall appearance? Are you wearing an alluring scent?
- When you are around him or her, do you feel like you're sixteen again?

- Do you find yourself thinking of this person frequently outside of the usual context of your contact?
- Do you purposely withhold some conversations, letters, or events from your spouse?
- Do you dread accountability times? Do you not even *have* a person to whom you are accountable for your thoughts and actions?
- Do you find yourself thinking of this person instead of your spouse when you watch romantic movies?
- Do you think of this person during romantic activities with your spouse?
- Do you talk about him or her more than about your spouse?
- Is the love you feel for this person infatuation that wants to possess or is it true love? Real love wants the other to be all he or she can be in Christ—a love that would never lead the loved one down a treacherous path away from God. Are you acting with his or her best interest at heart?

Let an application of the Golden Rule help determine the state of your relationship. Ask yourself: *Would I want someone else to treat me as I am treating his or her spouse, even if only in my heart?*

And there's one more factor to consider. Foster, who earlier suggested that we should not expect all our needs for intimacy to be met in marriage (we're talking here about our need for acceptance, respect, value, and appreciation at a personal level, *not* physical, romantic, erotic intimacy), qualifies his statement with the reminder, "We really must be sensitive to how our actions and even our thoughts affect our marriage."[4]

It may be easier for husbands to appreciate their wives' cross-gender friendships than it is for women to accept this in their men. In one piece of research on cross-gender relationships, when men imagined their wives committing sexual infidelity, their heart rates took leaps of a magnitude typically induced by three successive cups of coffee. They sweated and their brows wrinkled. Yet when they imagined a nonphysical, emotions-oriented friendship, they calmed down, though not to their normal level. For women, things were reversed—redirected love, not supplementary sex, brought the deeper physiological distress.[5]

In Song of Solomon 8:6 we read the bride's words to her groom:

> "Put me like a seal over your heart,
> Like a seal on your arm.
> For love is as strong as death,
> Jealousy is as severe as Sheol,
> Its flashes are flashes of fire,
> The very flame of the LORD."

A king's seal was commonly used as a sign of ownership, similar to the way cattle ranchers brand their livestock or our mothers wrote our names in our clothing before sending us off to camp. Yet Solomon used his seal to mark something priceless, and therefore something from which he would never part. Solomon's bride desires to be set as a seal on her husband's heart in the place of his affection. In other words, she is asking, "Let me own your heart."

In that context, we read, "Jealousy is as severe as Sheol." Sheol was the place of the dead. How strong is death? Strong enough that it never gives up its dead (until Christ returns). In the same way that death is permanent, the lover would not give up her beloved. This jealousy is a godly kind, the kind that would never allow the loved one to pursue the wrong path without warning. It is the opposite of indifference.

So are we saying a mate should be jealous? Yes and no. Exhibiting the kind of jealousy that desires to control one's spouse stunts the relationship's ability to grow and mature. We're not talking about a jealousy that stifles; nor are we encouraging the competitive jealousy we might feel when another receives a promotion or is honored in some way.

We're talking about the side of love that guards that which God intended to be exclusive. It protects the relationship's security. Sometimes an "outsider" can see the warning signs more clearly than the person in the midst of a situation. Consider that one of God's names is "Jealous God." Even Erica Jong, the siren of the sexual liberation in the 1970s, has conceded, "The great experiment of my generation was that people tried to abolish jealousy. It never worked."[6]

Yet aren't we supposed to trust each other? What about in 1 Corinthians 13 where we read that love "is not jealous" and that it "believes all things"? Paul is speaking there against having a controlling jealousy, not a protective one. Nor is he talking about the blind sort of belief that ignores the evidence. One pastor explained it like this:

> "Love believes all things": Then what if I'm disappointed?
> "Love bears all things": Then what if there's no change?
> "Love hopes all things": What if there's still no change?
> "Love endures all things. Love never fails."

The positive side of jealousy desires to protect something that is irreplaceable. What is love worth? Again, Solomon writes in Song of Solomon 8:7:

> Many waters cannot quench love,
> Nor will rivers overflow it;
> If a man were to give all the riches of his house for love,
> It would be utterly despised.

Consider the Robert Redford movie *Indecent Proposal*. The character Redford plays offers a million dollars to a husband and wife, who agree to let the wife sleep with the man. As the movie shows, it's not worth a million dollars to risk losing the exclusive husband-wife bond.

How do we stay faithful to our promise? It starts in our *thinking:* "Whatever is true, whatever is noble, whatever is right, whatever is pure, whatever is lovely, whatever is admirable, if anything is excellent or praiseworthy—think about such things," writes Paul in Philippians 4:8 (NIV). The battle to keep your marriage exclusive is won or lost in the brain before it proceeds to a bedroom.

16

WHEN DELIGHT BECOMES OBSESSION: SEXUAL ADDICTION

There are sixty queens and eighty concubines,
and maidens without number;
but my dove, my perfect one, is unique.
—Song of Solomon 6:8–9

E ventually he was bound to be caught. For years he committed adultery with coworkers. Then he started using the Internet to feed his appetite. Before long he was meeting strangers for sexual encounters. Like one of the nearly 7 percent of married clergy who use pornography, this man fell further and further into sin. When he accidentally corresponded in a porn chat room with a woman who knew him from church, he confessed his behavior to the senior pastor. Then he was shocked to find himself out of a job. His argument: "But I *confessed!*"

His wife, whose suspicions had been trivialized by others for years, joined a spouse's support group and found great encouragement through the process of rebuilding their marriage and establishing personal accountability.

We often hear it said that "Every sin is the same in God's eyes— They're all bad." And while it's true that the blood of Christ covers all, 1 Corinthians 6:18–20 suggests that sexual immorality is more grave for two reasons: First, it's a sin against the body. Second, we take the Holy Spirit with us when we commit sexual sin.

Flee from sexual immorality. All other sins a man commits are outside his body, but he who sins sexually sins against his own body. Do you not know that your body is a temple of the Holy Spirit, who is in you, whom you have received from God? You are not your own; you were bought at a price. Therefore honor God with your body. (NIV)

We see this noted, not only in God's special revelation of His Word, but also by noticing the world around us. A writer for *Elle* magazine made this observation:

Of all our appetites, it seems to me, sex is the most anarchic. It's where we feel our keenest sense of sin. The sexual impulse rides roughshod over our ethics and our desire to be just to other people. All over the world, people build these fragile structures called relationships and the single biggest fault line that can destroy nearly all that hard-won trust is the issue of sexual wantonness, or infidelity—the idea that one of the partners will look outside the relationship to satiate a sexual appetite he or she cannot control.[1]

With every other kind of sin we receive instruction about putting on armor so we can stand and fight (Eph. 6). Yet when it comes to sexual immorality, the scriptural advice is much different: Flee!

When describing the intimate relationship between Christ and the church, Paul uses the bride and groom relationship as the most fitting earthly analogy. God has chosen the most loving, intimate metaphor in the world to picture His relationship with us. He has apparently designed sexual intimacy as much for pleasure as for procreation (see Song of Solomon). So we can learn much about our Creator and His desire for us to experience delight from how He made us. Human sexuality represents a powerful aspect of our being that can bring some of life's greatest joys, but it can also generate enormous pain. And for some it brings an ongoing struggle with what many label as sexual addiction.

Some question whether such a "condition" even exists, or if it's really simply a series of bad choices. Medically speaking, the word *addiction* has a specific meaning—that substances taken into the body act on the brain in such a manner that their removal brings withdrawal symptoms. In that sense excessive sexual activity is not addictive. Yet we will use this term, as is done at the popular level, to describe those with sexual obsessions, compulsions, dependency, or increasingly unhealthy involvement.

Using this broader definition, experts in the field of Christian counseling, some speaking from personal experience, suggest that the condition exists. Its impact is considerable. Russell Willingham, in his book *Breaking Free*, defines sexual addiction as "an obsessive-compulsive relationship with a person, object, or experience for the purpose of sexual gratification."[2] His broad definition could include many behaviors, both pre- and extra-marital.

Self-described recovering sex addict Dr. Mark Laaser identifies loneliness as the driving emotion behind such behavior. He prescribes Christian fellowship as the "antidote." His research as a counselor suggests that traumatic episodes in early life play a significant role in the development of sexual addiction. According to his work, *Faithful and True: Sexual Integrity in a Fallen World*, 81 percent of sex addicts were sexually abused as children, 74 percent were physically abused, and 97 percent emotionally abused. He says most addicts have as a commonality the abandonment of "touch, love, nurture, and affirmation." Abandonment, or even the *sense* of abandonment through divorce or death of a parent, can represent significant risk factors for sexual addiction.[3]

The progression of symptoms suggests that such addiction comes close to meeting the criteria for a true addiction, not only in the frequency of acting out, but also in the escalation of activities to find sexual gratification. Like most addictions, "tolerance" develops as the conscience is seared, necessitating more powerful experiences to reach the same effect. Like a drug addict needing increasing amounts of his drug, the sex addict finds himself falling into increasingly sinful sexual behaviors to achieve the same thrill. Sex becomes a means of escape from reality as it provides a temporary sense of feeling "normal." For the afflicted person, the result is a double life that includes denial and often despair.

Exposure or public discovery may provide the needed motivation for the sex addict to seek help due to family pressure or law. And as with any addiction, the consequences of exposure may include financial problems, relational upheaval, job loss, and community shame.

The book of Proverbs has much to say about the consequences of sexually immoral behavior:

> Can a man scoop fire into his lap without his clothes being burned? Can a man walk on hot coals without his feet being scorched? So is he who sleeps with another man's wife; no one who touches her will go unpunished. (Prov. 6:27–29 NIV)

The sobering recognition of consequences can lead to a period in which the addiction seems under control, but a relapse will occur unless ongoing help is sought.

Most sex addicts are male, but certainly some women are similarly afflicted. They often relate stories of abandonment or abuse, and lack of affirmation by the males in their family of upbringing, followed by acting out. Their resulting response may include seductive behavior, adulterous acts, and serial sex partners. Some sex addicts move in the direction of homosexual behavior or fetishes to get the craved endorphin fix.

Certain core feelings surface in recovering sex addicts, according to Carnes in his book, *Out of the Shadows.* They include these thoughts: "I am basically a bad, unworthy person," "If you really knew me, you wouldn't love me," "I can't depend on others to meet my needs, so I must meet them myself," and "Sex is my greatest need." The resulting depression can put the addict at risk for a relapse in sexual "acting out" and even thoughts of suicide.[4]

As with any of God's good gifts, sexuality—created as a wonderful expression of covenant love and intimate bonding—can become a painful trap and a seemingly irresistible force. Its immense power finds its full expression within marriage—a committed, covenant relationship. When people seek sexual pleasure devoid of commitment, accountability, and responsibility for personal actions, they often find themselves in a downward spiral of self-destruction.

Some activities as part of this spiral are socially acceptable in many contexts. It may begin with frequent use of sexual humor and innuendo.

Turning every conversation in a sexual direction may be the first discernible clue of an underlying problem.

Consider the male choir member who made crude jokes about his wife's anatomy. A fellow believer asked him, "Jay, are you into pornography?"

Stunned, he said, "What makes you ask that?"

"Because you seem desensitized to what is appropriate."

His wife later confided, "He keeps a stash of magazines in a drawer beside the bed."

Easily accessible sexually explicit material draws an ever increasing number of willing participants by way of catalogs, magazines, TV with cable and satellite feeds, and now—one of the greatest dangers—the Internet.

One couple who had enjoyed a relatively good marriage for more than two decades split up after their grown son used his father's computer. There the son found a long list of pornographic favorites on the record of recently visited Web sites.

Access to the World Wide Web has the advantage of providing speed and access to all sorts of information, but it has proven dangerous to those prone to sexual addiction. Whereas one might hesitate to go to an X-rated movie or to buy inappropriate literature, the easy, in-home availability of online pornography has proved nearly impossible for many to handle. The sale of sexually degrading images has become a $10 billion-a-year industry, compared with the $10 million-a-year industry it was thirty years ago, according to the *New York Times*. The paper goes on to report that it's now easier to order porn into the home than pizza.[5]

The addict can rationalize about the progression of symptoms at first because the viewing of pornography and masturbation "doesn't hurt anybody." Many people fantasize about sexual activities. Yet according to Scripture, to engage in sexual fantasies about someone other than one's spouse constitutes adultery—clearly a sin to avoid if one is to "walk worthy" of Christ and His payment for our sins. This requires drawing on the divine power to demolish strongholds, "tak[ing] captive every thought to make it obedient to Christ" (2 Cor. 10:5 NIV), which becomes quite a discipline for the one immersed in sexual thoughts.

Sadly, involvement in sexual activity will escalate over time, and these individuals become "hooked on a feeling" that can only be chased, never permanently obtained. We read in Ephesians 4:27 (NIV) the exhortation not to give the devil a "foothold" through our anger. The same would certainly apply to starting down the path to immorality.

Many progress to voyeurism (gaining sexual pleasure from watching others engage in sexual behavior), exhibitionism (gratification from self-exposure), and certain types of fetishes. Those with fetishes derive sexual pleasure from a wide variety of objects, including women's clothing or shoes.

Most sex addicts follow a fairly predictable cycle of behavior, outlined by Arterburn in his work, *Every Man's Battle*. The cycle begins with a visual/emotional trigger usually followed by a struggle between the longings for sexual release and the desire to "do good." The fantasy may serve temporarily as an escape from emotional pain, but eventually a "plan" begins to develop to turn fantasy into reality.[6] We find in the book of James an explanation of how such a progression happens:

> Each one is tempted when, by his own evil desire, he is dragged away and enticed. Then, after desire has conceived, it gives birth to sin; and sin, when it is full-grown, gives birth to death. (James 1:14–15 NIV)

The planning may involve complex rituals, whether driving to get pornography, casing a store to verify that no familiar people are around, or driving great distances to avoid being recognized. The ritual provides a heightened sense of satisfaction while waiting for the opportune moment. The addict stalking his prey acts as a predator and, in some instances, it is precisely that.

Then he or she reaches the "goal"—the pornographic material, the affair, or the appointment with the prostitute—and sexual release takes place. Yet suddenly, deep shame and remorse quickly replace the sheer thrill of the act itself as the bleak reality of the post orgasmic state sets in and with it a sense of acute loneliness. Life has remained unchanged with only a brief escape, and now thoughts center on the risk of exposure—the legal, moral, familial, and health consequences. Additionally, for the Christian, the spiritual reality of moral failure can feel overwhelming. Consider David's description in Psalm 32 of how his bones wasted away and how guilt sapped his energy.

The addict then believes his or her own promises: "Never again." "If I don't get caught or contract some venereal disease, I will never fail again." Such promises, even couched in Christian jargon about forgiveness and restoration, are almost certainly doomed to failure without consistent Christian fellowship, personal accountability, and often, professional support. In the absence of these, the fragile addict awaits the next visual stimulus, and the awful cycle begins again.

The Bible speaks clearly about some issues, declaring certain behaviors sinful. These include premarital and extramarital sex, incest, bestiality (sex with animals), and necrophilia (sex with the dead; see Levit. 20:15ff). One must assume Scripture includes these prohibitions because there was a need to prohibit them. Romans 1 tells us that God's judgment sometimes involves His giving sinful people over to their sin. That is, sometimes His discipline allows people to continue in the downward spiral of sexual degradation. Historically, we observe from the great cultures of Egypt, Greece, and Rome, that sexual immorality became a large part of the social conscience and contributed to the dissolution of their prominence.

Some Christian couples erroneously believe that they can keep the "letter of the Law" by drawing the line at intercourse. They feel that as long as they abstain from vaginal penetration, even if they engage in something as intimate as oral sex, they have stayed within God's prohibitions against "sex" outside of marriage. The intense sexual emphasis in American culture (music videos, movies, and TV sitcoms) and even the example set by some political leaders help encourage this attitude of "take it to the limit." Couples who are truly following Christ from the heart, however, will not ask, "How far can I go?" but, "What is God's standard for sexuality and how can we most glorify God in this relationship?"

Those who counsel sex addicts recommend that they start by being honest with themselves that they have a problem. Then they must tell someone they trust about their addiction (James 5:16, Eph. 5:21). Next, as one young man who held a magazine-burning event with his accountability partner, the addict is encouraged to destroy all pornographic material, including sales catalogs if those pose a problem. If videos bring temptation, video stores of any kind must be avoided.

A husband who had struggled with pornography for years—one of the nearly twenty percent of married men who do—shared his recent experience of sitting outside a convenience store listening to the end of a favorite song on the radio after filling his car with gas. Suddenly he realized he had not even felt tempted to go in and buy a pornographic magazine. On his long journey toward godliness, he knew he had not yet "arrived," but he breathed a prayer of thanks for the small victory.

17

TROUBLESHOOTING MALE PROBLEMS FROM SIZZLE TO FIZZLE: WHEN HE'S NEVER IN THE MOOD

On my bed night after night I sought him whom my soul loves; I sought but did not find him.
—Song of Solomon 3:1

Many books and marriage conferences emphasize the common problem of the disparity between the husband and wife's interest in sex. While they usually focus on men with high levels and women with low levels, some couples have the opposite problem—he is never interested. Continually hearing that they are "different" in this way only adds to the frustration these couples feel.

Lanette is one of the most attractive women I (Sandi) have ever known, but it didn't take long to find out why she paid so much attention to her beautiful hair, flawless makeup, and stylish clothes. Her husband ignored her. She changed her hairstyle—sometimes the color, sometimes the cut—about six times a year, hoping that somehow she would find the right combination to catch his interest.

Laura sat across from me in her company's cafeteria. She picked at her food and periodically wiped tears. "I caught him masturbating," she told me. "I've gone six months without having my needs met. I've begged him to pay attention to me. And now this!" Laura's husband had a long history of alcohol abuse, causing periodic impotency. His insecurity about it made him avoid intimacy altogether, so she lived as a married celibate.

While other women complained that their husbands were always after them for sex, Laura listened longingly.

Candy called me on the recommendation of a friend. "We've been married for six months," she told me, "and the only time we did anything was on the first night of our honeymoon. The rest of the trip, he said he was too worn out from all the festivities. That was just the beginning of the excuses. Most recently I bought a new sexy nightgown for Valentine's Day. We had a special dinner together, but when it came time to 'be together,' he fell asleep on me. It must be so wonderful to be married to someone who expresses physical love. I can't imagine how special that would be."

A little more than a third of married women complain that "he's rarely interested."[1] Men can experience lack of interest in sex for a variety of reasons. Usually the greatest fear that enters a wife's mind is that her mate is having an affair with another woman, or worse as it turned out for Candy, with a man. These legitimate concerns must be explored. In addition, other reasons for low sexual interest in men include such health factors as diabetes, a high level of stress, and, as with both Lanette's and Laura's husbands, a history of alcohol abuse and self-gratification using pornography. Also, if brain serotonin levels are too high—as is true for many patients on antidepressants—he may develop sexual dysfunction.[2]

When the wife has a lower sex drive than her husband, she can still usually help him experience sexual release in a relatively brief time. It is much more complex when the one with the lower libido is the husband. Because sexual satisfaction for her generally takes longer, requires more concentration and ambiance, and is a reflection of the intensity of her feelings toward her man, the uninterested husband must involve himself for much longer to satisfy his wife. And her partner's enthusiasm is more closely linked to her ability even to experience ultimate satisfaction than it would be for many men with less interested wives. Nevertheless, it's still worth while to have intimate contact, if only to assure her of his love, affection, and concern for her welfare.

Sadly, many wives in this situation have spouses who care little about meeting their needs. Yet some of those whose husbands *are* trying to be sensitive have painful conversations that go something like this:

Him: "Do you need me to meet your needs tonight, sweetheart?"

Her: "It would be nice if you actually wanted me."

Him: "Hey, I'm doing the best I can."

Her: "I don't want some sort of sympathy session—doing it because you have to. You'd just be pretending."

Him: "Then what do you expect me to do? Lie and tell you I can't wait? I'm willing to meet your needs. That's the best I can do right now."

For the woman in this situation, the first place to begin is to pray for the Lord's guidance to help her have a difficult but necessary conversation with her husband. Together they need to explore the cause or causes of his lack of interest. Some women feel they are wrong or that they're being demanding to expect their husbands to meet these needs. Yet 1 Corinthians 7:3 makes it clear that the husband has a "duty" to his wife in the same way the wife has a "duty" to her husband.

The neglected wife will probably feel insecurities such as, "If only I were more beautiful" or "If only I were more sexy." Even if doctors can identify a medical cause for the husband's seeming indifference, these feelings are nearly impossible for her to overcome. As a result, she will probably find herself feeling especially vulnerable when other men show her attention. First Corinthians 7:5 gives the clear command not to deprive each other for this very reason—because it leaves one's spouse more vulnerable to sexual temptation. If your spouse refuses to obey here, you as the deprived spouse must recognize the additional moral vigilance that must accompany such difficulties in your life.

Ultimately, the way your spouse decides to respond to your need is largely out of your control. If he ignores your pleas despite attempts at communication, you must live as a celibate married person. In this case our Savior's submission to the Father serves as a source of enablement and encouragement: "When they hurled their insults at him, he did not retaliate; when he suffered, he made no threats. Instead, he entrusted himself to him who judges justly" (1 Peter 2:23 NIV). That is not to say you silently bear it, opting never to bring it up. Periodically express your ongoing desire for marital oneness. Yet recognize that if your husband fails to respond, it is out of your control. For many women, this is a source of ongoing grief, as sexual oneness was created as an essential piece in the marriage equation. If this is true for you, express your emotion to God, knowing He will honor you for exhibiting a quality that reflects the heart of God himself—loyal, faithful love that cares for the unloving.

The Lord understands the celibate life. In Ronald Rolheiser's book *The Holy Longing,* he notes, "When Christ went to bed alone at night he was in real solidarity with the many persons who, not by choice but by circumstance, sleep alone. And there is a real poverty, a painful searing one, in this kind of aloneness. The poor are not just those who are more manifestly victimized by poverty, violence, war, and unjust economic systems. There are other less obvious manifestations of poverty, violence, and injustice. Celibacy by conscription is one of them."[3]

18

SEXUALITY AND AGING

Let his left hand be under my head,
and his right hand embrace me.
—Song of Solomon 8:3

She was sixty-three years old when she conceived, using *in vitro* fertilization with donor eggs. Nine months later Arceli Keh became the oldest woman in the world to give birth—the modern world, that is. After all, Luke 1:7 tells us that Elizabeth and Zechariah were both "well advanced in years" when their son John the Baptizer was conceived. Sarah was ninety when she gave birth to Isaac (Gen. 17:17). And these folks had nothing on Methuselah, who after 782 years still had little ones calling him "Da-da" (Gen. 5:26).

Regardless of how many decades we medically extend the "childbearing years," the aging process—for all the money spent fighting it with facelifts, tummy tucks, and liposuction—is still occurring. Unless someone discovers the "Ponce de Leon" gene or another "fountain of youth" in the various wrinkle creams and herbal remedies, we will show advancing signs of age as the body's mechanisms for repairing itself fail.

Slowly, almost imperceptibly, the pounds accumulate, and the inches expand. Add wrinkles, bags, and sags, and—before you know it—loss of confidence will follow. One wonders if the diminishing eyesight that comes with aging might be God's way of keeping us from having to face the wrinkles!

While we Westerners tend to view aging as an enemy to be fought, the Book of Proverbs lends a different perspective when it describes gray hair as "a crown of splendor" (Prov. 16:31 NIV).

In 2 Peter, we find exhortations to grow in knowledge, self-control, perseverance, godliness, brotherly kindness, and love. The Scriptures teach us that as long as these are increasing, life has purpose and meaning. Aging provides the opportunity to grow in many areas. While some medical problems may arise, a life with purpose through deepening love for God can be joyful and satisfying. Hopefully, as we age we grow in wisdom and kindness. Certainly we need these traits to face the accumulated years' changes, particularly the ones that affect sexual functioning. Recognizing that satisfaction and performance have enormous mental components, it's easy to see that, for both men and women, the changes aging brings can generate some new challenges or bring old ones to the surface. Yet these challenges can provide wonderful opportunities to deepen intimacy and discover ways for a man and woman to delight each other in an atmosphere of ever deepening unity.

Many women feel unattractive and fear loss of sexual *desirability*. In contrast, men, though some do obsess over their looks, usually are most fearful of the loss of sexual *ability*. Performance anxiety issues, even impotence, develop for men who have rarely struggled to "rise to the occasion" in the past.

But, midlife can be an exhilarating time as well. Many husbands and wives draw closer, as the shared years and life experiences have "smoothed out the rough edges." As character, charm, and understanding flourish, couples find that physical appearance alone doesn't define attractiveness. For example, Lois and Oscar, both in their nineties, have spent many years together as husband and wife. They demonstrate a deep commitment and affection, developed through the complex pressures they have faced together. What couple in love doesn't talk of "growing old together"?

An interesting difference between men and women was reported in *Psychology Today*.[1] There seems to be a tendency for men, as they age, to retain a mental preference for the image of the "woman I married"— the young, attractive, blushing bride. With the passage of time, that girl of their dreams has morphed into a middle-aged woman, and men can experience difficulties in arousal and performance as a reaction.

The same study suggests that the average woman, as she matures, finds in her mate attributes that *become* "the ideal." That is, if her man puts on a little weight and thins out on top, she modifies her ideal to include a "plump, balding guy"—a nice adaptation. This difference in ideals can have significant impact on the marriage.

The man in a "midlife crisis" might leave his wife for a younger woman or have extramarital affairs to meet his perceived need to feel young and virile again. At the same time, though the wife feels content with her partner, she senses his distance and becomes hypercritical of her own appearance.

It doesn't have to be this way. Many couples find middle life quite satisfying. With the fear of pregnancy gone, years of history built together, and deep communication developed through years of observing each other, many couples report this as their best time. Feeling unencumbered with all the cares of youth, they enjoy lovemaking. It may take them longer, but no stopwatch ticks off the minutes. They have time to enjoy, to explore, and to learn more about each other. One woman in her seventies, after nearly fifty years of marriage, read a book on marital intimacy and told us, "I learned something new—but I'll be danged if I'm going to tell you what it was!"

"Midlife crisis" is not a mandatory stage. Men don't have to fit the stereotypical picture of the guy with the red sports car, shirt unbuttoned to the navel, leaving his marriage for a twenty-something blonde. Women aren't destined to be depressed, miserable, and hypercritical about their own appearance. Aging poses certain complex challenges, but with the support of spouse, family, church, and good medical care, midlife and beyond can be absolutely fantastic!

Perimenopause

Midlife alters the woman's hormonal cycle. The prepared woman knows changes are coming, and that they're part of the divine design. The complex synchrony of estrogen and progesterone wavers. Perimenopause, which typically lasts several years preceding menopause, includes unpredictable estrogen production. Other hormones change, too, so women in their late thirties and forties may experience symptoms that have an impact on their sexual responses. These include hot flashes, those bursts of "core meltdown." Add in sleep disturbances, night sweats, generalized moodiness, and at times profound depression, and you have a fragile condition.

A good medical exam and proper treatment can resolve most of these issues and women will find hormonal stability again. Various therapies, some available over the counter and some by prescription, can significantly alleviate these problems.

With fluctuating estrogen production, the vagina loses elasticity, lubrication fails, and sex can become painful, bladder function is less predictable, and ultimately, some sexual sensations change. Surgical procedures, such as removal of the ovaries, have an impact on female sexuality, as well. And discomfort from pelvic inflammatory disease, endometriosis, or prominent fibroids can also inhibit function and cause discomfort.

Libido is a complex combination of many factors, and many of them can be changing in perimenopausal women, causing negative ramifications in the bedroom. A health care provider can help by prescribing estrogen replacement therapy (ERT) or other treatments. While some women are candidates for estrogen replacement therapy, others may choose other strategies of treatment. Despite occasional complications, normal sexual function is not only possible in the forties and beyond for most women, but it is a vital part of life in good, healthy marital relationships. In fact, women often report increasing sexual pleasure during these stages.

Men and Midlife

From an actuarial standpoint, the segment of the population age forty-five and over is the healthiest age group in the United States. If the AARP, a non-profit organization for people over fifty, were to become a nation, it would be the thirtieth most populous in the world, slightly under the population of Argentina. More than half of the people in history who have reached age sixty-five are alive today.

Due to today's improved health care and living conditions, normal sexual function for men is possible not only in their forties but well beyond, continuing as a vital part of life. While men in midlife have no dramatic hormonal flux equivalent with "the change" in women, they often undergo some psychological changes that affect marital intimacy. Some suggest that, in the forties or fifties, men come to recognize they will never win an Olympic medal or even advance in their own vocation much beyond their current status. While this is certainly a broad generalization, those who focus on such a realization may feel depressed and disappointed, and this may affect their sexual functioning.

Yet with such a sense of limitation can also come freedom. The couple that has worked hard to raise their family well begins to enjoy the long-term effects of wisdom, experience, and truly "knowing" each other. Men who work to keep the romance alive, to woo their wives with tenderness, can find midlife a terrific time to be in love. Most husbands find lasting contentment in their faith and commitment to their family. Those who go looking outside the marriage bond usually find themselves feeling more empty than they did when they started looking. God alone can truly fulfill the deepest needs and bring peace and joy to the soul.

Occasional impotence, the inability to achieve or sustain an erection sufficient to permit satisfactory intercourse, becomes increasingly common as the years pass. But, greater sexual control and better understanding of his wife's needs and preferences often makes the older lover more satisfying to his spouse. Assuming good health and a strong relationship, many men can achieve erection and reach orgasm into their eighties and beyond. Though sexual arousal and climax may require more time, pleasurable sensations can be heightened for both partners. Satisfaction and gratification do not always have to be defined as "climax." Couples can find joy in the journey of relational intimacy and spiritual oneness.

Medical factors can have an impact on sexual performance and pleasure in midlife and beyond. Erection and ejaculatory problems may have a neurological cause, so a thorough examination might clarify any problem and generate practical suggestions for keeping romance alive. Medications interfere with normal functioning, particularly some targeted at hypertension and psychiatric difficulties. Alternative drug therapies may make an impact, so consult your physician if you develop sexual problems.

At a recent conference, several wives shared with us that sex for them had been "short, sweet, and fall asleep"—for *him*. Yet with their husbands' changes brought by aging, they reported new pleasures as their men seemed less in a rush to get to the ultimate experience, having learned how to bring pleasure to their wives. These women were genuinely happy over the new heights that they had achieved. Some even found that they were more responsive sexually than they had ever imagined they could be.

Menopause

Menopause brings with it some predictable obstacles. As we said, without estrogen, decreased elasticity and lubrication may cause painful intercourse, bleeding, and tearing of the vaginal tissues. However, painful sex is not limited to estrogen deficiency in a woman, but can be related to a number of vaginal conditions. Thus, a thorough gynecological exam yielding an accurate diagnosis must precede therapy. Pain should never be considered normal, and a good physician can present a variety of options (for more on menopause, see p. 113).

Surgery and Medications

In addition to difficulties that accompany chronic medical illnesses, surgical procedures can affect sexual expression in midlife. Male sexual dysfunction can happen as a direct result of radical prostate procedures and some abdomino-pelvic vascular procedures. In other cases problems may be less direct, such as those that may arise following abdominal surgery. For men whose impotence is purely anatomical, prosthetic devices, pumps, vacuums, and an assortment of appliances may restore sexual function. For those with secondary issues (*e.g.,* fear following a heart attack), the medical team can assess the true risks and make suggestions of ways the individuals should best approach sexual expression.

In women, a number of specific gynecological procedures may affect sexual comfort and responsiveness. With orgasm, many experience the gentle contractions of the uterus; for patients with fibroids or endometriosis this may actually cause pain. But after a hysterectomy the sensations change. Most post-hysterectomy women are fully responsive and adapt quickly without problems.

Medications may require some adaptation as well. One husband, his wife on tamoxifen following breast cancer surgery, noticed during a romantic interlude that his wife was becoming physically hot. He could feel the heat within his arms and noticed the sweat on her lips. Thinking he was perhaps the world's greatest lover, he was thoroughly disappointed to find that these responses were the result of a hot flash, not hot love. Couples—especially those armed with a sense of humor—can certainly learn to express their love after the myriad procedures people face over the decades in countries where good medical care is available.

Communication Is the Key

As we've said before, the number-one sexual difficulty couples experience is the inability to talk about it. This appears to be a pattern that continues through the years unless couples make a specific effort to communicate about their intimate lives. Physicians estimate that nearly half of their menopausal patients suffer from a loss of sexual desire or satisfaction. And while approximately two-thirds of the men have noticed a decrease in sexual activity since their partners entered menopause, only half of the couples have discussed these changes together.

So the first line of defense is communication. The second is knowing what to expect. The third is knowing when to seek help any time you experience discomfort or ongoing anxiety. Finally, focus on the benefits of loving well at each age. In their time of youth, couples experience new, exciting sensations and awaken to worlds of self-discovery. With maturity come skill, confidence, and deepening intimacy. In old age, couples bring to each other the wisdom and joy of love learned over a lifetime. As the authors of *Love and Sex After Forty* remind us, "Love and sex are twin arts, requiring effort and knowledge. Only in fairy tales do people live happily ever after without working at it . . . but sex does not merely exist after the middle and later years; it holds the possibility of becoming greater than it ever was."[2]

Like the bride in Song of Solomon who felt free to say, "Dark am I, yet lovely," we begin by working to create a secure atmosphere for each other. In that place, loving eyes look beyond physical imperfections and exclaim, "This is my lover; this my friend" (Song of Songs 5:16 NIV).

19

QUESTIONS FROM OUR READERS

May he kiss me with the kisses of his mouth!
For your love is better than wine.
—Song of Solomon 1:2

Questions About Desire

What natural herbs or foods can I take to increase my desire?

Many companies market herbs as aphrodisiacs or sexual response enhancers despite legal restrictions. Although some long-touted aphrodisiacs are being tested—including a derivative of chili peppers now in legitimate trials[1]—to date there is no such thing as a science-verified aphrodisiac. In 1989, the Food and Drug Administration officially banned the sale of "any product that bears labeling claims that it will arouse or increase sexual desire or that it will improve sexual performance."

If you believe that eating oysters or exotic herbs will put you in the mood, they probably will, considering the fact that the brain is the most powerful sex organ we have. The same is true of vitamin E. While drinking alcohol initially increases genital blood flow, by the third drink, alcohol impairs performance.

Perhaps the best way to stay sexually healthy is simply to have sex.

Will an oral contraceptive take away my sexual desire?

One patient wrote, "I'm pretty sure that the oral contraceptive I'm taking has decreased my desire. I'm a lot less frisky than I was two months before the wedding, and I noticed it before the wedding. I think my husband is afraid I'll go off the pill and get pregnant. So he's convincing himself that I'm just nervous from the stress of not getting the sex thing perfect. Basically, he thinks I need to relax—not just my muscles, but my mind."

The pill combines two powerful hormones, but at low levels. Ideally, these artificially produced hormones shut down the woman's own ovarian production of estrogen—a major contributor to her level of interest. There is no real surge in progesterone, and the small amount of testosterone made in the woman's ovary can be diminished. A fair number of women have noted a decreased sex drive while taking oral contraceptives. For these women, physicians can switch prescriptions to a combination that includes a slightly more "androgenic" (male hormone) type of progesterone. Production of these hormones can cause acne, oily skin, and weight gain, so it may take a few months to find the "happy median."

More Questions About "The Pill"

When I'm on an oral contraceptive, should I take a periodic break?

Many pill takers believe they need to take a periodic break from oral contraceptives. This is unnecessary. Medical evidence suggests that, if women take their pills correctly, taking time off from them does not lower the risk of complications or disease, and it may result in a surprise pregnancy.

Do oral contraceptives cause weight gain?

Not all birth control pills cause weight gain. As many women tend to gain weight as to lose weight while taking a birth control pill. How one woman might interact with a specific pill is anyone's guess, but diet and nutrition always play a role. The pill can't be responsible for a fifty-pound weight gain!

Do oral contraceptives cause abortion?

Oral contraceptive pills (OCPs) are designed primarily to prevent ovulation or egg release. Most pills are a combination of an estrogen and a progesterone derivative that cycle a woman artificially without allowing ovulation. In addition to preventing egg release, the pill thickens cervical mucus, making sperm penetration more difficult. It also changes the motion of the cilia (tiny hair-like structures) within the fallopian tubes, altering egg transport. And it thins the uterine lining, making it less favorable to implantation should fertilization occur. While each one of these effects actually increases the effectiveness of the pill in preventing pregnancy, the latter could, in fact, have an abortive effect if breakthrough ovulation were actually to occur.

Nevertheless we must be careful not to overly simplify this complicated scenario. Those who argue that the uterine environment is hostile to implantation while the woman is taking the pill are correct. But, if breakthrough ovulation takes place, it also changes all the hormone levels. It is *not* like "just being on the pill." The estrogen level has to be higher in the first place to permit an egg to reach maturity. Once ovulation has taken place, progesterone is secreted in normal, high amounts, even if the woman continues to take the pill. Thus, in the roughly seven days it takes for the fertilized embryo to reach the uterus and implant, the uterine environment would be "friendly" to implantation.

In addition, good studies using vaginal ultrasound to monitor ovarian egg maturation in people on the pill have not supported the claim that significant rates of breakthrough ovulation happen. The data would suggest that people taking the pill regularly simply do not ovulate very often. Thus, the potential risk described seems very low, though the possibility does exist. It is significant that the majority of Focus on the Family's Physician's Resource Council concluded in 1997 that there is no direct evidence that the pill causes abortions.[2]

Another type of OCP contains only the progesterone type of hormone. This pill clearly has a higher rate of breakthrough ovulation, increasing the risk of a fertilized egg reaching a perhaps more hostile uterine environment because there is not even the minimal estrogen in the pill to begin to grow the uterine lining. For this reason, in my practice I never prescribed the "progesterone only" pill, though the clear evidence that abortions occur is unimpressive even here.

What should we do? Know the medical risks as they are currently understood. Be willing to be teachable if new data reveals different risks. Then prayerfully decide if you can use pills until the question is more fully resolved. If you take them, do so carefully as we *know* that will diminish the risk. And be gentle with others who make choices that differ from yours.

In my own practice, I delivered some babies conceived on the pill. So I know from personal experience that if there is an abortive effect of the pill, it certainly cannot be 100 percent, but the answer at this writing is unclear. If you need absolutes, stay away from the pill, but stay informed and consult your own physician. For now, taking them appears to be an ethical option, but there are some unknowns for which we are awaiting further research.

Questions About Intercourse

What can we do about the fact that I ejaculate before she is ready for me to?

In the workbook we included the "squeeze technique," though we don't recommend it. Another suggestion was to have sex twice in one night. Here's another.

Know this first: Once a woman has had one orgasm, should she wish to pursue a second one, the time between the first and the next is relatively short compared to how long it takes from excitation to orgasm with the first. So seek to bring your wife to ultimate satisfaction apart from intercourse, whether through touching with your palm or fingertips, oral stimulation, external contact with the penis, or a combination of these. Take your time and enjoy the trip. As was said so succinctly in a *Newsweek* article, ". . . Nature did not design most women to climax reliably through intercourse, especially in the missionary position."[3] Many couples say that they prefer to save intercourse for after her orgasm, so she is more lubricated and engorged.

Once she has reached ultimate satisfaction and expresses that she is ready again, move to penetration and thrusting, with additional manual stimulation for her if she requests it. The time required for male self-control should be much shorter. In addition, if you ejaculate apart from satisfying her, she has already reached a degree of ultimate satisfaction, so she is not left completely frustrated.

Enjoy each other. If it works out that she has an orgasm via penetration, wonderful. But if not, enjoy the fullness of your own experience and realize you will both be satisfied.

What are the some of the special challenges unique to virgins?

One reader wrote, "After going to the doctor two months before the wedding, I came away thinking I was good to go. All the running, tampons, and the fact that I'm over thirty made me think my hymen was very flexible, if not gone. So I didn't do any stretching exercises. I could always feel my body responding when we kissed, so I imagined we'd have no trouble at all on the wedding night. I was shocked when it was so painful.

"I know everybody has baggage, but I think I pride myself on being a 'free from bondage woman' who understands God's perfect plan for beautiful sex within marriage. But it still really hurt at the initial entry.

"Even now, if he thrusts too deeply, it's painful. I know I'm headed for trouble if I can't get into this 'penetration thing.' I'm already getting an aversion to sex. I want to be close to him and sexual with him, but not intercourse."

Another wrote, "I used to cry and cry out of frustration for my loss of interest in sexual intercourse because it's so painful. But now I think it's hopeless to cry. We both are desperate. It may be something mental or physical with me. Now I become angry with myself for desiring something that may never come back (orgasm). Should I just forget about it? Should I just endure painful intercourse? Am I going to be part of the statistics of women who don't respond?"

Yet another said this: "We ended up having a sexless honeymoon because the pain was so great for me. We called the doctor and he prescribed a numbing cream, but that didn't help when it numbed my husband on contact! When we got home, the doctor gave us dilators and that helped a lot. I would insert them for about thirty minutes to stretch me before intercourse. I felt a lot of fear and guilt. I had always dreamed I would be this satisfying lover for my husband and I feel as though I've been one big disappointment. We had a great relationship before, but after that we started arguing a lot. I never realized how sexual intimacy would be such a core part of our relationship. Our love life is much better now, but it has taken time to make the adjustment."

The first patient in these three scenarios probably has a tight hymeneal ring, even if she can insert two fingers. Or perhaps she has a slight skin flap inside the vagina, possibly caused by a congenital problem. It's important to know that pain is abnormal except at the beginning when couples are adapting to one another, and for some a deeper pain occurs at the time of ovulation when the ovary is swollen and a bit tender. Discomfort associated with intercourse is medically treatable. Find a physician who will listen, and then with exercises, dilators, lubricants, and even surgery, the pain can be resolved.

Our runner friend said, "Now when I talk to other women who are entering marriage as virgins, I tell them that having low expectations is key—don't set yourself up for failure by thinking you have an exceptionally loose vagina. Also, hands and mouth are great alternate ways of stimulation. I encourage couples not to get caught up with 'I must get intercourse good before moving on to the rest.' Lubricant on top of the condom has helped—no dry condoms! In addition, it has been great to talk with women who are willing to talk. I have found that especially helpful."

Another shared something else that came as a surprise for her.

"I always imagined 'entry,' but I never thought beyond that to think that 'what goes in must come out.' This is messy, smelly business. In our first experiences, the bodily fluids from our lovemaking spilled all over the bed, and we'd end up trying to edge each other out for the dry spots when it was time to go to sleep.

"No matter how often a person might shower . . . well, tell the type A virgin that this is messy business, but 'the boy' doesn't seem to care. Who do you think thought up Jell-O and mud wrestling? I'm sure it was guys! Now we keep a hand towel in the nightstand by the bed for spontaneous encounters. When we plan ahead, we bring a warm, moist, scented washcloth and make cleanup part of the interaction. A few scented candles can mask the faint seminal smell, too."

Apparently, these ladies are not alone. In a survey of two thousand Christian women, published in his book *The Secrets of Eve*, Archibald Hart reported what women do not like about sex.[4] Thirty percent complained about the mess, 6 percent listed "partner's smell" as a turn off, 16 percent didn't like the inconvenience. For 8 percent, it hurts.

In order to minimize the adjustment to sexual intimacy, isn't it better to live with someone first to make sure you're compatible?

Between 1960 and 1998, the number of unmarried couples in North America increased by close to one thousand percent.[5] The *Houston Chronicle* reported that couples who live together before marriage have an 80 percent greater chance of divorce after they are married than those who don't cohabit first. A Washington State researcher discovered that women who cohabit with a man are twice as likely to experience domestic violence as are married women. The National Center for Mental Health revealed that the incidence of depression among cohabiting women is four times greater than that among married women, and two times greater than depression among unmarried women. In a survey of more than 100 couples who lived together, 71 percent of the women said they would not live-in again.[6] In practice, cohabiting couples who marry—many of whom already have children—are about 33 percent more likely to divorce than are couples who don't live together before their nuptials. Virgin brides, on the other hand, are less likely to divorce than are sexually experienced women who entered marriage.[7] The evidence strongly suggests that, while test driving a car might be a good idea, "trying out" one's future partner is not.

Since God prohibits intercourse before marriage, what's wrong with sexual release that doesn't involve intercourse?

An increasing number of couples—including many Christians—are engaging in mutual orgasm, sometimes including oral sex apart from intercourse, in order to technically keep God's law against fornication. Consider one woman's statement: "My high school boyfriend and I wanted to save intercourse for marriage, but that didn't stop us from having ecstatic sex. We explored ourselves and each other and learned how to fantasize and kiss and touch in very imaginative ways. Those intense sessions left us feeling like we'd been transported to hyperspace."[8]

It's important for these couples to know that the prohibition against "immorality" that occurs numerous times in the New Testament comes from the Greek word *porneia*. This broad term encompasses premarital and extramarital intercourse and also any intimate sexual activity outside of marriage.

In addition to the sin issues involved, couples engaging in such sexual behavior are at risk for contracting sexually transmitted diseases (STDs). Together, more than twenty-five of these diseases are infecting at least 12 million Americans annually. One in four sexually experienced adolescents acquire an STD each year.[9]

20

SOME FINAL THOUGHTS

Beneath the apple tree I awakened you.
—Song of Solomon 8:5

Ginger had had no sexual experience before she was married. Several months before her wedding she began taking birth control pills; they decreased her desire for sex. In addition, for the first ten years of her marriage Ginger endured painful sex due to a physical problem that would require surgery to correct. Both husband and wife wondered about her lack of interest in sex, thinking there must be some deeply rooted psychological causes they didn't understand. The situation was further complicated when they read several popular Christian books about sex that wrongly stressed that simultaneous orgasm should be a couple's goal, and also insisted, again incorrectly, that vaginal orgasms are "the only way to go." Because vaginal penetration caused Ginger pain, all these factors collectively led to a painful experience overall.

Eventually, further education about sex helped reshape this couple's thinking about "how it must be done," and surgery corrected Ginger's medical condition, which proved to be the final solution. After ten years together, Ginger and her husband began to have a dynamic, active love life. This is one of many examples in which physical intimacy develops after years of difficulty.

Sexual intimacy is one of God's most beautiful gifts to us, but learning to enjoy this gift fully is a process that requires time and experience. Together the two of you can reach heights in your relationship that most cannot even imagine. If you're married or considering marriage, we hope this book has supplied the encouragement and biblical instruction you need to find great fulfillment in your relationship. If you're a physician evaluating and working with couples, we have tried to make this book a useful tool. And we have endeavored to create a frank, even entertaining resource for pastors and counselors, with an underlying theme of hope.

No matter where couples find themselves on a scale measuring relational health, there is every reason to believe life together can improve. We are convinced couples can develop intimacy by gaining knowledge, and knowledge in turn can improve our thinking and living. My (Sandi's) younger sister jokingly volunteered to write an introduction for this book stating as much. She wanted to say, "My sister has come a long way since her prepuberty days when she told me it was illegal to have sex any way other than in the missionary position. She also told me a special brand of MP (missionary police) made it their job to check." Yes, I told her these and more myths. While we blame television for a lot, we certainly should never count out "The Sibling Factor" as a contributor to our ignorance. I'm not sure my sister's husband has ever forgiven me. (Fortunately, a little education has corrected the damage her "sexpert" sister had inflicted.)

A couple's depth of physical pleasure and lasting heart intimacy is founded on spiritual growth and maturity. God created us to know Him and worship Him, and our earthly relationships stand or fall on the security and intimacy we find in our relationship with our heavenly Father. A couple in our church who had a basically decent marriage believed all-out commitment to the Lord would mean a less exciting sex life for them. As they both began to grow spiritually and increase in sensitivity, kindness, and compassion, they entered into a whole new dimension to their lovemaking. To their surprise, they discovered that the opposite of what they'd expected had happened: Their spiritual growth led to a more fulfilling, more thrilling sex life. As couples grow spiritually, they grow in their ability to give themselves more completely to and for one another. This selfless giving, as opposed to less intimate sex that amounts to little more than a sharing of body parts, is a key to developing sexual intimacy.

We have included a lot of Scripture in this book, believing God is the ultimate expert. And we have incorporated a lighthearted tone at times, convinced that a sense of humor is essential in unraveling the popular "Hollywood" notions about romance. (At a recent conference a woman observed, "Thank God for 'quickies.' But you sure never see them in the movies. The only on-screen couples who have quickies are under the age of fifteen and worrying about getting caught. And honesty? Do you ever see a woman who's left unsatisfied?") We also want to encourage a healthy sense of curiosity and mystery about male and female sexual preferences and the more important individual husband/wife differences.

If you're experiencing sexual difficulty now, know that there's hope. You can adjust. Sexual drives change over time, and disparity between your desires and your spouse's may equalize. You adapt. You grow. The important thing is to keep seeking and exploring options, keep loving your spouse, and as our Texas-born friend insisted was the key to sexual happiness, "Y'all be *nice* to each other!"

Appendix A

EXERCISES FOR
DEVELOPING INTIMACY

A major sex survey commissioned by *Redbook* magazine included responses from approximately 100,000 women. The findings? Among the most important, it determined that strictly monogamous women experienced orgasm during sex more than twice as often as promiscuous women. And it found that highly religious women were more likely to describe their sex lives as "good" or "very good" than moderately religious or nonreligious women. Later, in what is probably the most scientific, comprehensive study yet, researchers found the same results: The women most likely to achieve orgasm each and every time (32 percent) are conservative Protestants.[1]

A healthy marital relationship and a high level of commitment to one's marriage seem to play a major role in the extent to which a person is satisfied sexually. This is why the best foundation for a satisfying sexual relationship is a loving, Christ-centered marriage.

In addition to that, there are things we can learn about each other that can help to enrich sexual intimacy within marriage. But first, its helpful to understand why a husband and wife don't always "connect" when it comes to sex. For starters, each person is sexually unique. Your partner's likes and dislikes aren't available on a computer printout that can be obtained on the Internet (which could be a sign of some really serious problems!). So we take our individual preferences and combine that information with the fact that God made men and women with differing sexual-response timing. It soon becomes clear that it's impossible to "intuit" what will satisfy your partner; you must communicate with your mate. Developing sexual intimacy requires transparency—being honest about the person you really are.

Have you ever seen the book *How to Satisfy a Woman Every Time and Have Her Beg for More?* If all men were marrying that author, I'd tell them to buy her book. Since they're not, I don't necessarily recommend it. Why? It operates on the assumption that all women want the same thing, the same way. God has made all women and men unique, with varying needs, interests, and "erogenous zones." What works for one person may be a disaster for another. In the movies, when a man kisses a woman on the ear, she swoons; your wife may giggle! We're all unique in our responses to stimulation.

To help your spouse understand what you do and don't like sexually, you have to communicate. If something pleases you, learn to say so; if you find something unpleasant, let your partner know. Recognize, too, that your desires may vary from year to year, or even from day to day (or night to night). So leave room for "updates." A key element in learning to be sexually intimate is learning to be verbally intimate.[2]

Some people find it easier, initially at least, to write down their thoughts rather than verbalize them. You may be trying to figure out how to tactfully say, "Honey, this is really dull; there *must* be more to it than this." Your wife may tend to be critical when you try to be honest. Or your husband may think he knows it all and could satisfy anyone with an array of sexual techniques derived from junior high locker rooms, *Playboy* magazine, or by watching lots of movies. Writing out your preferences, and your mate's, may help.

When you have completed this workbook, you will have your own personalized version of *How to Satisfy Me*. What do you like? What satisfies your spouse? Talk about it. And recognize that through your years together much will change, so leave plenty of room for growth.

We'd like to offer some suggestions about how to use the workbook. First, *do not try to do all these exercises in one sitting.* Give yourselves time to process what you've learned. You may want to try doing one exercise per week. Also, you don't need to do them in the order given. And finally, while engaged couples can complete *some* of these exercises, we have designed this section primarily for married couples.

♡ Exercise 1—Knowing My Own Body (for Women)

Explore your body. To help your husband give you pleasure, you need to be well enough acquainted with your own body that you can guide him. What you discover when you are alone can relieve some of the uneasiness that may be present when you are together. Get to know yourself and what you enjoy so you can communicate it. Incidentally, men generally have more knowledge of their genitals than women have of their own because men's are so "handy."

We recognize that you may not consider it "okay" to touch yourself and explore your own body for the purpose of improving your intimate times together. However, it appears that medically, theologically, and socially this is helpful rather than harmful.

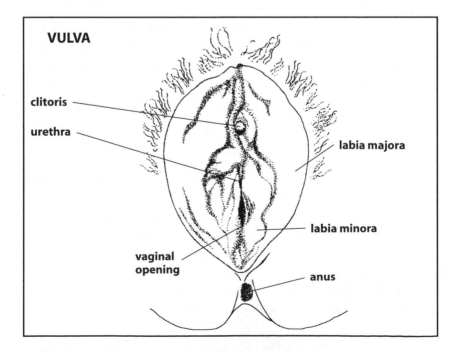

1. Hold the hand mirror and spread the outer lips (labia majora) so you can examine the rest of your external genitals.
2. Find the labia minora, or inner lips.
3. Next, look for the clitoris. If you are unsure of its location, touch where you think it might be. It is very sensitive to touch. (During lovemaking, some women prefer that their husbands touch around or near it, avoiding direct stimulation.) The purpose of this is to learn where the most pleasurable feelings occur for you. If you are more comfortable, find it while you are standing in the shower. When you are standing, it is at the "front most" point of your genitals. Remind yourself that God designed it only for receiving pleasure. Gently caress it and notice what sensations it brings. Remember that many men learn "this is what rings the bells," so your husband may rub or press too hard or too vigorously or too directly. What feels good to you?
4. Find your vagina. This is where you insert tampons if you use them. Using the moistened tip of your finger, try to find the opening. It may not be possible, as we saw in the story about the woman who had no vaginal opening. If not, make an appointment with your physician. If so, insert your finger into your vagina. Gently press on the vaginal wall. If you think of the opening of the vagina as a clock, start at the twelve o'clock position (nearest the front of the body) and slowly move around the wall of the vagina, pressing and stroking at every point of the clock. Try varying degrees of pressure and types of touch. Be especially aware of any points of pain or pleasure.
5. Now explore for sensation in the G-spot area. With your finger in your vagina, tighten the muscle you use to stop urinary flow. Keeping that muscle tight, move your finger in a little farther, just beyond the inner ridge of that muscle. Press, stroke, and tap toward the front of your body as though you are pressing the inside of your vagina toward your pubic bone, or "upward." This is the so-called G-spot area. Continue to massage using varying degrees of pressure. Note any sensations you might experience. Many women do not notice any different sensation here from that which is experienced in any other part of the vagina, and some feel pleasure here only when they

are already aroused. What you feel or don't feel is neither right nor wrong. Your goal is to become aware of these sensations in order to help both of you understand and discover.

6. Thank God for making you a sexual creature.

Now that you have a better idea of what does and does not feel pleasurable, set aside a time for doing this again with your husband present, guiding his hand to what does and does not feel good.

Do a stretching exercise. In the gynecologist's office the general standard is that a vagina should comfortably accommodate two fingers up to the second knuckle for comfortable intercourse. If this can't be done, we suggest gentle stretching while sitting in a warm tub of water. A warm massage with oil can also be used. Using your thumb or two fingers, you should apply gentle pressure posteriorly—that is, toward the tailbone—and maintain it for fifteen to thirty seconds; then relax and repeat.

You should repeat this exercise each day for about ten minutes, until you can do it comfortably using two fingers. Six to eight weeks of daily diligence will usually allow for comfortable intercourse and mastery at contracting and relaxing these muscles. If still a problem after marriage, the spouse can help by incorporating this exercise into their time of foreplay.

If a woman feels uncomfortable touching herself, she can use a plastic tampon applicator. Commercially available lubricants such as K-Y Jelly, Maxilube, Sensilube, and Replens are also useful.

♥ Exercise 2 — Exploring Pleasure for Men

After a bath or shower, focus together on his pleasure. He should guide her hand and communicate what he likes best—how hard, how soft, best locations for her touch, and types of motion preferred. Try to leave preconceived notions behind. Take for example a woman who read that the most sensitive part of a man's body is the head of the penis. As a result, she focused all of her attention there. Her husband had already told her this form of stimulation was too intense and that he didn't care for it. But she ignored him because some book told her otherwise. Later,

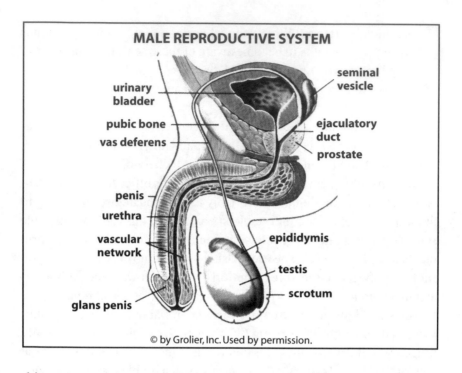

MALE REPRODUCTIVE SYSTEM

urinary bladder

seminal vesicle

pubic bone

vas deferens

ejaculatory duct

prostate

penis

urethra

vascular network

epididymis

testis

scrotum

glans penis

© by Grolier, Inc. Used by permission.

this man gently repeated his instructions, and he finally convinced his wife that even though it's the most sensitive place, the head of the penis has such sensitive nerve endings that for him, stimulation there brings a sensation not unlike pain. Most men prefer less-direct contact sometimes.

One of the women mentioned earlier told of her husband saying to her, "You're doing it wrong" when she tried to give him pleasure through oral sex. Many men have this complaint. If this is a practice in which you want to participate, gently share with her how you want her to go about giving you this kind of pleasure.

💙 Exercise 3 — Controlling Pleasure for Men

For men who tend to ejaculate before either the husband or wife is ready for this to take place, many recommend "the squeeze technique." Before sharing the "how to" on this, I want to say that I do not consider this the ideal solution for premature ejaculation.

One study suggests that men have difficulty "holding back" for more than three minutes once they have penetrated the vagina. Age certainly plays a role here, as does experience. Yet it is possible for a man to learn control that will enable him to hold back for as long as is necessary to regularly satisfy his partner. Still, for a young man having first sexual encounters with his gorgeous bride, I consider it more helpful for him to tell her, "You are so overwhelmingly exciting to me that I can't hold back, so let's make love twice. The first time, feel free to overwhelm me. The second time around I'll be there to satisfy you." Not only is this true and flattering to her, it allows him to mentally "stay with her," as opposed to distracting himself by rehearsing baseball scores to keep himself from getting too excited. (I especially want to avoid the type of "aversion therapy" one wife described: "When my husband gets 'too close,' I say, 'Green Berets.' This suggestion makes him imagine horrifying scenes of Vietnam so he can 'cool down.' ") Having sex a second time also allows her to be more expressive in her arousal without concerning herself that she will "make it too hard for him to control himself."

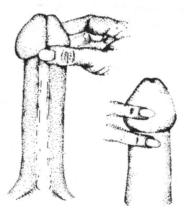

Now let's look at how the "squeeze technique" works. The woman sits straddling her husband's legs as he lies on his back. She places her thumb on the frenulum of the penis (see diagram) and her index and middle fingers just above and below the coronal ridge on the opposite side of the penis. She exerts a firm grasping pressure for four seconds, then abruptly releases her hold. She should always apply pressure front-to-back and not side-to-side. (For some reason this technique is considerably less effective when the man does it to himself.) Both partners should know this does not need to be painful; it should only bring a sense of pressure. She should repeat this technique every few minutes, making sure to use only the pads of her fingers. (If she used her fingernails, it would certainly remove his desire to ejaculate, but probably for a longer time than she had in mind.)

They should do this three to six times before attempting insertion. Couples who practice this technique for several weeks typically increase to approximately ten to fifteen minutes of vaginal containment with active thrusting. They usually need to continue this exercise for four to six months for permanent reconditioning.

💟 Exercise 4 — Helping Women Heighten Their Sense of Pleasure (PC Exercises)

Sexual stimulation within the woman's vagina relates much more to *pressure* than to *frictional* sensitivity. This makes sense because the related muscle group (the PC muscles) contains an abundant supply of pressure-sensitive nerve endings.

The wife needs to apply a firm, muscular squeezing pressure upon the penis within the vagina to give herself greater sexual stimulation. A larger object introduced into the vagina does not help increase sexual sensitivity, because sensitivity depends on contraction of the muscles, rather than expansion. Therefore, penis size has no direct effect on sensitivity for the wife. However, she can experience more satisfying stimulation when she tightens her PC muscles during thrusting of the penis. More stimulation results in reflex contraction of the vagina, which is part of the pattern that leads to orgasm for her.

Women can do these exercises easily, and some report *finally* being able to achieve orgasm after strengthening these muscles and then using them during lovemaking. (After childbirth, these exercises can more quickly help restore the tone of the vaginal muscles.)

The simplest way to find the PC muscles is to stop urine flow with the knees about two feet apart. Sit on the commode and let the urine flow, but then stop it without moving the knees. In nearly every woman, this procedure will exercise the PC muscles. Once you know which muscles you must contract, you can do this exercise while standing in line at the grocery store or sitting at your desk.

How often should you do them? Start with five to ten contractions in the morning plus the same number each time you use the bathroom. Hold each contraction for several seconds. You should work up to having enough control that you can release as little as a teaspoon of urine at a time. It gets easier.

After four days, increase the number to ten contractions, six times a day. Gradually, after four to six weeks, work up to about three hundred contractions per day. It will take a total of about ten minutes. By then you should begin noticing a difference.

After a total of about ten weeks you should have quite strong muscles, and you can stop doing the exercises. Occasionally check to see if you can still tightly squeeze one finger in the vagina. (If you can't, resume doing the exercises.)

Sexual activity itself also helps strengthen these muscles. If you will do some of these voluntary contractions during foreplay, you can heighten sexual tension. Your voluntary contractions help condition the PC muscles for the involuntary contractions of orgasm. *Not only can you experience more intense pleasure, you can shorten your response time by consciously contracting these muscles.*

Guidelines for the Communication
Exercises That Follow:

1. Listen. Try to understand your partner before explaining your own point of view.
2. Recognize that you do not need to agree.
3. Do not criticize, defend yourself, or apologize.
4. If you disagree but can understand how he or she sees it another way, say so.

5. When your spouse is finished speaking, summarize what you heard, and say, "Here is what it sounds like to me; I think you're saying . . ." (Just be careful you don't do this so much that you sound like an echo canyon or a wannabe psychiatrist.)

💙 Exercise 5 — Exploring Background Influences

Start talking about sex by answering the following questions:
* Think through your sexual attitudes from childhood through adolescence and adulthood. How did they form and change?
* From whom did you learn about sex? Was the information accurate?
* Do you tend to gravitate more toward the "Sex is a terrible, horrible sin" or the "Do it often, do it right, use a condom every night" mentality?
* What attitudes did your family communicate about sex? Was affection demonstrated openly in your home?
* Are you comfortable using the actual names for body parts or do you use euphemisms?

Read Psalm 139:1–18 together.

💙 Exercise 6 — Dealing with Past Sexual Sin

Consider Solomon's background. His father, King David, initiated an adulterous relationship with Bathsheba, Solomon's mother. The end result was the murder of Bathsheba's first husband and the death of the child produced from David and Bathsheba's first union. Then Bathsheba and David married and had Solomon. Solomon was a prime candidate for having "baggage" about sex from his family background. Yet God used him to write Song of Solomon, which presents the biblical ideal of sexual love in marriage.

Perhaps an important part of Solomon's background is the fact that his father openly acknowledged and repented of his wrong. David wrote

Psalm 51 after the prophet Nathan confronted him about committing adultery and murder. You too can break destructive family cycles that may have introduced wrong thinking or actions related to sex. The following suggestions may help:

- Mentally review your sexual history before the Lord; take inventory.
- Read Psalm 51—David's confession after committing adultery with Bathsheba. Pray through this Psalm, and confess your sin to the Lord.
- Assume your past choices will continue to have a lasting effect on you. If you have asked God to forgive you, know that you are forgiven; but realize that you may yet struggle with the consequences of those choices.
- Forgive any other person(s) involved.
- Determine if going back to ask forgiveness would cause more damage than healing. If it would help, make that contact.
- If you and your fiancé(e) have engaged in sexual sin before marriage, confess this to God individually and together if you have not done so before now. Take measures to stop. If you are married and the two of you were engaged in sexual activity before marriage, confess this individually and together if you have never done so.
- Determine how much to disclose. Before marriage, share about the past in general terms. (Avoid confiding details such as where and how you had sex, how often, frequency of orgasms, etc.) This conversation ideally should precede a commitment to marry. Your wife- or husband-to-be *does* have the right to know if you have been a practicing homosexual, if you have had previous marriages, and whether you are a virgin, for example.
- Determine what steps you can take to strengthen your moral purity.
- Recognize that guilt will probably recur and remind yourself of God's forgiveness when it does.
- If your sexual sin includes adultery, the decision of what and how much to disclose to your spouse goes beyond the scope of this book. However, we recommend these texts:

Torn Asunder: Recovering From Extramarital Affairs, by Dave
Carder with Duncan Jaenicke (Chicago: Moody Press, 1992)

His Needs, Her Needs, by Willard F. Harley, Jr. (Grand Rapids,
Michigan: Fleming Revell, 1986)

Recognize, too, that no book or conference can fully address your
specific needs. You may need qualified professional counsel.

- Determine how your background and past experiences have made
  you view sexual issues different from how God views them.
- Pray, thanking God for his grace and forgiveness. Ask Him to help
  you retrain your mind to think as He would have you think. (See
  Rom. 12:1–2.)

❤ Exercise 7 — For Wives: How Can I Improve Our Relationship?

- How do I make my marriage a priority?
- Can he trust me? Do I hold personal information in confidence?
  (E.g., I don't tell my closest friends his private thoughts if he wants
  me to keep them confidential.)
- How can I make meeting his sexual needs more of a priority?
- How can I make myself more attractive to him? Get rid of the nightly
  face cream? Change out of my pajamas or sweats before he arrives
  home from work? Do my hair on weekends?
- Are the two of us unified in how we view spending habits? Domes-
  tic responsibilities?
- How can I develop my potential for God's glory, fully using my
  gifts and talents so that he is married to a godly, interesting woman?
  (According to one survey, the greatest cause of stress is undeveloped potential; certainly, a significant cause of depression in women
  is undeveloped potential.)
- Do I speak well of him or do I refer to him in public as Boss Hogg?
- Do I withhold trust from him even in areas where he has proved

himself trustworthy? (Talking with other women, spending habits, etc.)

- Am I warm and supportive of him? Do I affirm his strengths and gifts?
- How can I be more fun to be with?
- Does my attitude of submission toward my husband reflect the relationship of the church to Christ?
- Do I demonstrate a gentle, quiet spirit?
- If someone were to ask my husband, would he be able to say honestly, "Being with this woman strengthens my relationship with the Lord"? Could he say, "I have seen the heart of Christ in her"?

List three of your husband's most admirable traits:

♥ Exercise 8 — For Husbands: How Can I Improve Our Relationship?

Take a minute to write down three of your wife's favorite things.

List three admirable traits.

Next, write three times when you felt strong feelings of love for her.

Now answer the following questions.

- Am I doing a great job of "bringing home the bacon" but sitting on the sofa like Porky Pig when I get home? When the kids get in the way, do I throw something or yell, "Honey, move the kids; they're blocking my view of ESPN!"?
- How can my actions demonstrate that I love my wife?
- Do I withhold trust from my wife even in areas where she has proved herself trustworthy? (Talking with other men, spending habits, etc.)
- How do I make my marriage a priority?
- Can she trust me?
- Do I love her sexually in a sensitive, understanding way?
- Am I doing all I can to make myself attractive to her?
- Are the two of us unified in how we view spending habits? Domestic responsibilities?
- Am I developing my potential for God's glory, fully using my gifts and talents?
- Do I help make it possible for her (by my financial and time commitments) to develop her potential and use her gifts and talents? Do I relegate her to household domestic duties?
- Do I speak well of her?
- Am I warm and supportive of her? Do I affirm her strengths and gifts?
- Am I fun to be with?
- How can I do a better job of conversing with her?
- Does my sacrificial love for my wife demonstrate the love of Christ for His church?
- Could someone point to how I treat her and say, "That's how Christ treats the church"?
- Is my love for my wife helping her grow in grace? In holiness? Do I pray for her? Do I tell her so?

- If someone were to ask my wife, would she say, "Being with this man has strengthened my relationship with the Lord"? Could she say, "I have seen the love of Christ in him; I've seen the dedication and his servant heart"?

♥ Exercise 9 — Questions for Couples About Leaving and Cleaving

What are some ways we have observed other couples do a good/bad job of leaving their parents?

In what ways have we left our own parents?

Are there any ways in which we have *not* left our parents? (List them.)

Are there ways in which we are not cleaving to each other?

What pressures do we feel that hinder us from leaving? From cleaving?

♥ Exercise 10 — Strengthening Your Communication

Answer these questions together:

* Most of what I know about relationships, I learned from . . .
* When it comes to interacting with people, I am pretty good at . . .
* I feel closest to you when . . .

On a scale of one to ten, rate yourself, then your partner, in these areas:

Listening. I pay attention when you speak, staying graciously attentive. I "stay with you" rather than "tune out." I refrain from interrupting or thinking of a quick answer while you're speaking.

Respect. I look up to you. I see you as a unique human being with legitimate viewpoints. I defend your right to be in charge of your own life. You can count on me to be on your team. I consider and often accept your suggestions. Your words have weight with me. I speak to you in a courteous tone.

Acceptance. I accept the way you are. I do not try to change your personality. I allow you to disagree without trying to force you to see things my way, getting defensive, or arguing. I give you freedom in friendships with others.

Being self-revealing. I am vulnerable with you about my feelings and fears, desires, dreams, and fantasies. I confide in you about my weaknesses as well as my strengths. I tell you when I feel embarrassed about something you have said or done. I let you in on what is going on with me.

Complete the following thoughts and discuss your responses.

When it comes to conversational intimacy, I see _myself_ . . .
  a. as being closed as a mall on Christmas Day. (I keep things well hidden.)
  b. open twenty-four hours a day. (I hold nothing back.)
  c. closed but beginning to open up more.
  d. sometimes open, sometimes closed.

e. open, but regretting it and finding the risk too great.

f. other:

When it comes to conversational intimacy, I see *you* . . .

a. as being closed as a mall on Christmas. (You keep everything well hidden.)

b. open twenty-four hours a day. (You hold nothing back.)

c. closed but beginning to open up more.

d. sometimes open, sometimes closed.

e. open, but regretting it and finding the risk too great.

f. other:

Some ways I avoid intimacy when we are getting uncomfortably close, are . . .

a. to laugh or crack a joke.

b. to shrug it off as though I don't care.

c. to get huffy or angry.

d. to analyze everything under a microscope, hiding behind a wall of intellectualizing.

Some ways it seems like you avoid intimacy when we are getting uncomfortably close, are . . .

a. to laugh or crack a joke.

b. to shrug it off as though you don't care.

c. to get huffy or angry.

d. to analyze everything under a microscope, hiding behind a wall of intellectualizing.

♡ Exercise 11 — Communicating About Anger

Thomas Jefferson said, "When very angry, count to 100." Mark Twain said, "When very angry, cuss." Most of us tend to gravitate toward extremes. We either hold it all in or we blow up. Which is more characteristic of you? Your spouse?

Circle each statement that tends to coincide with your attitude about anger.

- It's a sin.
- Only weak people get angry.
- It's a negative emotion.
- It destroys relationships.
- It indicates something is seriously wrong in the relationship.
- It clouds our ability to think straight.
- It's helpful for identifying problems and trying to solve them.
- It motivates us to good actions.
- It's inevitable in any relationship.
- It's not compatible with love and caring.
- It's immature. If the other is angry, it's a character flaw.
- Other:

Anger often interrupts intimacy. How do you deal with this emotion? How does your spouse deal with it? By . . .

a. external politeness but inner rage.
b. yelling at the dog, the kids, and other safer targets.
c. pretending it's not there. ("I'm not angry!")
d. bottling it up—Old Faithful ready to erupt.
e. filing it for future ammunition.
f. withdrawing to your cave.
g. stonewalling.
h. playing sports or doing aerobics to work it off.
i. translating it into other feelings (hurt, disappointment).
j. crying.
k. praying.
l. striking something.
m. striking someone.
n. screaming and yelling insults.
o. yelling and arguing for hours at a time.
p. other:

Rage destroys relationships, and Proverbs is full of references that speak against it. Yet, although it's more socially acceptable, holding in anger is also very destructive because your spouse has to try to guess what's upsetting you. In addition, anger turned inward leads to depression.

The Bible includes nearly 400 specific references to anger and most of them refer to the anger of God. Thus, we can conclude that anger by itself is not an evil emotion. It's what we do with it that can be sinful.

Anger includes a spectrum of emotions, ranging from frustration to rage. It can actually be positive if it moves us to right action. Picture Jesus driving the moneychangers out of the temple. These men were making a house of prayer into an unethical marketing venture. If you get upset about the plight of the poor, your anger may make you do something about it. If a child being abused makes you feel outraged, your feelings are righteous.

Everyone experiences anger. So the goal is not to keep from disagreeing, but to learn to "fight fair." Discuss these as possible guidelines for your times of disagreement before they arise:

- No lying. If your spouse asks, "What's wrong?" you shut down communication by answering, "Nothing," if something is bothering you.
- No slamming doors.
- No yelling or profanity.
- If you are extremely upset, you may leave the room, but you must say, "I need time to cool down, so I'm going to leave now. But I'll be back soon so we can discuss this."
- Don't let the sun go down on your anger. Agree that you'll never go to sleep with it still churning. This does not necessarily mean the entire problem with solutions must be hashed out between midnight and 4:00 A.M.; it means you've worked through it to the point where the anger has subsided and you have agreed that when you have more time, you *will* work it out.
- Ask for forgiveness. Even if you are only 2 percent wrong, say you're sorry for that part which is your responsibility. It will start the process of reconciliation.

Say, "I'm sorry *that I* . . . ," not "I'm sorry, but . . ." or "I'm sorry, if . . ." or "I'm sorry you . . ." Ask without strings, "Will you forgive me?"

- If someone asks for your forgiveness, never bring it up again unless he or she asks you to cite examples to help identify a specific pattern in his or her behavior.
- After you "make up," recognize that your emotions may need time to catch up with your mind. You may need some transition time before you feel you can snuggle or have sex. More women report having difficulty with this than do men.

Exercise 12 — Dealing with Resentment

Complete the following together.

Sometimes it's hard to let go of old hurts because it entitles me to . . .

a. feel angry.

b. create a situation in which *you* can "see how it feels."

c. withhold sex.

d. justify an occasional binge.

e. get my "Martyr Card" punched. I get sympathy from others.

f. experience depression that I can blame on you.

g. flirt or have an affair, if I ever want one.

h. other:

Sometimes it feels like you hold on to resentment because it entitles you to . . .

a. feel angry.

b. create a situation in which *I* can "see how it feels."

c. withhold sex.

d. justify an occasional binge.

e. get your "Martyr Card" punched. You get sympathy from others.

f. experience depression that you can blame on me.

g. flirt or have an affair, if you ever want one.

h. other:

Now take turns answering the following to determine the extent to which the two of you agree or disagree.

- One of the nicest things you ever did for me was . . .
- Something you did that hurt me and I've never forgiven is . . .
- Something you did that hurt me and I've forgiven but I keep getting reminded about is . . .
- Something you said that meant a lot to me was . . .
- Something you've done recently that hurt me was . . .
- Something you've done recently that I really liked was . . .
- Sometimes it seems you have never forgiven me for . . .

Do you need to ask for, give, and receive forgiveness for specific offenses? Remember that "forgive and forget" does not mean the memory no longer registers it. It means you make a conscious decision not to dwell on it or bring it up.

Now determine ways in which letting go of resentment might benefit you.

Releasing my resentment might benefit me by . . .

a. making me feel freer to relate to you as friend and lover.
b. allowing me to feel more open to improving our relationship.
c. providing a sense of release from the negative emotions that have a grip on me.
d. freeing my emotions, which are currently destroying me.
e. letting me discover that enjoying a relationship with you is better than resenting you.
f. other:

Commit together to break away from destructive patterns:

"This day we leave our resentments behind and make a new start."

Date: _____
Signatures: _____

_____

Now join hands and pray together:

"Dear Lord, thank you for your grace and forgiveness. Help us to extend that same grace and forgiveness to each other. We now release our past resentments, asking you to give us a new start and help us leave behind those hurts that could destroy our future together. Help us to learn to relate as friends and lovers. In Jesus' name, Amen."

In the future, other past unresolved conflicts may arise. While it's important to let go of the past, it's also helpful to sit down and go through the process of giving and receiving forgiveness for the specific offenses as they come to mind. You could start a conversation with something like, "Honey, I know we put the past behind us, yet it's hard to keep from continuing to feel hurt because I keep feeling upset that we never resolved [the specific issue of concern]. Neither of us said we were sorry; we just left it up in the air. Can we deal with that now?"

❤ Exercise 13 — Improving the Process of Sex

The Song of Solomon (SOS) is God's answer to our "SOS" about sexual difficulties. In this book of the Bible we see a couple expressing their love verbally and explicitly. In studies taken on failed marriages, sexual incompatibility was the third most common marital problem. This goes hand in hand with poor communication: If a husband and wife can't talk to each other, the intimacy in their marriage is stunted as well.[3]

Now that you've been working on your relational skills, begin moving toward a discussion of more intimate aspects of your lives. Each couple has their own love language. Consider the words Solomon says to his bride in 4:1–4:

> "How beautiful you are, my darling,
> How beautiful you are!
> Your eyes are like doves behind your veil;
> Your hair is like a flock of goats

That have descended from Mount Gilead.
"Your teeth are like a flock of newly shorn ewes
Which have come up from their washing,
All of which bear twins,
And not one among them has lost her young.
"Your lips are like scarlet thread,
And your mouth is lovely.
Your temples are like a slice of a pomegranate
Behind your veil.
"Your neck is like the tower of David
Built with rows of stones,
On which are hung a thousand shields,
All the round shields of the mighty men."

Solomon wrote this poetry about 3,000 years ago. Had he spoken these words to a gentile North American girl today, she might have run from the room crying. He uses some terms that we do not generally consider positive (hair like a flock of goats?), but knowing he intended his lovely bride to interpret his metaphors as supremely complimentary, we get the gist of what he was saying to her.

A friend drew the following picture to show what Solomon's bride would look like if we took literally everything he said about her.

The Bible is filled with Hebrew poetry, yet Solomon's small, beautiful wisdom book provides a graphic, poetic, descriptive demonstration of what it sounds like to be totally romantically, erotically head-over-heels in love with your spouse.

Read Song of Solomon to each other, trying to imagine how the writer intends his imagery to compliment his beloved. (Study Bibles and commentaries such as Jody Dillow's *Solomon on Sex* can aid here if you want further help in deciphering the language.)

♥ Exercise 14 — Write Love Letters

Solomon and his bride verbalized their feelings about each other's body. Do as they did, using your own terms. Write a love letter to your spouse, each of you describing your sweetheart's body. If you are at a total loss about how to begin, simply follow Solomon's outline:

Him for her:
How _____ you are my darling,
How _____ you are!
Your eyes are like _____.
Your hair is like _____.
Your teeth are like _____.
Your lips are like _____.
Your temples are like _____.
Your neck is like _____.
Your _____ [add your own favorite part(s)] is like _____.
And you are wholly desirable.
This is my beloved and this is my friend.

Her for him:
Your head is like _____.
Your eyes are like _____.
Your lips are like _____.
Your hands are like _____.
Your abdomen is like _____.
Your legs are like _____.

Your appearance is like _____.
Your mouth is like _____.
Your _____ [add your own favorite part(s)] is like _____.
And you are wholly desirable.
This is my beloved and this is my friend.

Now read them to each other.

♥ Exercise 15 — Sharing How You Feel About Your Own Body

Now that you've articulated what you feel about your spouse's body, talk openly with your spouse about your own body. Dim the lights or wear sunglasses if this is too difficult for you to do in broad daylight.

- Going from the top of your head to the bottom of your toes, talk about how you feel about each part. How do you wish it were different? What do you like about it?

Time and circumstances change our physical appearance (accidents, surgery, and gravitational pull all contribute to this). As Gypsy Rose Lee said, "I still have everything I had ten years ago—it's just a few inches lower." Wisdom suggests that kindness and grace are always appropriate and that the beloved can always find something to appreciate.

While your husband or wife is talking, listen without interrupting. Then summarize what you hear being said. Clarify or expand on what your spouse has heard.

In Song of Solomon 8:5, long after the lovers are married we read that the women of the city ask this:

> "Who is this coming up from the wilderness,
> Leaning on her beloved?"

The king and his wife are returning from a weekend away. Now she is so beautiful as to be hardly recognizable to them. Earlier they criticized her appearance. Now they ask, "Wow! Who's that?"

Think of the old movie *Rocky,* starring Sylvester Stallone. If you've seen it, you'll remember his girlfriend Adrian. She started out looking homely. But by the end of the movie, as she responded to his love, she had become beautiful.

- If people who knew you years ago saw you now, what would they say?
- Interact with this statement: "Now that I've got him (or her), I can 'let myself go.' "
- True or false: I make my physical appearance, my attractiveness to my spouse, a priority.
- True or false: People judge the ability and success of a man in terms of his wife's appearance.
- True or false: People judge the ability and success of a woman in terms of her husband's appearance.
- On a scale of one to ten, how important is it to you that your spouse find you attractive?
- List things you can do to make yourself more appealing to your spouse, both in private and in public.
- Read this quote from marriage counselor/sex therapist Marty Klein, and state whether you agree or disagree in terms of your own experience:

Although you might wish it weren't so, if you're like millions of women, your body isn't supermodel slim and probably never will be. In a perfect world, this is no big deal. Yet in my experience . . . I've discovered that an extra ten, twenty, or thirty pounds can have a troublesome effect on a woman's sex life. Interestingly, it's generally not the woman's partner who finds the weight gain a turnoff—it's the woman herself who allows her erotic pleasure to be held hostage by the number on the scale or a pair of too-tight jeans. This isn't to say that some husbands aren't put off by weight gain, particularly if it's substantial—say thirty pounds or more. But fortunately, very few men cite a gain or loss of ten to twenty pounds as the key to their partner's attractiveness. Instead, most men talk far more about how their wives feel about their weight.[4]

Now interact with this statement:

> Many women say "gross" when they see men wearing Speedo bathing suits. Still, women do have *some* visual orientation. And her man's hygiene and weight still factor in to her ability to fully enjoy his body.

End by expressing love and admiration for your spouse's body.

💝 Exercise 16 — Sharing How You Feel About Your Lovemaking

Work toward getting more and more comfortable talking about details of your love lives. The following topics are listed for you to discuss outside of the context of lovemaking. If you think of others, add them!

- The time of day we are usually together sexually is _____.
- Is that time optimal for both of us?
- The place where lovemaking usually takes place is _____.
- Place(s) where we would like it to happen are _____.
- We usually have _____ amount of light in the room when we make love. Could this be improved in any way?
- Some variety in lighting we would like to try is _____.
- Do hygiene issues ever inhibit our desire? (Four hours at the gym with the guys may have elevated his testosterone level, but like three-day-old fish, he stinketh!)
- Does one of us usually initiate more than the other? Is this the way we both want it?
- What are our unspoken signals that say, "I'm interested"?
- Are there other ways either of us would like to communicate interest or have interest communicated?
- What do we usually wear? (One wife in the Pacific Northwest shared, "There's a movement afoot in some local Christian subcultures. Some now suggest that women should not dress sexy for their husbands because this is the 'world's' way of viewing sex.

Flannel is the fabric of choice." We believe there is nothing spiritual about being dowdy.)

- How long does it usually take her to climax, from beginning to end? (This is where the husbands at workshops sometimes jokingly yell, "Hours!")
- How long does it usually take him to climax, from beginning to end? (This is where wives at workshops sometimes yell, "Seconds!")
- How do we want to be pursued? Hint and then back off? Hint and then try again in a different way? Hint and go for it? Other?
- How do we want to be directed? Discussion outside of sex? Gentle redirecting of hands? Verbally?
- How do we generally redirect? How does each of us feel about that?
- What kinds of caresses do each of us prefer? On what parts of the body? *With* what parts of the body?
- What positions increase excitement for each of us? What sustains desire? What decreases interest?
- Do we have any uncommunicated fantasies? Strip Monopoly? Showering together? Polaroids?
- What degree of dress or undress does each of us like?
- What are our preferred kinds and colors of apparel? (Some men actually don't like black nightgowns, but their wives have been buying them for years, operating with the mistaken notion that all hubbies find black exciting.)
- Are we each courageous enough to walk into a lingerie department and buy something we would enjoy seeing him or her wear?
- How can we draw the five senses into our lovemaking?
- Interact with this statement: "We're totally comfortable being naked together, but the surprise and delight of seeing each other nude no longer brings the erotic rush it did when we were first married." Is this true for you? What are the pros and cons of love "settling down and becoming more secure"?
- What sets the mood for him? For her?
- How much do you want left to the imagination?
- What elements enhance the whole experience for you?
- List an assortment of ideal atmospheres you'd like to try.

💙 Exercise 17 — Sexual Preferences

At a marriage conference, we handed out the following survey. Each partner was asked to state his or her preferences (there's one for each—first wives, then husbands). The husbands and wives then came together to discuss them. Please use this opportunity to do the same—respond to the survey separately, then talk together about your responses. We've included some "off the wall" possibilities to help relax the mood. Remember to keep a sense of humor!

Sex Practices—Her Preferences: Gross or Great?

Scale					
No way Gross I'd rather die		Okay, if you like but it does not sound "special"			Oh, yeah Gotta have it Gonna be great!
1	2	3	4	5	6

"Missionary position" only—limited to one position for life

   1   2   3   4   5   6

No one set position—more changes than a man with a TV remote

   1   2   3   4   5   6

Oral/genital foreplay—to do

   1   2   3   4   5   6

Oral/genital foreplay—to be "done unto"

   1   2   3   4   5   6

Oral/genital orgasm—to do

   1   2   3   4   5   6

Oral/genital orgasm—to be "done unto"

   1   2   3   4   5   6

Anal intercourse

    1   2   3   4   5   6

Man on top

    1   2   3   4   5   6

Woman on top

    1   2   3   4   5   6

Whipped cream on top

    1   2   3   4   5   6

Side to side

    1   2   3   4   5   6

Front to back

    1   2   3   4   5   6

Watching partner undress

    1   2   3   4   5   6

Being watched as I undress

    1   2   3   4   5   6

Cuddling only

    1   2   3   4   5   6

Mood lighting

    1   2   3   4   5   6

Black lights (with body paint)

    1   2   3   4   5   6

Only during solar eclipses

    1   2   3   4   5   6

See-through lingerie

1	2	3	4	5	6

Industrial-grade opaque flannel lingerie ("But it's *comfortable*")

1	2	3	4	5	6

Foreplay

1	2	3	4	5	6

Floor play

1	2	3	4	5	6

Assisted by sexual devices (vibrator)

1	2	3	4	5	6

Costumes—Brave Heart, Warrior Princess

1	2	3	4	5	6

Early morning (mouthwash on the nightstand)

1	2	3	4	5	6

Late night (No Doz on the nightstand)

1	2	3	4	5	6

Nooners (Who works?)

1	2	3	4	5	6

Before 10:00 P.M. (Some partners do want to go to sleep early!)

1	2	3	4	5	6

Anytime, anyplace

1	2	3	4	5	6

Desired frequency (*circle one*):

Tri-weekly   Try weekly   Try weakly   Other:

Actual Frequency (*circle one*):

Tri-weekly   Try weekly   Try weakly   Other:

Usual order in which I would like these "done unto me" (rank in order of preference):

___ Mouth to mouth kissing

___ Fondling breasts

___ Fondling vagina

___ Oral foreplay/sex

___ Intercourse

___ Orgasm

___ Other:

Interact with this statement: A woman's greater responsiveness does not appear to be connected to any special lovemaking technique. Instead, responsiveness and satisfaction are significantly affected by the relational context in which lovemaking takes place.

Sex Practices—His Preferences: Gross or Great?

Scale					
No way Gross I'd rather die		Okay, if you like but it does not sound "special"			Oh, yeah Gotta have it Gonna be great!
1	2	3	4	5	6

"Missionary position" only—limited to one position for life

 1 2 3 4 5 6

No one set position—more changes than a man with a TV remote

 1 2 3 4 5 6

Oral/genital foreplay—to do

    1   2   3   4   5   6

Oral/genital foreplay—to be "done unto"

    1   2   3   4   5   6

Oral/genital orgasm—to do

    1   2   3   4   5   6

Oral/genital orgasm—to be "done unto"

    1   2   3   4   5   6

Anal intercourse

    1   2   3   4   5   6

Man on top

    1   2   3   4   5   6

Woman on top

    1   2   3   4   5   6

Whipped cream on top

    1   2   3   4   5   6

Side to side

    1   2   3   4   5   6

Front to back

    1   2   3   4   5   6

Watching partner undress

    1   2   3   4   5   6

Being watched as I undress

    1   2   3   4   5   6

Cuddling only

| 1 | 2 | 3 | 4 | 5 | 6 |

Mood lighting

| 1 | 2 | 3 | 4 | 5 | 6 |

Black lights (with body paint)

| 1 | 2 | 3 | 4 | 5 | 6 |

Only during solar eclipses

| 1 | 2 | 3 | 4 | 5 | 6 |

See-through lingerie

| 1 | 2 | 3 | 4 | 5 | 6 |

Industrial-grade opaque flannel lingerie ("But it's *comfortable*")

| 1 | 2 | 3 | 4 | 5 | 6 |

Foreplay

| 1 | 2 | 3 | 4 | 5 | 6 |

Floor play

| 1 | 2 | 3 | 4 | 5 | 6 |

Assisted by sexual devices (vibrator)

| 1 | 2 | 3 | 4 | 5 | 6 |

Costumes—Brave Heart, Warrior Princess

| 1 | 2 | 3 | 4 | 5 | 6 |

Early morning (mouthwash on the nightstand)

| 1 | 2 | 3 | 4 | 5 | 6 |

Late night (No Doz on the nightstand)

| 1 | 2 | 3 | 4 | 5 | 6 |

Nooners (Who works?)

    1   2   3   4   5   6

Before 10:00 P.M. (Some partners do want to go to sleep early!)

    1   2   3   4   5   6

Anytime, anyplace

    1   2   3   4   5   6

Desired frequency (circle one):

Tri-weekly   Try weekly   Try weakly   Other:

Actual Frequency (circle one):

Tri-weekly   Try weekly   Try weakly   Other:

Usual order in which I would like these "done unto me" (rank in order of preference):

___ Mouth to mouth kissing
___ Fondling penis
___ Oral foreplay/sex
___ Intercourse
___ Orgasm
___ Other:

Interact with this statement: A woman's greater responsiveness does not appear to be connected to any special lovemaking technique. Instead, responsiveness and satisfaction are significantly affected by the relational context in which lovemaking takes place.

♥ Exercise 18 — Understanding Your Attitudes About Sex

Individually answer the following questions. You may wish to discuss some or all of your responses with your partner later.

If you are having a sexual problem, would you prefer that it have a physical, emotional, or interactional cause? Why?

What are the prerequisites for your becoming sexually aroused? What factors are physical? Do they seem to have changed in the last few years? If so, how? Why?

Do you feel comfortable keeping your eyes open during lovemaking? Why or why not?

Do you think of men and women as more alike or more different? Why?

What do you see as the greatest barriers to attaining satisfying intimate relationships?

Have you learned any lessons about yourself and the opposite sex the hard way?

If you had to lose one of your senses *for sex only,* what would it be and why?

Should contraceptive responsibilities be assigned or shared between men and women?

Do you remember trying to get answers about your body, sex, or similar topics as a young child? How did the person you asked respond? How did you feel?

Are you embarrassed by any lack of information you have?

How do you view sex and sexuality during this season of your life? In what ways is it different from five or ten years ago? Are there things you feel you have missed? If so, what?

Close your eyes and imagine a couple having a pleasurable sexual interlude. When you are finished, open your eyes. How old were they? How does this reflect on your perception of sex?

What did you learn from your mother about gender roles? Your father? Do you hold their views today? Have their views changed any? How do your views differ from theirs?

💜 Exercise 19 — Preventing Moral Failure

Your sexuality is a precious gift to be protected. You can prevent many future sexual difficulties by following God's guidelines for sexual purity. Read 2 Samuel 11–13, then answer the following questions.

- Is there a member of the opposite sex in your life about whom your spouse has expressed discomfort? Is his or her "radar" accurate?

- Spend a few moments dealing with any unconfessed sin in your thoughts. What time can you set aside for regular confession?

- If you were to develop deep affection for the wrong person, in whom will you confide?

- List some of the consequences of committing sexual sin:

- How might such sin affect your relationship with God?

Consider these words from the wife of a former member of the Clinton Administration about her husband's philandering:

I am trying very hard to understand. That doesn't mean I don't feel any pain or anger. I'm not happy about what he did, and sometimes I think about dismembering him, and good friends have offered to help me dig up the back yard and bury him. I'm not saying I'm standing by this man no matter what. I'm taking it day by day. I know one thing: I'm not going to leave someone who's been my best friend for twenty years. I was numb. I still am. I think any decision I make is highly personal, and there's no one formula that's right. This is a really horrible trauma for

everyone who has been touched by it, and answers don't come—
at least for me—immediately.[5]

- List ways unfaithfulness could affect your marriage and extended family.

- How could unfaithfulness affect your relationships at church?

- How could unfaithfulness affect your relationships at work?

- List those whom you would be ashamed to face if you were ever unfaithful.

- List how unfaithfulness would affect your thoughts about yourself and your future love life.

- List those who might be delighted over your moral failure.

- List how the other person involved might be affected by an affair.

- List medical risks.

- How can you strengthen the "glue" binding your marriage?

- What action can you take to keep or bring your thoughts in line with God's?

- Pray that God will cleanse your thoughts, bring your affections in line with His desires, and keep you from stumbling.

Though we included the following questions in chapter 15, they are important enough to add here for review: *Are you being tempted?*

- Do you make special trips past her desk or his house?
- Do you manipulate situations so you can be alone in secluded, private settings?
- Have you started taking special care of your dress and overall appearance? Are you wearing an alluring scent?
- When you are around him or her, do you feel like you're sixteen again?
- Do you find yourself thinking of this person frequently outside of the usual context of your contact?
- Do you purposely withhold some conversations, letters, or events from your spouse?
- Do you dread accountability times? Do you not even *have* a person to whom you are accountable for your thoughts and actions?
- Do you find yourself thinking of this person instead of your spouse when you watch romantic movies?
- Do you think of this person during romantic activities with your spouse?
- Do you talk about him or her more than about your spouse?
- Is the love you feel for this person infatuation that wants to possess, or is it true love? Real love wants the other to be all he or she can be in Christ—a love that would never lead the loved one down a treacherous path away from God. Are you acting with his or her best interest at heart?

Let an application of the Golden Rule help determine the state of your relationship. Ask yourself: *Would I want someone else to treat me as I am treating his or her spouse, even if only in my heart?*

Like a beautifully wrapped package under a Christmas tree, the gift of sexuality, that mysterious, exclusive gift you reserve for each other, becomes, remains, or can become again a celebratory expression of the love you share together. We read this in Song of Solomon 8:14:

> "Hurry, my beloved,
> And be like a gazelle or a young stag
> On the mountains of spices."

♥ Exercise 20—Warning Signs in Communication

A number of researchers studying marriage have identified several key negative responses in communication that are predictors of marital failure. If you recognize these in yourself and/or your spouse, seek help immediately.

Clam Up

Do either you or your spouse frequently "shut down" conversation with a perfunctory, "Yes, honey" or by getting up to make a sandwich rather than giving an answer. (Men tend to do this more than women without realizing that this approach damages intimacy.)

Blow Up

In the heat of conflict, do you try to outdo each other with caustic remarks? Do you have escalating conflicts? They start something like this: "Honey, you didn't take out the trash." Then they progress to, "Honey, you never take out the trash," to "Honey, you're too stupid to take out the trash," to " . . . and so is your mother!"

Shoot Down

Do you feel as though your spouse often negatively interprets an innocent remark? For example, he says, "I see you got your hair cut." She assumes, "He hates my hair cut. Otherwise he would have said he liked it." If she makes his favorite dinner, does he automatically assume she must be feeling guilty because she spent too much at the mall?

Put Down

Does your spouse sometimes make you feel that your opinions, preferences, and even you as a person are of no value and unworthy of respect? (This might present itself in vicious looks or caustic remarks.) If one says something as simple as "It's cold in here," does the other respond with, "It's not cold. You'd be cold in an oven"?

♡ Exercise 21—For Further Discussion

What is your strategy to maintain personal sexual purity?

How do you deal with loneliness?

What are your usual means of avoiding emotional pain?

Do you resent it when your spouse questions your wrong behavior?

In the last 20 years more and more sexually explicit material has appeared on TV. One survey reported that seven of eight intimate relationships on prime time TV were between non-married individuals. What impact will this have on the coming generation? What impact does it have on you?

To whom are you personally accountable?

Many movies, magazines, and TV shows portray homosexual relationships as an "alternate lifestyle." What is your response?

What risk factors for sexual addiction do you have?

Does your church have a ministry to sex addicts? Who will help the spouses of the addicts?

How might understanding the "fear of the Lord" (Prov. 2:5) and knowing you've been "bought with a price" (1 Cor. 6:20) affect your thought life?

Appendix B

CONTRACEPTION?
OH, BABY . . . MAYBE

A *garden locked is my sister, my bride,*
A *rock garden locked, a spring sealed up.*
—Song of Solomon 4:12

One way to prepare for a fulfilling love life with the one you'll marry is to decide what you believe and want to do about contraception, if anything. This subject is surrounded by controversy and strong opinion. Contraception ideally involves using a drug, device, or method to prevent sperm from fertilizing a woman's egg. (We reject methods of birth control that allow fertilization but prevent implantation.) Couples should seek God's wisdom about such issues as the spacing of children and the number of children you wish to have. Contraceptives can be to lovemaking what Nutrasweet and "salt-free" are to food. These substitutes may not taste as good in cheesecake or potato chips as the real thing, yet the health and lifestyle advantages of using them for some may outweigh the benefits of caution-free living. And at least people using them are eating.

When a pastor friend in Virginia sits down with couples during one of their premarital counseling sessions, he asks them to sit with their backs touching each other. Then he tells them, "Without looking at how your partner is answering, hold up the number of fingers for how many children you want to have." It's always interesting to find out whether couples have discussed this, if they agree, and how they plan to reach their goal without "going over." Couples frequently run into conflict in this important area, so it's best to resolve differences as early as possible. A mutual friend of ours remains single today because the young man with whom she was in love told her when he proposed that he did not want children.

In Christian circles, two primary schools of thought exist. The first holds that because Psalm 127 says "children are a gift of the Lord" (v. 3), avoiding this "gift" hinders God's blessing. Thus they consider it inappropriate to use any premeditated method to avoid conception. Many of these patients do, in fact, maintain a rigorous schedule of cycle monitoring to "abstain electively" during the fertile period. This strikes us as being a contraceptive method (in fact, it is called the "rhythm" or "sympto-thermal" method of contraception). It requires charting a woman's temperature to determine the time of ovulation; it also includes observing bodily indicators, such as changes in vaginal discharge and the cervical opening. Generally, the "safe zone" is considered the time from one week before menses through five days after menses. This method is not absolutely effective in preventing pregnancy, and it may even violate the spirit of these people's convictions. It may also violate the guidelines for biblical abstention given in 1 Corinthians 7, where Paul writes that the only time to refrain from sexual relations within marriage should be . . .

1. by agreement
2. for a short time, and
3. for the purpose of devotion to prayer.

(All three stipulations need to be met—it is not "multiple choice.") The Old Testament includes additional times of abstinence: seven days during menses, seven days after menses, the evening before worship, and forty to eighty days after the birth of a child. However, reverting to these dietary and ceremonial laws violates the New Covenant (see Acts 10:1–16; 1 Cor. 8:8; and 1 Tim. 4:3–4). Peter says that taking people who are under the New Covenant and subjecting them to Old Covenant rules adds encumbrances that weigh them down. Some have followed Levitical requirements to abstain during menses and seven days following. Shall we observe all ceremonial and dietary laws of the Old Covenant?

A few stalwart theologians (but certainly not all) who hold this view believe that engaging in sex primarily for pleasure, as opposed to reproduction, is "unnatural." They base their argument on Romans 1:26, which says, ". . . their women exchanged the natural function for that which is unnatural." Please note, however, that the next verse clarifies that Paul is talking about homosexuality here, not reproductive function: ". . . Also the men abandoned the natural function of the woman and burned in their desire toward one another, men with men committing indecent acts."

A look at the Song of Solomon, God's poetry book on marital sexual love, shows us that God intended sex for pleasure. Solomon filled the book with images that focus on pleasure. Yet in its eight chapters it never mentions children or reproduction even once.

The second school consists of those who consider choosing contraception and family planning appropriate as long as they respect the sanctity of human life. This entails avoiding methods that may permit conception but cause spontaneous abortion. Intrauterine devices (IUDs) probably fall in this category, as does one type of progesterone-only birth control pill.

Couples deciding they will use contraception should acquaint themselves with what is available and then prepare to discuss their options during a premarital appointment with their physician. It's asking a lot to expect a doctor to explain each method in detail—how it works, and its pros and cons. However, by studying the options and "narrowing the field" before the appointment, good understanding and a suitable method of contraception should result.

But discussing methods of contraception might be premature. Deciding if they should even *use* contraception, and if so, what type, remains one often-overlooked yet critical issue for engaged couples to talk through. A patient named Shelly made a medical appointment to talk about contraception two weeks before her wedding. Up to that point, she and her fiancé had given it little thought. Their limited education came from high school health class and medical reports on morning talk shows. Unfortunately, they had left almost no time for any of the hormone-related methods to take effect. This greatly limited their immediate options. A good rule of thumb is for couples to have their premarital medical visit three months before marriage if they plan to use oral contraceptives. This allows enough time for the medication to take effect, to correct any breakthrough bleeding, or "spotting," and to move the cycle away from the wedding date.

Generally the woman visits her family practice doctor or Ob/Gyn. We strongly suggest that the future husband attend the consultation portion of the appointment so he can hear the medical explanations and ask any questions that might help the couple arrive at a suitable solution.

Sometimes doctors prescribe Nitrofurantoin or a similar antibiotic during this visit, for the bride to take with her on the honeymoon. A woman having intercourse for the first time may experience pain and blood in the urine from a bladder infection related to sexual activity (the so-called "honeymoon cystitis"). Antibiotics can help clear up this infection. The medication can be especially useful for couples planning to honeymoon far away from medical facilities—it's probably better to have it and not need it than to need the antibiotic and not have it.

Methods

Abstinence. Some say this is the only 100 percent effective method of birth control. Actually, this is technically not true. As in the case of the couple whose story we shared in the first chapter, along with similar cases I've seen, some couples get pregnant via "outercourse," without ever having sexual intercourse. Nevertheless, this is certainly the most effective method of birth control, though it is not supported scripturally within marriage.

Marrying a partner who has a sexually transmitted disease may require periodic or complete abstinence, and it is possible for these couples to have mutually satisfying sexual experiences without sexual intercourse. Nevertheless, abstinence does not appear to be God's original design for the "one-flesh" marriage relationship.

Withdrawal. This involves having sexual intercourse but then withdrawing the penis right before ejaculation. We do not recommend this method for a number of reasons. First, the psychological one. It's sort of like sitting down to a nice dinner in a restaurant, eating your salad, cutting your steak, but then having the steak pulled away just as you're about to take a bite.

From a contraceptive standpoint, sperm is in the seminal fluid that a male releases before ejaculation. So sperm often enters the vagina even if ejaculation does not take place there. In addition, a man cannot always control the time of ejaculation. Thus, the husband may find that, though he had good intentions, it's "too late"—his timing is off a little—and ejaculation takes place prior to withdrawal.

Some claim the Bible condemns this method based on the Onan story in Genesis 38. As discussed earlier, God did not condemn Onan merely because he interrupted the act of sex, as some have suggested. (Others base their condemnation of masturbation on this passage.) Rather, the text indicates that Onan invoked God's wrath because he disobeyed the biblical command to give his brother an heir.

Douching. This involves trying to flush the seminal fluid out of the vagina immediately following intercourse, using one of a number of liquid substances. Not only does this occasionally upset the sensitive chemical balance of the vagina, it also is an ineffective means of preventing conception. Sperm begin swimming toward their destination long before a woman has a chance to stop them by using this method, and many have safely reached the "sanctuary of the cervical mucus" before any liquid could "hose" them out, drown them, or destroy them.

Chemical barriers. These include foams and jellies. They contain spermicides—chemicals that kill sperm. Chemical barriers work only fairly well by themselves; doctors usually recommend their use in conjunction with condoms or diaphragms. Chemical barriers cause minimal side effects. Some men and women have allergic reactions that cause burning or swelling, but this can often be remedied by changing brands. Foams and jellies are relatively inexpensive and can be purchased without a prescription. Some require insertion up to fifteen minutes before intercourse; others work instantly. Foams have a slightly higher success rate, but without a barrier (condom) they do not reduce the likelihood of transmitting a sexually transmitted disease; nor do they provide sufficient protection against pregnancy.

Oral contraceptives. The most commonly prescribed contraceptives are birth control pills—or "combination oral contraceptives." The word *combination* means the pill contains both estrogen and progesterone in various dosages. Therefore, it is designed to inhibit ovulation (prevent egg release) and artificially control the menstrual cycle (that is, generate a light flow). Different women require different combinations to avoid breakthrough bleeding—"spotting"—which is a common side effect that normally can be expected to disappear after several cycles. Some may also experience the complete absence of menstrual flow. Though this generally is not considered a serious complication if the woman has taken her pills regularly, there often is some concern that she may be pregnant, so she should at least contact her physician's office. The newer low dose pill works effectively, but it may cause some side effects also. Your physician will explain the possibilities, as will the package insert that accompanies each new package of pills (although this lengthy fine-print document defies careful reading by most patients).

The pills cost approximately twenty to thirty dollars per cycle, and most health insurance companies deny coverage for them. A woman must take her pills daily as prescribed to effectively prevent conception. One of my patients, a teenager, borrowed her friend's pills thinking, *If I take one just before having sex, I won't get pregnant.* She got pregnant.

It's important to note the effect that oral contraceptives may have on a woman's interest in sexual activity. Because they artificially regulate the female menstrual cycle by overriding the woman's own hormone production, these low-dose pills cause a low estrogen state and also block the ovaries' production of testosterone. Testosterone, as we said earlier, is the male hormone that stirs the libido (or sex drive). A definite percentage of otherwise normal women find that while taking birth control pills they have virtually *no* sex drive. As one pill user said, "Being on the pill certainly prevents pregnancy for us. But not so much because it's effective. It's because it has decreased my interest so much that I desire sex only about once a month." Often, switching to a pill with a slightly different combination of hormones will solve this problem.

Another side effect derived from the pill's decreasing estrogen level is a decrease in vaginal elasticity and ability to lubricate. This simply means that intercourse while taking the pills may be uncomfortable without the addition of a vaginal lubricant. Anyone can buy lubricants without a prescription, and they are a wise investment, especially for newlyweds. When women stop taking the pill, they often stop needing/ requiring lubricants.

It is important to know whether the pills are "combination" or "progesterone only." The progesterone-only pills have a higher level of break-through ovulation, which theoretically might permit conception but prevent implantation, thus allowing an abortion to occur. This phenomenon is rare with combination pills taken correctly, but may factor into a couple's decision about which type of contraception works best for them.

Some medications, such as certain antibiotics, reduce the effectiveness of birth control pills. Check with your physician whenever additional medication is required. Certain patients experience side effects such as bloating, nausea, and headaches. If these cause significant distress or concern, consult your physician or, at minimum, read the FDA insert that comes with the packaging.

The intrauterine device (IUD). The IUD is quite effective but I don't recommend it. The IUD is merely a formed piece of plastic placed within the uterus. It apparently works this way: Conception occurs in the fallopian tube, just as if one were using no contraception. Yet when the so-called pre-embryo—the tiny developing baby—reaches the uterus, it is unable to implant (attach to the wall of the uterus). Thus, it aborts without the woman ever knowing it. The abortion risk, coupled with a risk of infection within the uterus that can lead to infertility, renders this method unacceptable, in my view. Some research has suggested that the IUD may work in some other way than I have described, and that it actually prevents pregnancy rather than terminating it. However, until we have more data, I would recommend erring on the side of caution.

Norplant. The Norplant System costs several hundred dollars and it involves implanting small plastic rods, usually under the skin of the upper arm. It functions by the slow release of progesterone from these rods. When supplied to the body continuously, progesterone will block the normal cycle and eventually prevent the release of any eggs. Once the system is in place and has had time to function (approximately a week), ovulation and pregnancy are quite rare. Unfortunately, some patients have unpredictable bleeding during the five-year period of use, which can cause distress and dissatisfaction. A physician can remove the plastic implants at any time, and some women do opt for removal rather than tolerating the breakthrough bleeding. Fertility is usually restored within a cycle or two.

Progesterone injection. A different strategy involves receiving a slow-release progesterone injection. Protection is usually reliable for three months. Once injected, it cannot be removed. Afterward, the return to normal cycling and fertility is rather unpredictable (and may take up to six months). Side effects with progesterone include possible spotting, bloating, and moodiness in some women. It is effective, but not quite as effective as Norplant or the combination pill.

Barrier Contraceptives

Condom. Available over the counter, condoms (or "rubbers") prevent sperm from ever reaching the egg by placing a latex rubber "boot" (which looks like the finger of a glove) over the erect penis before it enters the vagina. The condom is currently the best barrier for preventing some sexually transmitted diseases (STDs), although the media has greatly overstated its effectiveness in this regard. Statistics vary from a three to 12 percent failure rate with typical use. Many men complain of decreased sensitivity from wearing a condom. Also, condoms can break, leaving the woman without any protection. Thus condoms are more effective when used in conjunction with chemical barriers and are really not reliable protection against STDs.

The condom is currently the only temporary contraceptive available for male use (as opposed to vasectomy, which though reversible in about 75 percent of cases, is considered "permanent"). Scientists are always trying to develop injections and medications that inhibit sperm production, but to date nothing effective enough to recommend is available.

Female condom. The female condom has never caught on in the United States. Besides being bulky and messy, it has been described as being "like having a romantic encounter with a zip lock bag." Some research suggests it is also slightly less effective than the male condom.

Diaphragm. Approximately the size of the palm of the hand, the diaphragm is a round latex "hat" that a woman places over her cervix. Diaphragms come in several sizes, so a woman planning to use one must see her doctor for fitting. The cost of this contraceptive is the cost of the medical office visit and of the diaphragm itself (which is usually twenty to thirty dollars, including its case and a tube of gel). Unfortunately, clever sperm can find their way around the edges of the diaphragm, making "chemical warfare" necessary in conjunction with this approach. (In other words, it necessitates putting some spermicidal foam or jelly made for diaphragm use inside and around the edges of the diaphragm.)

The diaphragm should remain in place for eight to ten hours after use. Once removed, wash it in soap and water, dust it with a fine coating of talc, and store it in its case. (I had one patient who did not use her case and her dog gnawed on her diaphragm.)

Diaphragms with holes should be discarded. To find holes, rips, or tears, hold the diaphragm up to a light source to see if any pinpoints of light shine through. Next, fill it with water to make sure it doesn't leak. Because some researchers suspect a possible talc/ovarian cancer link, wisdom would suggest rinsing the diaphragm before applying cream and inserting.

A woman using the diaphragm has about a 5 to 10 percent chance of conceiving in a year. A lot depends on how vigilant she is about using it regularly and correctly. Many diaphragm users simply insert it every evening, and if romance happens they are "prepared." They must reapply the diaphragm gel if more than two hours have elapsed since insertion. Likewise, more gel is recommended for each additional "romantic interlude" that evening. This does not mean the diaphragm should be removed. Leave the diaphragm in place and add more cream to the vagina.

Cervical cap. The cervical cap is more popular in Europe than in the United States. In fact, doctors here must order it from a single source in California. Like the diaphragm, a physician must fit it to the patient. Yet it is more difficult to insert, and it can irritate the cervix. The cervical cap is approximately as effective as the diaphragm, although it is slightly less likely to dislodge.

Sponge. Approximately two inches in diameter, the sponge comes filled with spermicide. When the wife inserts it before intercourse, it provides protection for up to twenty-four hours, even with multiple encounters. However, she must leave it in place for at least six hours after intercourse for effective prevention of conception. It has a 75 to 88 percent effectiveness rate per year. (It seems to be less effective for women who have been pregnant.) Insertion instructions come with the packaging. It differs from the diaphragm in several ways: It's available at the local drug store, it has "one size fits all" fitting, and it is disposable. Available internationally, it has been off the market for a while due to manufacturing problems that are being remedied; it should return to the marketplace soon, if it hasn't already.

Major drawbacks of both physical and chemical barriers include messiness, clumsiness, and elimination of "spontaneity." Most couples get around the lack of spontaneity and the awkwardness of stopping to apply cream or use a condom by having a vibrant sense of humor. Making a team effort can ease some tension while preparing for intercourse with contraception.

Sterilization

When a couple feels certain they want no children or no *more* children, they may want to consider surgical sterilization. While surgeons sometimes can reverse these procedures, individuals should refrain from sterilization unless they feel certain by decision and conviction that they desire no future childbearing, even considering the unlikely scenarios of death, divorce, or other catastrophe. A couple must prayerfully come to the place of mutual, settled conviction concerning biblical principles of childbearing, family planning, and "filling the earth."

For women. Sterilization generally involves interrupting the fallopian tubes to prevent sperm from reaching the egg. While oophorectomy (removal of the ovaries) or hysterectomy (removal of the uterus) also result in permanent sterility, most doctors steer away from recommending these more extensive procedures for contraception because of risk and side effects, not to mention a quite high expense that many insurance companies do not cover. Since the tubes are located in the abdomen, tying or blocking them requires making an incision to do a surgical procedure, allowing access to the abdominal cavity.

There are a variety of techniques available: tying the fallopian tubes, cauterizing them with electricity, and blocking them with plastic clips or rubber bands. Individual doctors and circumstances dictate the procedure of choice. These may include use of the laparoscope (so-called bandaid surgery) that the surgeon inserts through a small incision at the navel, as well as other instruments that are inserted at the pubic-hair line. Patients generally tolerate these procedures well and can undergo them on an outpatient basis. They bring moderate abdominal discomfort and occasional significant shoulder pain, which are normal responses to the carbon dioxide used to inflate the belly for visual exposure and to provide room to operate.

Often patients elect to have tubal sterilization immediately following childbirth. It is accomplished with a small incision below the umbilicus, taking advantage of the anesthesia used during childbirth. The laparoscope is not used in these cases because the increased uterine size brings the tubes near the umbilicus. These procedures have low failure rates—approximately one (or fewer) in 400. Following recovery from surgery, few side effects remain. However, occasionally during the procedure on the tube, some of the blood vessels that supply the ovaries are disrupted. This may account for menstrual disturbances in some patients.

If the patient has carefully weighed the pros and cons of permanent sterilization and decides on a tubal procedure, the freedom from fear of conception can be very liberating. Many couples have reported a dramatic rise in frequency of intercourse and satisfaction following this procedure. On the other hand, I have had several patients who regretted sterilization decisions made at a young age. Fortunately, for many, a tubal reversal using microscopic techniques can often restore fertility. However, it is costly, and it will not always work. Thus, couples should be certain before choosing sterilization options.

For men. Vasectomy, the sterilization procedure in the male, involves surgical interruption of the vas deferens. This is the tube that carries sperm from the testicle to the storage gland, the seminal vesicles. Because of the external location of the testes within the scrotal sac, patients can have this procedure done in the doctor's office under local anesthesia. It costs less than tubal sterilization in the female and usually has few side effects after the surgical incision has healed. In light of the male anatomy, patients should remember that this operation is performed in a location before the "storage gland." In other words, fertility remains after the vasectomy until these storage tanks are empty. Thus, couples should use alternate protection for several ejaculations. Safety demands a zero sperm count before a couple can rely on the vasectomy. This takes usually a month or two. After that time, the failure rate is quite low—less than 1 percent. Medical investigation linking vasectomy with prostate cancer will require clarification in the years to come. At this writing no research has established a *clear* hazard. However, patients should consult with the urologist or family practice doctor who performs the procedure to explore the current status of this research.

Finally, after trying to prevent conception for years, one in six couples find themselves faced with a fertility problem once they start trying to build their family. Others find that once they have a child or two and want more, they have difficulty conceiving. Couples considering the use of contraceptive methods must realize that increasing age can play a contributing role in this problem as well. "I never dreamed during all those 'how to prevent pregnancy' lectures in health class that I might someday be unable to get pregnant," says the president of an infertility support group. "I wish I had not taken my fertility for granted."

At the opposite end of the spectrum, it may interest you to know that, according to the *Guinness Book of World Records*, the "Fertile Myrtle Award" goes to a peasant woman from Moscow who gave birth to sixty-nine children (sixteen sets of twins, seven sets of triplets, and four sets of quadruplets). A more typical couple has about an 85 percent chance of conceiving per year if they pay no attention to the monthly cycle and enjoy a vigorous, contraceptive-free love life.

 **Contraception Alternatives Worksheet**

Discuss these matters together:

- What are your thoughts on contraception? Are you satisfied that your views can be supported biblically?
- If contraception is an option, which contraceptive method seems best to you at this point?

Write out the pros and cons of each of the following methods of contraception.

abstinence _____

_____

_____

withdrawal _____

_____

_____

douching _____

_____

_____

chemical barriers _____

_____

_____

oral contraceptives _____

_____

_____

IUD _____

_____

_____

Norplant _____

_____

_____

low-dose progesterone injection _____

_____

_____

male condom _____

_____

_____

female condom _____

_____

_____

diaphragm _____

_____

_____

cervical cap _____

_____

_____

sponge _____

_____

_____

sterilization for him _____

_____

_____

sterilization for her _____

_____

_____

- Which method now seems best after weighing all the pros and cons?
- How many children do you both want?
- What about age spacing?
- Is there any reason to suspect you might have a fertility problem?

Appendix C

TO HELP ME FEEL
CLOSE TO YOU, . . .

At our marriage seminars we have surveyed women, asking what helps put them "in the mood." Here's what they said:

- Do all these things during the day, not just at night.
- Be attentive when I talk.
- Show interest in what's going on with me through conversation and thoughtfulness.
- Provide me with lots of emotional/verbal communication.
- Don't focus constantly on "downer" circumstances at work.
- Compliment me during the day on both inner and outer beauty.
- Say affectionate things.
- Avoid barbed comments.
- Give or mail me a love note—personal romantic thoughts from the heart.
- Take me out to dinner.
- Hire a babysitter.
- Brush my hair.
- Give me a massage.
- Take me out once a week.
- Hold hands with me.
- Walk together outside.
- Pray with me—more than just the dinner blessing.
- Slow dance with me. You don't need lessons; just hug me to music.

- Watch romantic movies. Yes, these are chick flicks. You married a "chick."
- Have candlelight dinners at home—no waiter to interrupt.
- Share personal romantic thoughts from the heart.
- Take weekend getaways at least once a year.
- Make a big deal of our anniversary.
- Tell me what you find romantic. Beach? Mountains? Dirt biking?
- Kiss me for real, not just little pecks, puckers, or air kisses.
- Hug for real. Go for the full face-to-face deal.
- Take your time at foreplay. God did not give us all this skin for nothing.
- Talk to me about what you want during sex.

NOTES

Chapter 2: What Is Sex?

1. Glen Gabbard, M.D., and Roy Menninger, M.D., eds., *Medical Marriages* (Washington, D.C.: American Psychiatric Press, 1988), 101.

Chapter 3: The Male Anatomy

1. Lisa Bannon, "Growth Industry: How a Risky Surgery Became a Profit Center for Some L.A. Doctors," *Wall Street Journal*, 6 June 1996, 1.
2. Clifford Penner and Joyce Penner, *The Gift of Sex* (Waco, Tex.: Word, 1981), 70.

Chapter 4: The Female Anatomy

1. Herbert Miles, *Sexual Happiness in Marriage* (Grand Rapids: Zondervan, 1976), 70.

Chapter 5: The Sexual Response Cycle

1. Clifford Penner and Joyce Penner, *Restoring Intimacy*, 106, as quoted in Marjorie Hansen Shaevitz, *Super Woman Syndrome* (New York: Warner Books, 1984), 57.
2. Vickie Kraft, *The Influential Woman* (Dallas, Tex.: Word, 1992), 72–73.
3. In the famous "Attractive Stranger" experiment, good-looking men and women approach the opposite gender and suggest a dinner date, offer an invitation to the stranger's apartment or make a flat-out proposition. The study has been replicated many times, each with the same results: Men overwhelmingly (in the area of 70 percent or higher) agreed to the sexual invitations—even more often than they agreed to the dinner date—while women overwhelmingly said yes to dinner but no to sex. (From Chi Chi Sileo, "Studies Put Genetic Twist on Theories About Sex and Love," *Insight,* July 3–10, 1995, 36–7.)
4. Mark Clements, "Sex in America Today," *Parade*, 7 August 1994, 4–5.
5. Stephen Perrine, "Secrets of the Male," *Glamour*, February 1996, 172–75.
6. Harold Wahking and Gene Zimmerman, *Fulfilled Sexuality* (Grand Rapids: Baker, 1994), 38.

7. Richard Foster, *The Challenge of the Disciplined Life* (San Francisco: HarperCollins, 1991), 154.

8. Hebrew scholars S. M. Lehrman and Franz Delitzsch agree that the curves of the hips refer to the swaying motion as she dances before Solomon. Mahanaim was a small town from which David fled as a fugitive from Absalom (2 Sam. 17:24). The allusion here seems to be the appearance of the angelic host to Jacob at Mahanaim on his return to the Promised Land. Possibly Solomon is telling his bride that he considers her dancing angelic.

9. Chris Vognar, "Culture Crash," *Dallas Morning News*, 29 March 1997, 7C.

Chapter 6: The Wedding Night and Beyond

1. Kathy Peel, "Great Sex!?" *Today's Christian Woman* [magazine on-line], 1995; available at http://www.christianity.net/tcw/ on the Internet.

2. Henri Troyat, *Tolstoy* (New York: Dell Publishing, 1967), 568.

3. S. Craig Glickman, *A Song for Lovers* (Downers Grove, Ill.: InterVarsity Press, 1980), 106.

4. Jody Dillow, *Solomon on Sex* (Nashville: Thomas Nelson, 1977), 153.

5. Gary Inrig, *Whole Marriages in a Broken World* (Grand Rapids: Discovery House, 1997), 185.

6. Joseph Adelson, "Sex Among the Americans," *Commentary,* July 1995, 26–30.

7. Bill Farrel, Pam Farrel, Jim Convay, and Sally Convay, *Pure Pleasure* (Downers Grove, Ill.: InterVarsity Press, 1994), 117–18, as quoted in Inrig, *Whole Marriages*, 197–98.

Chapter 7: Questions About Varying Levels of Interest

1. As reported in an untitled sidebar in *TV Guide*, 8 February 1997.

2. Philip Elmer-Dewitt, "Now for the Truth About Americans and Sex: The First Comprehensive Survey Since Kinsey Smashes Some of Our Most Intimate Myths," *Time,* October 17, 1994; 62–66, 68, 70.

3. Dillow, *Solomon on Sex*, 120.

4. W. W. Meade, "Sharpen Your Sexual Senses," *Redbook,* March 1994; 104, 118, 120.

5. Karen Scalf Linamen, *Pillow Talk: The Intimate Marriage from A to Z* (Grand Rapids: Revell, 1996), 190–91.

6. Robert Bruce and Debra Bruce, *Reclaiming Intimacy in Your Marriage* (Minneapolis: Bethany House, 1996), 110.

7. According to studies, about 96 percent of people fantasize. According to Dr. Ethel Person, M.D., author of *By Force of Fantasy* (Basic Books), the Romantic Fantasy is women's number one fantasy. This is the fantasy of loving someone and being loved in return. See Stephanie von Hirschberg, "It's All in Your Head," *New Woman,* September 1995: 114, 118–19, 140–41.

8. Bruce and Bruce, *Reclaiming Intimacy*, quoting William H. Masters, et al., *Masters and Johnson on Sex and Human Loving* (Boston: Little, Brown & Company, 1985), 304.

Chapter 8: Questions About Orgasm

1. Walter Wangerin, "Sex Held Hostage," *Marriage Partnership* (summer 1992): 43.

2. Jack and Carole Mayhall, *Marriage Takes More Than Love* (Colorado Springs, Colo.: NavPress, 1978), 208.

3. Herbert J. Miles, *Sexual Happiness in Marriage* (1976; reprint; Grand Rapids:

Zondervan, 1996), 67.

4. Clifford Penner and Joyce Penner, *Restoring the Pleasure* (Waco, Tex.: Word, 1993), 117.
5. Mayhall, *Marriage Takes More Than Love*, 208.
6. Penner and Penner, *Restoring the Pleasure*, 97.
7. It may interest you to know that the most orgasms reported in an hour by a male was seventeen; the most prolific female subject has 134. See "Are the Sexes Out of Synch? A Health/Gallop Poll," *Health,* July/August 1994: 52–58, 60.
8. Wahking and Zimmerman, *Fulfilled Sexuality*, 60.
9. Ibid., 61.
10. Ibid., 62.

Chapter 9: Other Questions Couples Ask

1. Rachel and Leah scrapped over mandrakes. See Genesis 30:14–16.
2. Willard F. Harley Jr., *His Needs, Her Needs* (Grand Rapids: Revell, 1986).
3. Linamen, *Pillow Talk*, 46.
4. Ron R. Lee, "The MP Interview: Sexual Greed," *Marriage Partnership* [magazine on-line]; 1995; available on the Internet at http://www.christianity.net/.
5. Joseph Adelson, "Sex Among the Americans," *Commentary,* July 1995: 26–30.
6. Gary Chapman, *The Five Love Languages* (Chicago: Moody Press, 1992).
7. Bruce and Bruce, *Reclaiming Intimacy*.
8. Ibid., 112.
9. Due to these and other factors, about 45 percent of both men and women said they enjoy sex after age thirty-five more than when they were younger. The percentage of women who achieved orgasm during lovemaking "always, often, or sometimes" increased as a woman approached middle age, from a low of 79 percent among those in their twenties to a high of 88 percent among those in their forties. Men remained fairly constant in their experience of orgasm during lovemaking, from 96 percent in their twenties to 98 percent in their forties. (Taken from a telephone poll of 1,002 adults, as reported in "Are the Sexes Out of Synch? A Health/Gallop Poll," *Health,* July/August 1994: 52–58, 60).
10. David Schnarch, Ph.D., "Joy: With Your Underwear Down," *Psychology Today,* July/August 1994: 38–43, 70, 74, 76, 78.
11. Kathy Peel, "Great Sex!?" *Today's Christian Woman* [magazine on-line], 1995; available at http://www.christianity.net/tcw/ on the Internet.
12. Mark Clements, "Sex after 65," *Parade*, 17 March 1996, 4–7.

Chapter 10: What Is Marriage?

1. Bruce and Bruce, *Reclaiming Intimacy*.

Chapter 12: A Word to Wives

1. Zig Ziglar, "Building Winning Family Relationships," *Dallas Texas 2000* 1, no. 8 (1997): 1.
2. Arlene Dahl, as quoted by R. Ruth Barton, *Becoming a Woman of Strength* (Wheaton, Ill.: Harold Shaw, 1994), 85.
3. Kraft, *The Influential Woman*, 22.

Chapter 13: Celebrate or Celibate?

1. Troyat, *Tolstoy*, 578.
2. Perrine, "Secrets of the Male," 175.

Chapter 14: Protecting Your Sexuality

1. Dave Carder with Duncan Jaenicke, *Torn Asunder: Recovering from Extramarital Affairs* (Chicago: Moody Press, 1992), 54–55.
2. Various writers, "Adultery: The New Furor over an Old Sin," *Newsweek*, 30 September 1996, 58.
3. Ibid.
4. Ibid.
5. William Griffin and Ruth Graham Dienert, comps., *The Faithful Christian: An Anthology of Billy Graham* (New York: McCracken Press, 1994), 60.
6. Carder with Jaenicke, *Torn Asunder*, 55.
7. Philip Yancey, *The Jesus I Never Knew* (Grand Rapids: Zondervan, 1995), 118–19.
8. Gordon MacDonald, *Rebuilding Your Broken World* (Nashville: Thomas Nelson, 1990), xvii.
9. Ibid., 53.
10. Ibid., 47.

Chapter 15: Developing a Loyal Heart

1. "Adultery: The New Furor over an Old Sin," 58.
2. Harley, *His Needs, Her Needs*, 12–13.
3. Foster, *The Challenge of the Disciplined Life*, 161.
4. Ibid., 162.
5. "Adultery: The New Furor over an Old Sin," 58.

Chapter 16: When Delight Becomes Obsession: Sexual Addiction

1. *Elle* magazine, May 1999, 170 ff.
2. Russell Willmingham and Bob Davies, *Breaking Free: Understanding Sexual Addiction & the Healing Power of Jesus* (Downer's Grove, Ill.: InterVarsity, 1999).
3. Mark Lasser, *Faithful and True: Sexual Integrity in a Fallen World* (Grand Rapids: Zondervan, 1996).
4. Patrick Carnes, *Out of the Shadows: Understanding Sexual Addiction* (Center City, Minn.: Hazelden Information Education, 2001).
5. Read it by visiting www.nytimes.com/2000/10/23/technology/23PORN.html.
6. Stephen Arterburn, Fred Stoeker, Mike Yorkey, *Every Man's Battle: Winning the War on Sexual Temptation One Victory at a Time* (Colorado Springs: WaterBrook Press, 2000).

Chapter 17: Troubleshooting Male Problems from Sizzle to Fizzle: When He's Never in the Mood

1. From a *Redbook* magazine survey of more than one hundred thousand married women, cited in Dr. Janet Wolfe, *What to Do When He Has a Headache*.
2. Irwin Goldstein, "Male Sexual Circuitry," *Scientific American*, August 2000, 70.
3. Ronald Rolheiser. *The Holy Longing: The Search for a Christian Spirituality*. New York: Doubleday, 1999, 210–11

Chapter 18: Sexuality and Aging

1. Jill Neimark, "The Beefcaking of America," *Psychology Today*, November/December 1994, 32ff.
2. Robert Butler, M.D., and Myrna Lewis, ACSW. *Love and Sex after 40* (New York: Harper and Row, 1986), 132.

Chapter 19: Questions from Our Readers

1. Jack Hitt, "The Second Sexual Revolution," *New York Times Magazine*, February 20, 2000, 34ff.
2. Joel Goodnough, MD, "Redux: Is the Oral Contraceptive Pill an Abortifacient?" *Ethics & Medicine*, Spring 2001, 48.
3. John Leland, "The Science of Women and Sex," *Newsweek*, May 29, 2000, 48–52.
4. Archibald D. Hart, Catherine Hart Weber, Debra Taylor, *Secrets of Eve: Understanding the Mystery of Female Sexuality* (Nashville: Word, 1998).
5. David Popenoe and Barbara Dafoe Whitehead, *The State of our Unions: The Social Health and Marriage in America*, June 1999 and 2000,
6. Cited in *Christian Single*, September 1999.
7. *U.S. News and World Report*, May 19, 1997, 56-60, 62, 64.
8. As quoted by Rebecca Chalker, *Ms* magazine, November/December 1995, 49–52.
9. Gracie Hsu, "America: Awash in STDs," *The World & I*, June 1998, 56ff.

Appendix A: Exercises for Developing Intimacy

1. Philip Elmer-Dewitt, "Now for the Truth About Americans and Sex: The First Comprehensive Survey Since Kinsey Smashes Some of Our Most Intimate Myths," *Time*, October 17, 1994, 62–66, 70.
2. One Health/Gallop Poll found that those who talk explicitly with their partner about their desires were more than twice as likely to enjoy satisfying love lives. (From "Are the Sexes Out of Synch? A Health/Gallop Poll," *Health*, July/August 1994: 52–58, 60.)
3. Bruce and Bruce, *Reclaiming Intimacy*, 102.
4. Marty Klein, "Is Weight Wrecking Your Sex Life? The Naked Truth Is That Women, More Often Than Men, See Extra Pounds as a Turnoff," *McCalls*, as quoted in *Dallas Morning News*, 20 March 1996.
5. "Adultery: The New Furor over an Old Sin," 58.

INDEX

270